CILT Rep

Confidence
THROUGH
Competence
IN
MODERN LANGUAGE
LEARNING

An international view of some contemporary issues

edited by
Reinhold Freudenstein
& C Vaughan James

*Mit guten Wünschen für den
neuen Lebensabschnitt,*

Ihr

Reinhold Freudenstein

16. 10. 1987

Centre for Information on Language Teaching and Research

Published by CILT on behalf of the Fédération Internationale des Professeurs de Langues Vivantes (FIPLV). CILT wishes to acknowledge the material support given by FIPLV, and the contribution of the editors, Professor Reinhold Freudenstein (University of Marburg, Federal Republic of Germany) and C Vaughan James (Passim Ltd, Oxford, United Kingdom).

First published 1986
ISBN 0 948003 316
Copyright © 1986 Centre for Information on Language Teaching and Research

Printed in Great Britain by Warwick Printing Co Ltd

Published by Centre for Information on Language Teaching and Research, Regent's College, Inner Circle, Regent's Park, London NW1 4NS

All rights reserved. No part of the publication may be reproduced, stored in a retrieval system, or transmitted in any form or by any means, electronic, mechanical, photocopying, recording, or otherwise, without the prior permission of the Copyright owner.

CONTENTS

	Page
Editors' Preface	v
INTRODUCTION	1
Language learning today Christopher Brumfit	2
PART ONE: CREATIVITY AND LANGUAGE LEARNING	11
Creativity, brain and language Matti Bergström	14
Creativity and interactional competence in foreign language learning Els Oksaar	23
PART TWO: THE TEACHER AND THE TAUGHT	37
Learning to communicate in a foreign language Denis Girard	40
The teacher's role in communicative teaching Christopher Brumfit	58
Tailoring teaching to the pupils Christoph Edelhoff	66
Negotiating language in foreign language classrooms Claus Faerch	79
PART THREE: INNOVATION AND LANGUAGE TEACHING	97
In defense of innovative methods Charles Parish	100
Music in teaching French by suggestopaedia Ludger Schiffler	117
PART FOUR: COMPUTER-ASSISTED LANGUAGE LEARNING	131
A linguist looks at computer-assisted instruction Frances Karttunen	133
Micro-computers in language teaching Åke Hägg	146

PART FIVE: EXAMINATIONS AND TESTING 155

    Language awareness, communicative competence and testing 158
    Matti Luukkainen

    Evaluating speaking ability 184
    Ray Clifford

CONCLUSION 211

    Where do we go from here? 212
    Sauli Takala

APPENDIX 231

    The International Federation of Modern Language Teachers 231
    (FIPLV)

Editors' Preface

The fourteen papers included in this volume have been carefully selected from the great number presented at the Helsinski World Congress of the International Federation of Modern Language Teachers (FIPLV: see Appendix) in July 1985. The volume should therefore be regarded not as a random collection of conference papers but as a thoughtfully structured book with its own internal organisation and rationale. Drawing contributions from six countries, it can truly claim to be international and to achieve several useful aims, not only treating a number of universally important issues but bringing together information, experience and opinion from a wide range of sources in Europe and the USA.

In his introductory paper, Christopher Brumfit gives an overview of the state of language teaching today, thus providing an informed background for the discussion of five major issues. Each thematic section opens with a largely theoretical paper, followed by more practically orientated papers, thus outlining problem areas in a clear and easily intelligible manner and then looking at attempts to tackle them in real teaching situations. Finally, Sauli Takala - beginning also with a review of past and present - gives some shrewd and positive indications for the future.

Several of the papers have been translated (from French or German) and all have been edited for presentation in this volume. We are confident that together they constitute a useful contribution to the literature and will be especially welcomed by those many teachers who do not normally have the time or energy to devote to reading the mass of monographs that are now on the market. We are most grateful to the Centre for Information on Language Teaching and Research for making publication possible.

Reinhold Freudenstein
Vaughan James

INTRODUCTION

Language learning today

Christopher Brumfit
*University of Southampton,
United Kingdom*

Introduction

In this paper I propose to give an overview of current views about the state of language learning. I shall interpret this theme broadly, looking at language learning as a psychological and a social phenomenon, for we need to recognise that the process of language learning arises out of our systems of schooling and the expectations of our societies, as well as out of the psychological structure of the human mind.

The acquisition of language

Psychologists, linguists and others have been investigating the processes of language development for many years, but the ways in which they have done so have reflected the assumptions about language of their times, as well as the state of theory in their own disciplines. It is possible to distinguish at least three major orientations in attitudes to language development: a concern with language and concept formation, a concern with language and social interaction, and a concern with language as an autonomous and describable system. Such different concerns inevitably affect the attitudes of researchers, and lead them – in their search for procedures simple enough to be investigated – to ignore certain aspects of language at the expense of others. Thus psychologists have frequently been concerned with the link between concept and symbol, linguists with languages as generative systems, and sociologists with languages as value-laden indices of social relations.

But language teachers are concerned not with any limitation of this kind, but with the totality of language as a human resource. Children and adults are aware of using language, but they are rarely concerned with the limitation of language function to empirically identifiable aspects that is necessary for systematic observation to proceed. So we have to draw on a wide rather than a narrow account of the nature of language if we are to see it as it will appear to our learners. We are forced more into eclecticism and interdisciplinary interpretation than into theoretical tidiness and disciplinary purity, for a theory is an attempt to formulate a problem in solvable form, and a discipline is a construct to enable students of language to limit their subject matter to areas where problems can be identified and solved. We cannot afford any such limitation since we are constantly confronted by students who need help with language acquisition now, whatever the state of our understanding, and who perceive language as a natural phenomenon which is not isolated from other activities and modes of behaviour.

Nonetheless, it is clear that a view of language has developed over the past decades that clarifies the process of language acquisition, even if it does so by revealing how complicated the process must be. This view sees language as a system of meaning among other communication systems, and draws upon anthropology, sociolinguistics and social psychology for its inspiration. Simplifying somewhat, from anthropology has come a view of how language systems interact with particular social contexts, sociolinguistics has shown how language variation in natural speech may be systematic, and social psychology has offered some ways in which motivation for such variation may be accounted for. All of these must be recognised in a rich account of language acquisition, and all have to be recognised by teachers as significant factors in classroom activity.

For many years it has been recognised that a major difference between first and second language acquisition has been that in some sense first language acquisition is simultaneously the acquisition of the 'faculty of language', while second language acquisition is either the superimposition of a further system on an already developed faculty, or the extension of repertoire, depending on one's view of the nature of second language learning. And this general statement seems valid as a simplification, providing we recognise that the concepts 'first' and 'second' language are both potentially confusing, and that most children in the world grow up as more or less multilingual learners, with access to several languages for different purposes in their lives.

Recent work in first language acquisition has been increasingly concerned with pragmatics and the acquisition of discourse. Language has thus been seen as a process of interaction between social norms reflected in the language of parents and siblings, the rapidly developing knowledge of the world of the child, and the innate capacity of the child to learn. Whether this innate capacity is uniquely a language acquisition capacity, or merely part of our ability to understand the world around us becomes less important to us than to researchers, the more we recognise an intimate connection between the acquisition of understanding of the world and the acquisition of language systems. The more we take up an interactionist position on language development, the more important the quality of learning outside the language system itself becomes. Wells (1981) has shown in detail how the total interactive context is enormously important for children. They appear to operate by a process of gradual approximation in which meaning, function and structure develop side by side, and the observed world increasingly comes into linguistic focus, so to speak. Halliday has expressed this position with most sophistication:

> Meaning is at the same time both a component of social action and a symbolic representation of the structure of social action. The semiotic structure of the environment - the ongoing social activity, the roles and statuses, and the interactional channels - both determines the meanings exchanged, and is created by and formed out of them. This is why we understand what is said, and are able to fill out the condensations and unpeel the layers of projection. It is also why the system is permeable, and the process of meaning subject to pressure from the social structure... The reality that the child constructs is that of his culture and sub-culture, and the ways in which he learns to mean and to build up registers - configurations of meanings associated with features of the social context - are also those of his culture and sub-culture. (Halliday, 1975: 143)

Socialising children in this way is clearly a complex task, and it is one which therefore influences the ways in which adults interact with children. There are observable tendencies for adults talking with children to produce significantly different organisation from that of adult-adult speech. Thus speech is more closely contextualised to the immediate environment, utterances are shorter and are spoken slower, there is less structural variation, more repetition and more limited vocabulary. Untrained adults, that is, operate with children in ways similar to those we demand from trained teachers of languages.

Second language acquisition

The recognition that first language acquisition involves acquiring a general language faculty at the same time forces researchers to see a link between understanding of the world and development of the language system - and, more especially, development of the ability to use the language system. But where does this leave second language acquisition? It would certainly be possible to argue that if knowledge of language and knowledge of the world have already been acquired to a considerable degree, then the process of second language development could be seen as - in principle - separate. But at the same time this requires us to accept a model of first language learners, discretely defined, followed by second language learners, discretely defined, and as we have seen this does not reflect the reality of the world for most learners. It is hard to imagine that we acquire first languages with a close relation between social demands and language, but do something totally different with second languages.

Yet the current thriving activity in second language acquisition studies (SLA) does reflect a divide along these lines. At the seminar in April 1984 for the retirement of Pit Corder, it was clear that interlanguage studies were divided into those which sought an autonomous drive towards the acquisition of second languages with a structure which was at least partially predictable, and those which were concerned more with social environment and the stimuli for language development. On the one hand we were presented with a car with wheels and no engine, and on the other a car with an engine but no wheels. Neither seems a very appropriate model for language use, which is presumably our major concern in the language classroom.

What I have characterised as the 'autonomous' view tended to stress the product of language acquisition, and looked to a universal system. The assumption underlying this view was that context was not in itself crucial, but that the observed similarities between acquisition sequences of different learners reflected the nature of the human mind when confronting the human phenomenon, language. The research evidence is therefore assumed to be text, the product of language use, compared with the text produced in language use by advanced native speakers.

This is quite different from the alternative, 'process' view. Here, there is more interest in interlanguage as an indicator of how learning takes place than as a reflection of the nature of language. For people who hold this view, the nature of classroom discourse becomes important, and the internally motivated drive to move through observable stages is only significant when the criteria for triggering off each stage of development can be identified.

I have referred to interlanguage studies as a general field, because it is important that we recognise the contribution of research to our understanding of second language acquisition. But the seminar reported on (Davies, Criper and Howatt, 1984) made it clear that this is a field which lacks complete unity - a sign no doubt of its vibrancy. It is by no means clear to educationalists, though, that the findings of such studies have any precise significance for language teaching and learning. Hypotheses may be generated for further research, and some of this research may be usefully reflected in classroom experimentation, but even if an identifiable sequence of morpheme acquisition is accepted by all researchers, and even if generalisations with considerable power can be made across languages, it is unclear what teachers should do with such information. So many years of trial and error by teachers (some of whom have been strongly motivated by the undoubted attractiveness of potential commercial returns!) have failed to produce any reliable and painless method for the teaching of foreign languages, and it is unlikely that research will reveal a sudden panacea for all our problems. We shall still have to sort out the motivational difficulties that confront us in our classes all the time. The best we can hope for from research results is that they should give us some indication of what not to do to conflict with normal systems of language acquisition, so that we do not actually make the task more complicated than it already is.

What is clear, though, from many studies in second language acquisition, is that creative strategies of the kind made by mother tongue learners may be operated also in the use of second languages. Littlewood (1984) summarises a survey of this area as follows:

> The most important of these strategies seem to be generalisation, transfer and other forms of simplification. However, we do not understand the learning process sufficiently well to be able to state which strategy is most likely to be applied at a particular stage or in particular domain of language. In any case, in their deeper psychological reality, the strategies are probably not distinct from each other. (Littlewood, 1984: 35)

The fundamental question, for current methodological theory, is the implication of claims that there are similar strategies to be adopted in first and second language learning. Does this mean that we should expect learners to acquire second languages in the same kind of classroom organisation as that provided for first languages? Does it mean that we should replicate as far as possible the conditions of first language natural acquisition? What are the significant differences between first and second language activity?

What is interesting, is that teaching methodologies have often appeared to throw informal light on the concerns of researchers into the process of language acquisition itself. It is to this issue that we shall now turn.

Language learning methodologies

Much discussion of language teaching has assumed a fundamental distinction between language 'learning' and language 'acquisition'. While not denying the usefulness of this distinction, I have blurred it in the discussion so far. This is mainly because the relative places of conscious and unconscious learning, both in first and second language work, are by no means clear. As we saw earlier, caretaker talk is structured in ways not dissimilar to those used by language teachers, and anyone who has brought up a small child knows that there is a considerable degree of self-consciousness in a child's acquisition of mother tongue. Questions are constantly asked about meaning, and sometimes about form and function as well. Children's metalinguistic awareness is widely attested. And in second language work there is increasing recognition of the role of unconscious strategies.

Changes in language teaching, and therefore in our expectations about the nature of language learning, have responded to general educational theory of course, as well as to views on the nature of language. Thus the 'communicative' movement can be seen as part of the shift towards progressive education as reflected in such diverse traditions as British primary education and education for political action as seen in the work of (e.g.) Paulo Freire (1971). This has been particularly clear in the methodological response to the demands of communicative teaching. In contrast to the syllabus tradition (van Ek, 1975; Wilkins, 1976; Munby, 1978), methodological writers (e.g. Allwright, 1977) were not so much concerned about the definition of needs or the specification of syllabus content. They saw the changes necessary as emerging from the management strategies of the teacher, the organisation of the classroom, or the relationship between teacher and students. Such concerns also underlay a number of packages of language teaching techniques which became widely popular during the 1970s, though most of them had been developed before. These include The Silent Way, Counselling Learning, Total Physical Response, and Suggestopaedia. Although these vary in a number of important ways, the motivation for grouping them together in people's minds was often their apparent freeing of learners from limitations imposed by conventional school expectations about language learning. Particularly, procedures such as the creation of a relaxed (or conversely an intense) environment enabled learners to increase their capacities for incidental and unconscious learning, and devices such as role-plays, physical activities and imagination-provoking visual stimuli increased interest and thus the naturalness of the inherently unnatural classroom setting.

But in general teaching, too, teachers' expertise was having an impact. Good teachers develop an instinct about when to abdicate responsibility as well as accept it. They know that they should withdraw sometimes, in order to give learners freedom, that they should interact simply as communicators as well as teach formally, and that their role is not simply to act as arbiters of correctness. This feeling within the teaching profession has been supported by some of the more theoretical and research-based issues already referred to. There may not be a great deal to be learnt precisely from general views about the systematicity of learner second language development, but the general principle of systematicity and partial predictability is extremely suggestive. It particularly links with current feelings about the role of uncorrected activity. As long as we recognise that constant correction distorts the process of language acquisition by placing too much emphasis on the formal medium rather than the substantive message, we shall be a little suspicious of too much correction. But of course there is a stronger point to be made once we acknowledge that there is a limit to what can be done about language acquisition through the medium of teaching. If we are not completely in control, and if the prime necessities for effective language learning are not strong control of input and strict regulation of learner behaviour, then our attitudes to learner activity which results in casual errors will change considerably. The process of creative construction is incompatible with a view of language learning in which errors simply reinforce more errors.

Yet learners regularly demand to be corrected, all teachers feel the need to provide some sort of feedback, and there have been striking successes in language learning by students whose methods have been highly formal and error-correction centred. We cannot be completely dismissive of correction, even the most formal and traditional. As so often in pedagogy, the question becomes one of how to define and use a particular strategy most appropriately, rather than one of whether to use it.

It may be helpful here to distinguish between formal pre-acquisition activity and informal acquisition itself. For while we may accept that the process of language use demands a close integration between language structure, world knowledge and strategies for use, we have to acknowledge that the tokens of the system for a foreign language are in no way familiar to many learners before they start (by 'token' here I mean any element in a system, lexical, phonological, structural, cultural, pragmatic or whatever). The process of using tokens as a system may require the integration referred to above, and - as with all complex activities - the best way to learn to do something is to do it in a reasonably safe environment with opportunity for support and general feedback. But the tokens themselves in language learning are often initially entered into a user's system by more or less formal and artificial means. The most obvious example of this is in the use of wordlists, which are often learnt, decontextualised and by rote, by many sophisticated learners.

It has been fashionable in teacher training circles to deplore this, but I suspect we are actually being faced with a definition problem. To see such activity as language learning proper is a confusion: such learning must be integrated and use-oriented. But to see such activity as a form of pre-learning which will enable learners to have tokens available for subsequent use more readily than they otherwise would makes complete pedagogic sense. The implication for language teaching, though, is that genuine language use needs to be incorporated into regular classroom activity on a fairly large scale, not that all non-genuine activity has to disappear. It is this need that has led to the emphasis on accuracy and fluency as basic distinctions for teaching in a number of people's work (Brumfit, 1984).

This is only one example of an area where teaching practice has independently arrived at a position consistent with recent developments in language learning theory. But we can see similar connections in most recent developments in pedagogy. The emphasis on defining needs derives from a concern for the predictable social contexts of particular language acts. Syllabus design based on functions and notions similarly attempts to integrate significant learning categories with the purposes for which learners use language. The use of groupwork is partly to create natural conditions of language use in class, rather than the formal setting of whole-class activity, and attempts to engage students' genuine feelings and interests arise similarly out of a dissatisfaction with language as a purely cognitive or decontextualised activity.

What is clear from all this is that there is a coincidence, though at a fairly abstract level, between the preoccupations of language teachers, and those of language researchers. Language teaching is not the same as language learning, but it is helpful when they are compatible with each other. Indeed, in some ways understanding language teaching is more important than understanding language learning, for we can do something about language teaching quite directly, through our programmes of training and certification of teachers. What we can do about language learning is more indirect, and harder to explore. But, of course, teaching must be the servant of the process of learning. There is no point in understanding teaching except for the light it throws on our understanding of learning, for without learning, teaching must become merely decorative and exploitative.

Nonetheless, a consideration of language learning today must recognise that much language learning takes place in direct contact with language teaching. We are fortunate that the two are often not too far apart.

References

ALLWRIGHT, R L. Language learning through communication practice. ELT Documents, 76/3, 1977.
BRUMFIT, Christopher. Communicative methodology in language teaching. Cambridge: Cambridge University Press (1984).
DAVIES, A, C Criper and A P R Howatt (eds). Interlanguage. Edinburgh: Edinburgh University Press (1984).
FREIRE, Paulo. Pedagogy of the oppressed. New York: Herder and Herder (1971).
HALLIDAY, M A K. Learning how to mean. London: Edward Arnold (1975).
LITTLEWOOD, William. Foreign and second language learning. Cambridge: Cambridge University Press (1984).
MUNBY, J L. Communicative syllabus design. Cambridge: Cambridge University Press (1978).
VAN EK, J. The threshold level. Strasbourg: Council of Europe (1975); reprinted Oxford: Pergamon Press (1981).
WELLS, Gordon. Learning through interaction. Cambridge: Cambridge University Press (1981).
WILKINS, D A. Notional syllabuses. Oxford: Oxford University Press (1976).

PART ONE: CREATIVITY AND LANGUAGE LEARNING

We open the first section of this volume with perhaps the most technical of the papers, which lies somewhat outside the normal purview of the language teacher but which is nevertheless shown to be of direct relevance, particularly in the heyday of the communicative language teaching movement. The essentially anarchic nature of creativity poses problems of operating within a formal institution etc, and in view of the relationship shown to exist between thought and language, the responsibility of the language teacher in influencing the whole development of the young learner is seen to be very great.

In the second paper, Oksaar takes every use of language to be an act of creation – even listening or imitation. But the sending of verbal messages is only one part of the process of communication, which comprises also non-verbal and extra-verbal media and depends very much on socio-cultural congruence if the speaker's intention is to be unambiguously interpreted. The effective user of a foreign language must be as aware of the culture of the foreign language community as he is of the grammar and lexis of the language, and this must be reflected in his communicative behaviour.

Bergström begins with the popular supposition that language and creativity are interrelated and looks for evidence in the functioning of the brain. If creativity is defined as behaviour in which the individual produces something 'new and unpredictable', this presupposes a factor that cannot be explained by rational logic. The problem is to identify a brain function in which this is possible. Bergstrom describes the operation of the brain stem as a random power-generator and of the cerebral cortex as an information-generator, moving on to the principle of information <u>selection</u> in the brain which gives rise to the possibility of creativity, requiring a high level of consciousness of the sort that leads to the type of behaviour that is discouraged in an orderly school system, and a suppression of the information-generator and other inhibitory factors. Creativity is inhibited by high information pressure and rigid rules or laws, etc. (Bergström comments that creative ideas often appear absurd in their social environment – a point perhaps worth remembering in our later discussion of 'innovative methods' in section IV!) Mental processes (thinking) conform with neurophysiological processes in the brain, and language mirrors the structure of thinking. Language has two roots: the rational – conscious, containing order, stability, etc and the irrational – unconscious, containing disorder, chance, etc. It is the conflict between the two that produces creativity, which thrives therefore on disobedience and nonconforming. It involves choice and is achieved only at the cost of predictability. The incidence of unpredictability in creative thought is echoed in the creation of the 'new and unpredictable' in language, in which the dynamic role of the verb is vital in facilitating choice and therefore creativity. The more our students are encouraged to become mere information-mongers, the less will be their faculty for creation.

Bergström describes the function of the left (rational) hemisphere of the brain and of the right (irrational) hemisphere. The predominance of one over the other varies in individuals and groups, and this can be affected by educational pressures. The language teacher can thus either 'create creativity' or suppress it.

Oksaar makes a plea for a more learner-centred approach to language teaching, with greater attention to the socio-culturally dependent behaviour patterns in language use. The argument is based on four principles: a language must be considered (and taught) as part of a larger entity - a culture; language changes and deviates from theoretical norms, and this is reflected in learner language, in which the creative element is too often neglected; language use differs in different situations; each learner is an individual and brings his own creative characteristics to the learning and communicating process. Discussing the meaning of creativity and its relationship with knowledge and learning, Oksaar takes issue with Chomsky, maintaining that the ability to create an infinite number of never previously heard sentences does not mean an equal ability to comprehend, since the lexicon of a living language is open-ended. She examines the relationship between creativity and imitation in the context of the concept of interlanguage or learner language, but the main thrust of her argument is directed toward the need for a more systematic account of the non-verbal and extra-verbal elements that can constitute a form of interference from one culture to another which inhibits communication no less than linguistic interference from one language to another. Communicative competence subsumes interactional competence, in which the verbal message is matched by culturally dependent paralinguistic, non-verbal and extra-verbal signals. In a communicative act, this whole range of features is brought together, and the communicator's ability to create sentences must be paralleled by an equal ability to accompany them with gestures, body movements, etc appropriate to the foreign language culture. This is especially important in teaching to learners whose acquisition of language may be inhibited by non-language factors. Knowledge of a culture (in abstract units - culturemes) is manifested in units of behaviour (behaviouremes), which facilitates systematic study and learning. If a verbal message is accompanied by behaviour which, in the target culture, contradicts that message, the result is misunderstanding or confusion. All the signals must therefore be in harmony (congruent), and effective communication requires creativity in far more than a narrow linguistic sense.

Creativity, brain and language

Matti Bergström
University of Helsinki, Finland

Introduction

Language and creativity are concepts which are often regarded as mutually interdependent. For this, however, direct, empirical, neurophysiological evidence is lacking. Since creativity is of such importance for the development of man as a species as well as of the individual, it is necessary to analyse the brain function in order to look for this interdependence. Such an analysis may be based on what is known of the human brain as a system. An empirically founded model of a developing brain (Bergström 1969) is especially suitable here, since the development of the brain system is closely connected with language development. Also, creativity in its more advanced forms depends on the individual's maturation and consequently on the maturation of the brain.

Here, creativity is considered as a form of behaviour, in which physiological category speech and language are also to be classified. Moreover, creativity is considered to be a form of behaviour in which the individual is producing something 'new and unpredictable'. This definition represents a view that there is an irrational factor connected with this kind of activity (see e.g. Clark, 1979). Creativity can consequently not be explained by rational logic. That it could be simply the ability to produce something 'new', e.g. new associations of known facts, is not held to be a good definition, since man-made machines such as computers are able to do this. The term 'unpredictable' in connection with the possibility of being useful for human development raises creative capacity above man-made, deterministic constructions to its proper value as a special function.

The task here is to look for a brain function in which the production of 'new and unpredictable' material is possible. For this, we may recll the neurophysiological process which controls the consciousness. Consciousness is known to be an activation of the cerebral cortex so that it is able to perform its cognitive and willed motor activities. The activation itself is initiated in the brain stem. Conscious behaviour thus needs the co-operation of both systems. On this co-operation we can base our model of the developing brain, which allows us to look for the connections between creativity and language.

Neuro-darwinism

The brain can be viewed, from the systemic point of view, as consisting of two poles: the primitive 'power-generator' of the brain stem and the highly developed 'information-generator' of the cerebral cortex; the two generators interact (Fig. 1) and control behaviour, including language and speech. The brain stem discharges mainly non-ordered, non-informatory nerve signals towards the cerebral cortex, and the cerebral cortex discharges informatory signals towards the stem. The effect of the power generator can thus be defined as entropic; it conserves disorder, whereas the information-generator has a negentropic effect; it conserves order, information. The power-generator, also known as the **formatio reticularis**, might equally well be called an entropy or random generator.

The sources of these generators are the vegetative system and the non-specific part of the sensory channels (for example the proprioceptive system and vision), feeding to the power-generator, and the information content deriving from genetic sources and from the environment via specific sensory channels, feeding to the cortex. The adequacy of these sources and adequate transfer capacity of the corresponding feeding channels are prerequisites for the efficient operation of the generators and, consequently, of behaviour.

The physiological system of the brain forms the basis for mental functions. The effect of the power-generator is manifested in the intensity of mental activity, that is, in the strength of consciousness and vigilance, which is in turn a prerequisite for the intensity and forcefulness of behaviour, as in speech and movement. The effect of the information-generator appears in the informatory content of our psyche (hereditary and acquired information), with which we control our behaviour. It also gives the informatory content of language and speech.

The behaviour control system thus contains special levels of power and information. Both have 'generators' of their own, ensuring that the activity controlled by information is carried out. Since the brain contains a great deal of information, however, it must be able to select what applies to each environmental situation from the vast choice available. This calls for an efficient system of selection in order to make it possible to classify information according to its value in each specific behaviour situation. Such a system is in fact known to exist in the the brain (see e.g. Hyvärinen, 1982), although its precise location and operation have not yet been established. Behaviour control, also working in the control of creativity, language and speech, can be illustrated with the following diagram (Bergström, 1980):

$$V \rightarrow I \rightarrow E \rightarrow M$$
V = selection (value), I = information, E = energy (power) and M = matter (environment)

An interesting question is how the selective operation in the brain works. 'Selection' and 'value' are among the highest categories of human psychology, and are linked with such areas of the psyche as creativity, motivation, emotion, chanelling of interest, etc. Since all these are connected with the present topic, we would do well to examine the principle of information selection in the brain. This principle also gives rise to creativity.

The dynamics of what happens in the brain in the interaction of the generators is the same, in principle, as what happens in Darwinian natural selection. The information discharged by the information-generator is subject to random changes, just as the genetic material in nature. In nature this random element derives from cosmic irradiation; in the brain its source is the brain stem power-generator, which can also act as a random generator. The random generator of the brain can give rise to 'mutations' - or variants - and 'errors' in the more or less stable information structures of the brain. These stable structures, originating from the stable environment, the cultural inheritance, etc, are also operative concepts in thought and behaviour control.

Continual variation of information is thus possible in the brain, and gives rise to new, unpredictable types of information. We might call this true creativity, in which the new information is unpredictable and cannot be logically deduced from the old. This explains the capriciousness of our thinking and the production of entirely new ideas. For the new, randomly produced matter to take over in the brain, it must compete with other information, especially the old, stable kind. This competition is a genuine struggle for survival, a 'natural selection', analogous to the way new species struggle for survival in nature. The struggle which takes place in the brain is for synaptic space, in which the new configuration of information must gain foothold in order to be reproduced, and thus survive. (For 'physiological competition' in neural systems, see e.g. Hyvärinen, 1982). This is a genuinely Darwinian struggle for living space: a case of neuro-Darwinian selection (Bergström, 1981). Information which has strength and vitality and has potential to control the behaviour of the individual successfully, survivies the struggle. The ultimate criterion is the social and/or natural environment. This selective pressure is exerted through the information-generator, which represents the environment and also the influence of genetic and cultural inheritance.

The crucial element of the process is the constant battle waged in the brain between various information structures. Psychologically, this takes on the form of thought and competition between concepts in our mind. We know that not all thought consists of the logical processing of old information, which is a dynamic mode of the information-generator; sometimes it creates new, unforeseeable situations in our minds. Aspects of this are evaluation, the mental struggle between alternatives, mental conflicts and selection of the best alternative.

Creativity

From the above analysis, based on the brain function (Bergström 1969, 1980), we can see that besides the 'logical' instrument the brain consists of an 'irrational' instrument. It is the interaction between these two which is interesting from the point of view of language, since the logical part represents the order principle in the brain and the irrational part represents the disorder principle. Since order and disorder do not mix with each other (like negentropy and entropy in thermodynamics), they are involved in a continuous interactive process, which acts as a 'motor potential' for all of our behaviour. So it also acts as a 'primus motor' for language and speech. With its potential of creative behaviour, it also ensures the connection between creativity and language at a deep mental and organic (brain) level.

We can see, therefore, that creativity - the production of new and unpredictable material in our behaviour - stems from the random and irrational element in brain activity. The irrational mode shows itself in competition, which as a dynamic principle is based on unpredictability and not on consequent, logical thinking. From neurodarwinistic dynamics it follows that creativity needs a high level of consciousness, i.e. a high degree of mental intensity. Such a high intensity is typical of creative people and is also typical of children, that is, before we depress them in our educational school system, which does not favour this kind of behaviour.

A further factor which enhances creativity is a depression of the information-generator, which lowers the selective pressure of the environmental standard information. A depression of the information-generator occurs also in sleep, which is known to be an important factor in the mental development of children. Imagination, too, and daydreaming, are connected with a relatively low degree of consciousness, but entirely free from the inhibitory influence of the brain cortex and environmental informative factors, which enhances creativity.

Creativity is strongly inhibited by high information-pressure acting on the brain through sensory channels. This can be explained by an enhancement of the selective pressure acting through the information-generator. It is also known that the brain's ability to handle information (information tolerance) decreases with pressures which are too high or too low (Lindroos, et al, 1984). Against this background we understand that creativity is also inhibited by social factors such as laws, regulations, rules and too rigid social organisations and institutions. Children should never be exposed to such influences during the critical periods of their development.

It is interesting to note that from the physiology of the brain it also follows that new ideas always seem to be 'absurd' if looked at from the point of view of social environment. This is due to their unpredictable and irrational nature. Therefore, new ideas always meet resistance and are exposed to destruction.

Despite the fact that creativity often causes conflicts (Cole, 1969), it is necessary for the development of mankind: the new and unpredictable future has to be compensated by new and unpredictable material in our mental power. This material is produced by the interaction of the two generators, which is the basis of creativity. But, as can be concluded from the above, creativity has a high price: the predictability of the future. This is something to think about for the futurologists. The more we are able to predict our future, the more we depress our creativity.

Language

We have to assume that the mental processes which we call 'thinking' conform with the neurophysiological processes in the brain. Since thinking needs a high level of consciousness and exhibits both rational (logical) and irrational elements, it is obvious that for mental thoughts to appear in the brain, interaction between the two generators is necessary. This would explain the oscillation of our thoughts between clear, exact logistic activity and more obscure, intuitive activity. It also seems clear that the latter mode would form the base for all mental acts (e.g. Taylor, 1963), whereas logical activity only differentiates the outcome of the holistic, intuitive mental view.

It is obvious that language mirrors the structure of thinking. Language therefore must also include, besides a logical informative structure, an irrational structure, which stems from the competitive principle of brain function. This structure must preserve the new and creative material of language.

In fact, we do have such a structure in language – the verb. The verb, in its usual transitive form, describes a competitive act, where a certain state 'wins' the struggle and another state 'loses' it; for instance, in the sentence: <u>I go out</u>, 'being out' wins over 'being in'. The verb 'go' thus expresses the competitive process. In intransitive verbs the continuous flow of the power-generator's action is shown. The verb 'be' is an expression of this flow in its purest form, the flow of consciousness. Verbs seem to be the basic tools for creativity, whereas substantives represent stable states of the information-generator. Creative individuals are of 'verb-type', whereas the non-creative are of 'substantive-type'. Both, of course, are needed.

When David Bohm, the well-known physicist, stresses the importance of verbs for a more holistic behaviour of man (1980), he is right, but his explanation of verbs as describing a 'flow', a 'movement' or a 'change', seems to need – in the context of the brain function – something additional to explain the force causing the movement: this is the competitive force inherent in the created, new and unpredictable material of the brain. The new concepts, appearing in the brain as informational signal configurations, live their own, independent life in the brain. They have to struggle for their life, to reproduce themselves (copy in the memory) and to adapt to selective pressure. It is no wonder that C G Jung describes thoughts as living their independent life in our mind 'like animals'. This also might explain the fact that languages live their own life, also seemingly independent of the individuals who are using them. It is, as it were, as if words preceded human beings – an idea which is found in several religions. In St John's Gospel we read: 'In principio erat verbum, et verbum erat apud Deum, et Deus erat verbum.'

Language has two brain roots: the rational and the irrational. The rational root is conscious and contains order, safety, stability, necessity, information and differentiated parts. The irrational root is unconscious and contains disorder, destruction (risks), liability, chance, uncertainty, undifferentiated wholeness. All this material has to be included in a mature, developed language. It usually is not, because the educational system of our schools suppresses the irrational root and prefers the rational, which is considered as the only suitable one for an information society. This philosophy therefore suppresses creativity in the children, who obey the rules. Creativity seems to live on the basis of disobedience, which may cause problems among children and young people. From brain development we know that in children the deeper, irrational part of the brain is the first to be matured. Since the irrational root of thinking and language works with probabilities, the individuals who are creative and use this source of their mental performance seem to be uncertain and often confused. A teaching system based on strict rules and certainties does not suit them, and it therefore classifies them in a secondary category.

The interaction between the two roots results in competitive behaviour, inner conflicts, emotions and creativity. A language using both sources is a living language used for survival – physical as well as mental progress. It seems that speech has especially this aim: to test the viability of new ideas and personal mental acts. The ancient, classical concept of rhetoric, which was included in the education of all young individuals, included this wisdom of language and speech. We, inhabitants of the modern information society, believing in techniques more than in humanism, consider language merely as a method for mapping sensory observations. Since language depicts our psyche, we are, with this method, encouraging our children to become mechanical, rational information robots.

Teaching language

Teaching a language has to include all kinds of mental properties in the process. It also has to take into account the neurodynamic properties of the brain. We have seen that a **dramatic mode** is inherent in language in the competitive factor. An **epic mode**, again, is due to the continuous flow of the consciousness via the power-generator. A **lyric mode** might also be seen in the struggle, from which the emotions in the brain originate. These three modes - dramatic, epic and lyric - need teaching in every language, so that the learners' aesthetic expression can develop to maturity. Without these properties a language cannot fulfil the needs of an individual in his different life situations.

It is not only the arts that preserve aesthetic behaviour. Aesthetic behaviour is also connected with a holistic mode of human life. This kind of holistic behaviour originates from the integrated action of the primitive power-generator, from the irrational brain root. The fact, that holistic and aesthetic behaviour also is represented in the right cerebral hemisphere (Sperry, 1983), might originate from a 90 degree rotation during development of the core-shell axis of the brain (see Fig. 1). This is an important view, since we know now that the right half of the cerebrum has its own 'pictorial, holistic dialect'. Apparently this dialect works as a 'postural' frame in language, too, like postural motor activity of the left hand in manipulative motor actions, which is controlled from the right hemisphere. The more differentiated 'dialect' in our speech is controlled from the left hemisphere, from its speech centres. Thus, this latter language 'dialect' (the rational root) does not work properly without the necessary frame given by the right hemisphere dialect (the irrational root). It is as in conscious willed movements, which are impossible without the co-operation of the more or less unconscious postural motor activity.

It is obvious that individuals, as well as whole nations, differ as to which 'dialect' - rational (left) or irrational (right) - is more natural for them. Education also contributes to this difference, as do cultural and political background. This may explain the lack of understanding between different groups of people, and also between 'East' and 'West'. Here language teaching has an important field to cover.

Figure 1

The physiological background of creativity

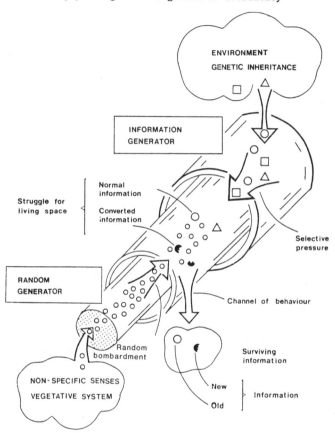

Since the interaction of the two generators in the brain provides it with great amounts of information, words, concepts, mental contents, etc, we have to select the word, thought or content, which we feed into the speech (motor) channels. This means that the brain contains a huge amount of possibilities, which can be used for actual speech and language. But, as soon as one 'word' is chosen and expressed as speech, the other possibilities disappear. Thus, each word appearing in our speech makes millions and millions of other possible words collapse. Silence, again, preserves these possibilities. This shows the responsibility we have for the use of words and for teaching a language. This 'collapse' function of the brain has its interesting counterpart in the Schrödinger function, used by the physicists in order to predict the appearance of an electron in certain experimental conditions. As the quantum particle seems to gain its real value from the field of probabilities in the experiment, so the differentiated word in our speech seems to gain its value from a field of possibilities in the brain. It is likely that the analogy between the spoken word and an observed electron does not occur by chance: the thought process, as well as language and speech, determine all aspects of human activity - aesthetic as well as scientific.

Therefore, since in modern society the word seems to destroy more than to construct, to kill more than to give new life, it may be of value for mankind not to underestimate the importance of language teaching and learning: it can 'create creativity' and thus secure the future for our species.

References

BERGSTRÖM, R M. An entropy model of the developing brain. Developmental Psychobiology, vol 2, no. 3, 1969, p 139-152.
BERGSTRÖM, R M. Brain, behaviour and ageing. Geron XXIII Year Book 1980-1981. Helsinki: Societas Gerontologica Fennica (1982: 7-13).
BOHM, D. Wholeness and the implicat order. London: Ark Paperbacks (1980).
CLARK, B. Growing up gifted. Developing the potential of children at home and at school. Ohio: Charles E. Merrill Publishing Company (1979).
COLE, H. Process curricula and creativity development. Journal of Creative Behaviour, vol 3, 1969, p 243-259.
LINDROOS, F. Overstimulation, occipital/somesthetic cerebral corical depth and cortical asymmetry in mice. Developmental Psychobiology, vol 17, no. 5, 1984, p 547-554.
SPERRY, R. Science and moral priority. New York: Columbia University Press (1983).
TAYLOR, C. Clues to creative teaching: the creative process and education. Instructor, vol 73, 1963, p 4-5.

Creativity and interactional competence in foreign language learning

Els Oksaar
University of Hamburg,
Federal Republic of Germany

In the literature on this subject, a **foreign language** is usually defined from the point of view of the context and order of acquisition and the 'relative importance of various languages' (Nold 1983, 71). The term foreign indicates that it is not the first acquired language and implies, in general a different learning situation. How it is acquired is the subject of a number of hypothesis – Contrasting Hypothesis, Identity Hypothesis, Input Hypothesis, Pidginisation Hypothesis, etc. Untested hypotheses are not infrequently raised to the level of fact (for example, Krashen's Monitor Model).[1] This is a methodological error that handicaps both research and practice.

On the other hand, the resulting galvanisation of the research scene is beneficial because it opens up possibilities of drawing closer to the important aim of knowing how people of different age-groups learn foreign languages and thence how they can most effectively be taught in a variety of contexts. The fact that the human being and not the model should be central, i.e. that we should be primarily learner-orientated, is unfortunately still not taken for granted. A humanistic, individual-centred approach to language teaching is indeed difficult, but it is more realistic than a theoretical model approach.[2]

Methodological questions and definitions

My aim in this paper is to widen the communication-orientated approach to foreign language acquisition research. This approach has been mainly syntax-orientated or, in the current orientation toward communication, the language has been classified predominantly as a structure and we have not considered the socioculturally dependent behaviour patterns in language use to be a problem in learning to communicate.[3] The essential difference between spoken and written language has hardly been operationalised; the use of non-verbal and extra-verbal media remains neglected or unintegrated.

The development of the communication-orientated approach should, on the contrary, be directed toward a shift of paradigm in linguistics. It has progressed in the last two decades from a form-related basis via semantics to the investigation of more complex contexts which may be described as functional, notional and cognitive. In contrast to a sentence-orientated, static and monological understanding of language, a text-orientated, dynamic and nowadays discourse-orientated understanding brings the interactive behaviour of the speaker and listener into the focus of investigation.

The empirical foundation of my argument derives from three long-term projects carried out at Hamburg: the Bilingual Language Behaviour project (twelve years) in Australia, USA, Canada and Sweden, completed in 1980; the current, ten-year Multilingual Language Acquisition project, involving children growing up with two, three or four languages; and the investigations of the language situation and questions of identity of minorities in Singapore and Hawaii (Oahu). The linguistic knowledge gained from these projections can also bear fruit in foreign language teaching. It shows, among other things, the importance of the sociocultural and affective features of the individual learner in relation to his motivation.[4] In the centre of the analysis is the **communicative act** (Oksaar 1975), in which the speaker and listener are each in their own way equally active; this is where they express their creativity in the use of language.

At this point we must define the terms relevant to my theme, which will also provide a structure for that theme. We shall do this via discussion of four principles which I have shown elsewhere (Oksaar 1983, 1985) to be methodologically useful in analysis of human language use.

THE PRINCIPLE OF THE WHOLE AND THE PART

Here I would like to stress the problem of too early isolation of language units from their socio-cultural framework, since language is always part of a larger whole - culture. In this respect it has a quite specific relation to culture, being on the one hand itself culture-dependent, and on the other hand a means of reflecting and defining that culture. Like Sofietti (1955), I use a general definition of culture, which I see as the 'ways of a people' i.e. all that specifically characterises a person or group, including not only material and spiritual aspects, but behaviour patterns as well.[5] These form information-bearing systems and become habits, like language itself.

Investigating spoken language, linguists have in most cases taken their data from purely verbal elements, without considering that non-verbal and paralinguistic data can influence those elements. The verbal message from the auditory channel appears simultaneously with other information signals via other channels, such as visual, tactile and olfactory, and are in many cases interpreted in conjunction with them. These other signals are culture-bound. For instance, **yawning** and **blushing** are biologically dependent, but in our culture – in a communicative act – they could be interpreted as signs of boredom, embarrassment, shame or pleasure.

THE PRINCIPLE OF CHANGE AND VARIATION

In certain areas, language use changes, and special attention must be paid to the variants as phenomena undergo such change. The teacher must be aware of these areas, which are usually socioculturally dependent. In the morphological system of modern German, changes in the area of feminine terms relating to professions can be observed over several decades (Oksaar 1976, 73-91). One needs only to compare the following:

a) Frau Müller ist Lehrerin, Ärztin
   (only the form with -in is possible)

b) Frau Müller ist Professor/Professorin, Minister/Ministerin
   (both forms are possible)

c) Frau Müller ist Kapitän/Schuster
   (the form without -in is the only one possible)

In the learner's language, communicative behaviour that deviates from the norm should be examined from the point of view of communicative adequacy and creativity (see Principle of individuality, below). What means does the learner use? In what way does his language use vary? What does he invent in order to convey the contents in a way understandable to his partner: When? Where? In what connection?

THE PRINCIPAL OF HETEROGENEITY

There are no homogeneous groups and no homogeneous language usages; they are all heterogeneous. In foreign language acquisition research, we should begin more than we previously have with case studies, and should not neglect them for considerations of 'representativeness.' It is here that the limitations of quantitative methods are especially visible; heterogeneity requires also qualitative methods. Over-emphasis on tests as reliable instruments of measurement is a great methodological weakness. As Guildford (1950, 1970/16) pointed out, easily 'objectivisable' tests and evaluation procedures often cause test designers to ignore the creative element, and such tests can deflect from what ought really to be measured.

THE PRINCIPLE OF INDIVIDUALITY

This derives from the previous principles and is especially important to the teaching situation, to which each learner brings varying experiences and prerequisites. Such differences also include the

ability to create. The term 'creativity' is now used increasingly
often in language teaching contexts, especially since the aspect of
process in language acquisition is receiving more attention at all
levels. But what does it mean? Guildford (1970) pointed out the
various definitions of creativity and the difficulties of defining
the concept precisely, depending on the criteria applied. In his understanding, it is a potential firmly established in the personality
and dependent on motivational and temperamental qualities. The important point (Guildford 1970,17) is that the creative act is a case
of learning, because it represents a behavioural change. 'A comprehensive learning theory must take account of both insight and
creative activity.' Guildford points out that the development of the
creative personality is a highly individual matter (1970,22). From
the point of view of learning and teaching, what is especially important is that 'no creative man can progress without previous
experience or knowledge; he never creates in a vacuum' (1970,23).

In this connection it is important to draw attention to the creative
aspect of Wilhelm von Humboldt's application of rules. Conte (1976,
622) has pointed out that in this context Humboldt was concerned
with the semantic aspect. Meanings are produced at the moment of
speaking; this is what constitutes the creativity of the individual
speech-act, not the combination of previously acquired elements of
language. Creativity as 'independent of the previous language activity of the speaker' is seen by Lanacker (1968, 1971, 14) as a
central characteristic of language use. He indicates that 'almost
every sentence that comes up is new and has never appeared before
... man possesses the ability to make up an infinite number of completely new sentences and to understand them'. Here we recognise the
Chomskian claim for 'an explicit formulation of the creative process
of language' (1965, 1969,19). I have already shown (Oksaar 1972,130)
that on his premises this is not possible in relation to natural
language with an ideal speaker/listener in a homogeneous language
community. The question of creativity in language use as described
by Chomsky, Langacker and others cannot be the same for the speaker
and the listener. If one is able to make up an infinite number of
never previously heard sentences, this does not mean that one can
also understand an infinite number of never previously heard sentences. Even the 'ideal listener' may get into difficulties, because in
a homogeneous language community the lexicon is an open system
(Oksaar 1972,131). One single word can make the understanding of a
sentence difficult or impossible. The statement 'an infinite number
of never previously heard sentences' must be relative as far as the
listener's role in the concept of creativity is concerned.

Creativity and imitation

During the 1970s attention was focussed progressively on systems
which the learner develops on the way to acquiring a second language. These systems were given various names: interlanguage,

approximate system, transitional competence, idiosyncratic dialect, etc.[6] In the concept of learner language, ungrammatical statements are not considered as disturbing deviations from the second language norms but as part of independent systems (Nemser 1971, Selinker 1972). They are the result of rule-governed behaviour. Learner language is seen as an independent system developing toward the norms and rules of the second language in a creative process specifically inherent only in man. Whether in this case one can separate creativity from imitation in a strict dichotomy, as is often attempted,[7] must be questionable, since this is impossible without a precise definition of terms. There is, however, no uniform definition of imitation. In psychology, imitation is generally accepted as a process 'in which behaviour is acquired by reproducing a model' (NcNeil 1974,14), whereby we can differentiate between spontaneous and non-spontaneous imitation. In the acquisition of phonetic and phonological systems, as well as vocabulary, imitation in this sense plays a central role. It is, however, connected always with the imitator's own individual activity, which can also be seen as creative. The question whether one learns by imitation or creation is unreal, since 'all learning processes presuppose creative participation' (Hüllen 1984, 108). Similarly, Guillaume (1925) pointed out that no imitation is completely passive: there is always selection. And Roman Jakobson (1972,8) emphasised that 'each imitation requires selection and thus a creative deviation from the model.'

We know from research on first language acquisition that with children there are various phases on the scale of complete imitation to original formulation.[8] Schneider (1978,276) points out analogies in second language acquisition in schools with children aged ten-fourteen. He states that 'the ability to imitate does not necessarily grow with the duration of the learning process', but that it can, especially in the early stages, be ascertained. Later 'the interruptions and contraventions of rules can, in general, increase and affect already acquired and established learning'.

In discussions of creativity versus imitation we are always referred to verbal means of expression, but we should also investigate paralinguistic and kinesic means, especially as we know that the interaction between speakers is most clearly visible in this field. In the communicative act, certain aspects of the partners' behaviour are taken over spontaneously: speaker and listener frequently adjust to each other in their gestures. This fact, known as interactional synchronism (Kendon 1970), can be observed in a number of paralinguistic phenomena: if one partner speaks quietly, the other does not maintain his normal sound intensity and also begins to speak more quietly.

The function of imitation in natural interaction should also be examined in respect of learning ability, and not only in test situations. Spontaneous imitations can have a communicative function as part of the phatic function. As our tests have shown, they not only mark difficulties of comprehension but also they may express emphatic agreement with the speaker or mutually shared emotion (Ryan 1973). On the other hand, it is different with expressions which are part of the manifestation of the cultureme. Greetings such as <u>Guten Tag</u> or <u>Auf Wiedersehen</u> only seem to be imitation or repetition; in fact they are conditioned by sociocultural norms which are situation-dependent. Such norms are not ascertainable by the learner in the same way as purely linguistic norms. Since they are not always codified, their appropriate use must first be 'discovered': for instance, in by no means all situations can the greeting <u>Tschüss</u> replace <u>Auf Wiedersehen</u>, despite its widespread use in Germany.

Non-verbal and extra-verbal elements

Non-verbal and extra-verbal communicative elements must also not be disregarded in analysis of spoken language, as they frequently relate back to behaviour patterns in the first language culture, producing situational interference. We are concerned throughout not only with language contact but with culture contact. Variants extend from first to second language and from first to second culture.[9] If, in a situation when it is expected of me, I do not shake hands in greeting, this may be interpreted as a signal I did not intend to transmit, even though I may make the greeting verbally.

In the last few years, discussion of learner language was concentrated on three main areas: the linguistic system, the learning process in the formation of learner language, and the communication process in its use. This places us at a disadvantage, since the other communicative means, mentioned above, are not taken into account.

Difficulties in this field are caused mainly by the fact that in learner language we have to deal with a high degree of variability and a continuum. Methodologically, Corder's programmatic statement (1978,73) '... we can locate learners ... along the continuum of change or development' has by no means been resolved, even though we work with variables rules and the implication scales. Because the learner varies his learner language behaviour according to his task, we lack long-term research into these variables. But his personal disposition is decisive in each case. Besides, we should take into account that there are also variations in the second language.

In spoken language we can describe language units through two models of expression — the normative and the spontaneous (Oksaar 1979,396).

The spontaneous model, which is characterised by deviations from the two-part Subject+Predicate type of sentence, is frequently found in learner language, but it is not realised that when he uses this model in dialogues, for instance in answer to questions, the learner is behaving like a competent speaker of the second language: e.g.-

    A. Wer kommt?   B. Eine Frau.
    A. Was macht er da?   B. Bastelt.
    A. Wo ist Vater?   B. Draussen.

In the spontaneous model dialogue, redundancies are avoided. From the point of view of form and content, the answer - with the question - comprises a rational unit in which speaker B does not express everything that is already known to himself and to speaker A: the theme is not repeated and the rheme is formulated.

Recent research interest has been focussed increasingly on processes and strategies which already held a central position in Selinker's Interlanguage Model (1972). But the possibility of distinguishing between the various strategies - learning, communication, production and reception - is methodologically still uncertain.[10] The positive feature that must be emphasised is that the individual as an active learner has been moved into the centre of interest.

Therefore we must now make a new, integrated start, in which all types of human communicative behaviour will be taken into account.

Linguistic and cultural behaviour

INTERACTIONAL COMPETENCE

Acquisition of language is culture learning (Oksaar 1981, 58). When one acquires a language, whether first, second or third, one learns more than a mastery of pronunciation, vocabulary and grammar rules. One learns to grasp reality and to structure it, and one learns to identify communicative relations, norms and situations, which become important component parts of the communicative and interactional competence of each language carrier. As I pointed out more than ten years ago, we must make a differentiation in the term 'communicative competence' (Hymes 1967). If we assume, with the Prague school, that it is important to consider written and spoken languages as two different codes, then we must specify a special competence for the use of the spoken language in face-to-face interaction. In this, the verbal message cannot be considered the only information signal. It is always connected with other, culturally dependent paralinguistic, non-verbal, kinesic and extra-verbal information carriers. I have described this competence as 'interactional competence' (Oksaar 1977, 140). Interactional competence is the ability of a person in an interactional situation to carry out verbal, paralinguistic non-verbal and extra-verbal communicative actions and to interpret them in accordance with the socio-cultural rules of the relevant group. We shall now look in greater detail at this type of competence from the viewpoint of foreign language acquisition.

THE COMMUNICATIVE ACT

The starting point for an assessment of learner language is an approach which integrates all the above factors and takes into account the relationship between them, as well as the perceptive, cognitive, affective and social behavioural system of the learner. The analytic unit of this integrated approach is the communicative act. By 'communicative act' I understand the complete action framework in which the speech activity takes place (Oksaar 1975, 738). Its component parts are not only the factors already mentioned, concerning verbal signals and other communication carriers, but also the partner, the topic of discussion and all the behavioural characteristics involved. For instance, the paralinguistic element **loud voice** or the kinesic element **raised hand** need not, of itself, express an effect. Only in combination with body movement and mime do they, for instance, signal danger. The creativity of language use is expressed in the communicative act.

If in the creative aspect of language use we see the ability of the speaker/listener to form never previously heard sentences and to understand many of them, then we must make this concept broader and more specific in order to deal with spoken language. From the point of view of interactional competence, the creative aspect in language use may be described as the ability of the speaker/listener to make up never previously heard sentences and to understand many of them, and to continuously produce new paralinguistic, non-verbal and extra-verbal information-carrying behaviours and to understand many of them.

This creativity is also important for the teacher in teaching situations. If he wants to create an atmosphere that will motivate the learners, he must understand the communicative means they have at their disposal. Since many of our schools now have ethnically heterogeneous classes, this is a very important question, because not all teachers have interactional competence in various different cultures.

For many learners, the language barrier is also a culture barrier if they are faced with foreign behaviour patterns in teaching situations. Conversely, familiar interactional patterns in teaching make learning easier. Tests with Polynesian children in Honolulu have shown that better learning was achieved in the American schools when the interactional behaviour patterns used in the classroom for narrative techniques were taken from their own culture (Au/Jordon 1981).

CULTUREMES AND BEHAVIOUREMES

This is a significant area of interactional competence, which includes the behaviour patterns connected with the verbal signal and other independent communicative behaviour patterns. From cultureme theory (Oksaar 1979, 1983) it is evident that these behaviour patterns can be systematised through the culture model. Culturemes are abstract units which are realised through behaviouremes. This means that in a given society we can empirically determine certain of the behaviour patterns of our fellows - that one greets another, or not; one thanks the other, or not; etc - according to various situational norms. If we can isolate them, the question arises: **How** does one greet the other? **How** does one thank the other? **How** does one ask for something? etc. The question **How?** concerns the behaviouremes which, for instance, with the cultureme **greeting** are structured differently according to temporal, social and spatial variables: from <u>Guten Tag, Herr Konsul</u> to <u>Hallo, Max</u>. However, we can also use only non-verbal behaviouremes to signal a message: a certain hand or head movement, a bow... Verbal and non-verbal behaviouremes may also be combined: <u>Auf Wiedersehen, Frau Meyer</u> + handshake. Knowledge of culturemes brings communicative harmony; lack of knowledge can lead to misunderstanding and even conflict. Good pronunciation and mastery of grammar do not help much. One interlocutor usually evaluates the behaviour of the other according to his own situational norms. These refer always to the non-verbal (glance, mime, gesture, body movement) and the extra-verbal, which includes culture-specific temporal and spatial factors, including - among others - punctuality, distance between speakers, etc. Silence can also be communicative: if speaking is expected when one keeps silent, and silence when one speaks, this can influence the attitude of the listener toward the speaker. And the quantitative question - **how much** one says, when, where and to whom - is also not without importance. Different forms of evaluation from different languages are indicated, for example, in such formulations as: <u>Redseligkeit</u> (German)/<u>Pratsjuka</u> (Swedish)/<u>love of chatting</u> (English).

If one comes from a culture in which it is customary to speak only when one has something important to say, and otherwise to remain silent, such behaviour may be misunderstood in another culture. In a culture where one is expected to talk, and where small-talk has an important social function to perform, e.g. in USA or France, silence can be misunderstood as a token of lack of interest, distance, presumption or stupidity, etc. If, in addition, one speaks slowly, with thoughtful pauses and no display of emotion, this may - in a culture system where the opposite behaviour is expected - lead to misunderstandings in people's assessment of oneself and one's behaviour. In this connection, there are significant differences not only between countries but also within them.

Elsewhere (Oksaar 1983a, 1984) I have given numerous examples of realisations of culturemes in verbal and non-verbal areas and have shown how difficulties can arise in spite of correct use of grammar and lexis. For example, the head movement that we describe as a nod will in many countries signal agreement, but this can easily be confused with the backward movement of the head which, in Turkey, Greece and Bulgaria means **No** and is synonymous with our shaking of the head.

Through disregard of the rules of behavioureme usage, situational interferences can arise. Interference research has so far limited itself mainly to linguistic aspects and dealt with written language. But if one examines communicative acts, i.e. spoken language, it becomes evident that it is above all human behaviour patterns that constitute communication and can be transferred. For instance, the realisation of the cultureme **Thanking** according to set rules: eye-contact, smile, handshake. What is taken for granted in our culture - e.g. eye-contact in thanking or greeting - may in many situations be considered impolite in Asia. In such situations a European normally behaves according to his own norms, which causes situational interferences. An expression such as <u>'Sie würdigte ihn keines Blickes</u>' (She did not even glance at him) would meet with very little comprehension in Asia because a glance would not be considered so usual there. Situational interference is by no means limited only to contacts between foreign languages and cultures, since the speakers of one language may also be multicultural. Individual differences, within the limits of acceptability, must also be considered in an analysis of the realisations of culturemes.

In structuring interactional competence in foreign language teaching, we must pay attention to the culture-specific, varying composition of direct and indirect expressions. Some may be difficult to recognise, such as the phatic function in invitations of the type '<u>Kommen Sie doch bald wieder bei uns vorbei</u>' (Come and see us again soon). In fact, expressions such as '<u>Ich melde mich</u>' or '<u>ich rufe Sie bald wieder an</u>' by no means necessarily constitute promises, and this can increase the difficulty for a foreigner, cf. 'I'll be seeing you' or 'See you later'. An American colleague living in the Federal Republic reports that at first he took such remarks as '<u>Wir laden Sie bald ein</u>' (We shall invite you soon) more literally than they were intended. In this social sphere of invitations, quite different behaviouremes may be usual. In South Asian countries it is customary for members of a lower social stratum to invite those higher up the social scale, while in the USA the reverse is usual. But in Korea, for example, such an invitation must be several times declined and several times repeated before it can be accepted (Kim 1977,13)

PRAGMATIC AND SEMIOTIC CONGRUENCE

Languages have, among other things, been called the keys of the world. Undoubtedly they do open doors to foreign nations, but they do not guarantee that one can walk across the foreign floor without slipping. Mastery of foreign behaviouremes can bring instant help.

What the learner needs can be made clear through a congruence model, which embraces not only the traditional congruences of grammar and semantics, but also takes in two others, the pragmatic and the semiotic.

By pragmatic congruence I mean congruence of the content of verbal, paralinguistic and non-verbal signals (Oksaar 1979, 395). If one says **yes** but at the same time shakes one's head, this congruence is ruptured. By the sentence '<u>Das ist eine schöne Geschichte</u>' (That's a fine story) one can express the precise opposite by breaking the pragmatic congruence: if the paralinguistic elements are not used in congruence with the verbal ones, then <u>schön</u> (fine) can have a quite different meaning of 'bad' or 'unpleasant'. The ironic use of the word can only be recognised through awareness of pragmatic congruence.

Semiotic congruence refers to the congruence of behaviour patterns in time, space, relationship and activity. The whole communicative act must conform with situational norms. If you call someone '<u>Du</u>' when the '<u>Sie</u>' form is the norm, you rupture the congruence. Insults, for instance, are broken semiotic congruences. How, in a given structure of the communicative act - i.e. on the micro-level - the norms are interpreted, cannot always be foretold. The tolerance limits in cases of breach of the norms and rules of pragmatic and semiotic congruence vary from one language community to another, as well as within them.

IMPLICATIONS FOR THE TEACHER

The professional and pedagogical expertise of our teachers has been dealt with in numerous publications, but I should like to draw attention to the question of their interactional competence. Are they in fact equipped to understand learners from other language communities and other cultures? The majority of children in the world today are taught through the medium of a language that is not their mother tongue (Tucker 1982,97). I have earlier referred to the culture barriers with which learners may be confronted, but we know very little about the culture barriers which teachers also encounter. Are they aware of the learners' cultural assumptions? Do the learners come from a culture in which silence and reticence or modesty are considered virtues, and free expression of one's personality and self-assurance must be suppressed - as, for instance, in many Asian countries? Can their active performance in class be properly measured by European or American standards?

Conclusion

In view of the multitude of socio-culturally dependent behaviour patterns, the following should be emphasised with regard to language use in interactions:

1. In language behaviour which deviates from the group norm, we should anticipate also deviations from the group cultureme realisations expressed via behaviouremes.

2. Whereas correct pronunciation and knowledge of the grammar and lexis of a foreign language are obviously of great importance, they do not guarantee understanding of the transmitter's intentions if the socio-culturally dependent behaviour patterns do not conform with the norms anticipate by the receiver. The better one knows a language, the more one is expected also to know the situation-dependent behaviour patterns prevailing in the relevant language community.

3. We should therefore concentrate our teaching on the creation of sensitivity to inter- and intra-cultural communicative behaviour patterns in diverse situations.

During the last few decades we have become far more environment conscious than ever before. It is now time for us to pay more attention to the spiritual environment of which foreign language teaching is an important part. Education in communication and tolerance between nations through knowledge of foreign languages, reflected in a more conscious experience of the mother tongue, should become an appropriately important factor in European education policy, and this should begin much earlier than it now does in many European countries.

Notes and References

1 See van Els et al. (184,35), Bausch and Kasper (1979), Bausch and Königs (1985), Lightbown (1985), Krashen (1985).

2 Oksaar (1984,243,262) and see Hüllen (1984).

3 See Littlewood (1981), van Els et al. (1984,274) and the discussion of the problem in various articles in the Applied Linguistics Yearbook 6, 1985 and earlier.

4 See Oksaar (1983a)

5 For analysis of the concept of culture see Kroeber and Kluckhorn (1952,149) and Oksaar (1984,25).

6 See Bausch and Kasper (1979), Knapp-Potthoff and Knapp (1982,50).

7 See the discussion of the Chomsky school in Oksaar (1977,148), van Els et al. (1984,27), Schneider (1978,150), Penzinger (1985, 10).

8   Oksaar (1977,148), Schneider (1978,151).

9   Oksaar (1983a, 1984).

10 Knapp-Potthoff and Knapp (1982,134), Bialystok (1978) and the detailed discussion by Badger (1985, 36).

PART TWO: THE TEACHER AND THE TAUGHT

The largest section in our volume comprises four articles from four European countries - France, the United Kingdom, the Federal Republic of Germany and Denmark. They combine neatly to encapsulate much of contemporary thinking on the aims and objectives of language teaching/learning, the roles of the teacher and the learner, and the relationship between the two. The role of the researcher is also discussed. Girard, while emphasising the importance of oral communication, makes a plea also for due attention to written communication and stresses the vital role of the teacher. Brumfit elaborates on an earlier assessment of what is expected of the teacher in a communicative language course, and Edelhoff tackles the problem of placing the learner at the centre of the process. Finally, Faerch develops the concept of **negotiation** in dialogue between researcher, teacher and taught.

Having broadly sketched the antecedents of the communicative approach to language teaching, Girard takes three topics: learning to communicate orally; learning to communicate with a written text; teaching these two kinds of communication. Assertions that second or foreign languages are acquired in the same way as native languages are untenable, since several of the characterisitcis of mother tongue acquisition could only recur in quite exceptional circumstances. School children taking a language not of their choice have no desire, need or even opportunity to communicate in it. But languages are a part of a basic education, and school age is the optimum time for study. Successful teaching depends on devising activities appropriate to the pupils' personal dispositions; these are discussed and reference made to Don Byrne's (1984) Interactive Model. Written communication involves a different sort of interaction, and Girard examines this theme with reference to different kinds of written text, journalistic and literary (he welcomes the return of literature to the language class). Citing Widdowson's work for the Council of Europe, Girard quotes the situation in France, where modern languages in the school curriculum have three objectives - communicational, linguistic and cultural: endorsement of a functional/notional approach does not imply the exclusion of grammar; concentration on the spoken language does not involve neglect of written communication; emphasis on communication does not justify disregard of the linguistic and cultural objectives. Many classroom activities are preparation for communication rather than the real thing, but learners' motivation requires the pleasure of actually communicating with others. Ultimately it is the responsibility of the teacher to create learning conditions in which this becomes possible.

Responding, as it were, to Girard's last point, Brumfit takes eight characteristics required of a good language teacher and places them in the context of a communicative syllabus. Teachers should naturally be clear of their own ideas on teaching and learning, principled but flexible, well-informed, constantly trying to improve and suitably humble about their own achievements and ready to acknowledge those of others. Their relations with their students should be governed by an understanding of their needs and a liking for them (or, at least, a disguising of dislike!). They should be free and approachable at all times by both students and colleagues. This eminently civilised and democratic code becomes less easy to apply than it might at first seem to be if the communicative exchange demanded by current approaches to language teaching/learning is to be genuine and convincing, which is essential for success.

Taking up Girard's call for the creation of learning activities appropriate to the nature of the learners, Edelhoff opens with a warning that becomes something of a refrain throughout this volume: language study is a means to an end, not an end it itself. Success may indeed depend on motivation, but since each pupil is an individual with his or her own peculiar characteristics, how can classroom teaching – sometimes in large groups – cater for these differences and still maintain interest? Edelhoff looks at 'autonomous learning' as developed by Holec for the Council of Europe, which he interprets as learning how to be independent and learning how to learn –– taking charge of one's learning. This he relates to the capacity of the learner to communicate, looking next at teacher-pupil relationships, having regard to the pupils as individual personalities, how they learn and how they interact with each other, the teachers and the subject. In the sense that the pupil is a social being, his freedom is restricted by the freedom of others; similarly, learning within the constraints of an institution must militate against autonomy. Edelhoff examines the curriculum implications of these apparent paradoxes and the problem of evolving pupil-orientated strategies and materials, leading to a more realistic definition of pupils' needs and of real-language tasks as exemplified in the 'Airport' project at Frankfurt, which is then described. The ultimate aim is to create the trust from which linguistic competence grows.

Discussing Widdowson's work for the Council of Europe, Girard refers to the 'relatively new term **negotiation**', and it is this concept that Faerch takes as the theme of the final paper in this section. He identifies two strands – negotiation between teachers and learners, which he illustrates with detailed examples of classroom discourse; and negotiation between teachers and researchers, for which he offers various models. Working out a relationship between these two kinds of negotiation should be fruitful and constructve for all parties concerned. This closely argued paper will be welcomed by the many teachers for whom the term 'negotiation' as applied to language teaching has hitherto lacked such a clarification.

Learning to communicate in a foreign language

Denis Girard
Academy of Sciences, Paris

Since the beginning of this century, when in many countries the Direct Method (teaching a foreign language in that language) has been progressively replacing the old Grammar-Translation carried over from the teaching of dead languages, the teaching of languages rightly called 'living' has always taken as an important objective that of leading the pupil to **communicate** in the foreign language, enabling him to **learn to communicate** in that language.

In the applied linguistics of the 50s and 60s, many linguists propounded a theoretical justification for this basic preoccupation. We may cite, for instance, what André Martinet wrote in Eléments de linguistique générale (1960):

> The essential function of the **tool** we call language is that of **communication**. French, for example, is first and foremost the tool which enables French-speakers to enter into an understanding with each other. We can see that if a language becomes modified in the course of time, it does so in order to satisfy the communicative needs of the community that speaks it as economically as possible.

Martinet realised that language also has other functions, two or three of which he indicated. Roman Jakobson distinguished as many as six (Essais de linguistique générale, 1963). But it is not surprising that for thirty years or so such language didacts have consistently awarded Martinet's 'essential function' pride of place without even waiting for researchers and theoreticians to give us sufficient information about this concept of communication.

In one version, language is approximated to other 'communication systems' which, according to communication theory, admit of a 'transmitter', who transmits information to a 'receiver' by means of a 'code' in a dual process of 'encoding' and 'decoding'. In this version, the essential element is mastery of a common code. In audio-lingual and audio-visual methods, which gave priority to speaking, the main problem was to assure good audio-discrimination and a pronunciation as close as possible to that of native speakers. Hence the importance given to faithful imitation of models recorded by native voices, which was the sole means of entering the foreign 'community'. The semantic contents of the messages being exchanged were, of course, considered important, but we did not know how to analyse or classify them as elements of communication.

Audio-visual pedagogy had at least the merit (somewhat in advance of fundamental research) of attaching particular importance to the communicative **situations** which largely condition the form and contents of oral exchanges — according to the place, circumstances, speakers and their interrelationships, theme and aim of the exchanges, etc.

The concept of communication was considerably refined by the research conducted by the Council of Europe on the definition of communicative needs and functions, and of the general and specific semantic-grammatical categories. These have been the subject of numerous publications since Trim et al, Systems development in adult language learning (1973) and a whole series of 'threshold levels' have appeared since J van Ek's Threshold level (1975) and D Coste et al, Un niveau-seuil (1976). The Council of Europe experts took as their starting point the work of the Oxford linguistic philosophers, R L Austin (1962) and J R Searle (1969), and certain sociolinguistic aspects of communication as recently defined by J J Gumpertz and D Hymes, who opposed 'communicative competence' to Chomsky's abstract notion of 'linguistic competence' (Gumpertz & Hymes, eds., 1972).

Language teachers are now better armed to teach their pupils to communicate; they have a better understanding of what speaking means. But the difficult transition from teaching to effective learning remains unaffected and it is for this reason that we now find it interesting to put ourselves in the place of the learner. What does 'learning to communicate' entail? How can it be achieved? If we can reply rather better to these questions we shall be able to draw more realistic conclusions as to what **teaching** foreign language communication should mean.

First, however, we must be aware of the unsatisfactory aspects of the theory that continue to exist even after more than ten years of basic research which have produced innumerable applications and repercussions. Up to now the emphasis has been placed on oral communication: can one also learn to communicate with the written language (other than in an exchange of correspondence)? Is the role of the 'receiver' exactly the same in oral and written communication? Is it restricted to a passive role? What is the contribution, in this respect, of the notion of 'negotiation' in the sense in which certain authors have already made such interesting use of it?

We shall base our argument on three lines of thought:

—   Learning to communicate orally.

- Learning to communicate with a written text.

- What teaching is required for each type of learning?

Learning to communicate orally

There is no doubt that for every individual learner (child, adolescent or adult), learning a foreign language means above all learning to speak it in order to communicate in the language. This is perfectly natural; the one experience of language that we all share in this life is that of our mother tongue, which has enabled us from a very early age to integrate into the linguistic community in which we were born by communicating with it.

For a long time we have contrasted the miraculous process of natural **acquisition** of a mother tongue with formal foreign language **learning**, which is extremely artificial. Certain new theories (Krashen 1981) consider that in foreign languages, as in mother tongue, nothing can lead to mastery of a language as a tool of communication except a process modelled on natural acquisition. Without wishing to enter into this contentious debate, I propose to linger for a moment on what experience has taught us about the acquisition/learning polarisation as teachers of foreign languages who have had to learn at least one foreign language at a time when our acquired mother tongue had already been consolidated.

The characteristics of natural acquisition are:

- it is achieved virtually without external constraint on the means, form or content of what is acquired;

- It applies without exception to the language (or languages) spoken within the micro-society of the family;

- it corresponded in the early stages to our fundamental needs: the need to eat and drink (vital needs) and other natural needs· to attract attention, obtain aid, receive affection, etc;

- it afforded satisfaction of the doubtlessly equally important innate need to make early use of our speech organs for the pleasure of playing with the noises and sounds they produce; of modulating them, either to imitate other human sounds we have heard or to invent new ones (little babies are extremely creative in this respect);

- it has been a powerful aid, beyond these early stages, in discovering the world (one's own body, one's surroundings and the circumstances of one's life) and subsequently in obtaining explanations of how things function (a child's curiosity is inexhaustible);

- it has enabled one to make known in an increasingly precise way one's own wishes, tastes, preferences, likes and dislikes in an early manifestation of independence and of all that will contribute to the make-up of the personality;

- it has rapidly led (within two or three years), without apparent effort, to a remarkable communicative competence.

We know that some of the characteristics of the discovery of language through the mother tongue will never recur (need for survival, discovery of oneself and of the world). Only the early transplanting of a child into another linguistic community could recreate the conditions necessary for natural language acquisition in a sort of linguistic rebirth. For the adult immigrant it is a more difficult matter (although the need to survive in a foreign, sometimes hostile, milieu can reproduce something like the needs of the baby); the results depend enormously on each individual's personality, and systematic study of the new language in an institutional context can often provide an indispensible aid.

I should like now to turn my attention to what formal learning of a foreign language (from the age of ten or eleven, which is the case in most European countries as well as in other parts of the world) can do to ensure that a child learns to communicate orally, taking into account that conditions are far less favourable than those which facilitated the acquisition of the mother-tongue.

Take, for example, the eleven-year-old French child who is beginning secondary education:

- he has to study the first foreign language for four hours a week, following a fixed timetable, according to a national syllabus and a textbook chosen by the teacher and his colleagues in the school;

- his communication needs are completely satisfied by his mother tongue;

- the mother tongue has enabled him early on to discover the world and the society in which he lives; ever since he began school, all his studies have been conducted in it, both spoken and written.

It is not easy to see, a priori, what could evoke in him the need to learn to communicate in another language, and he might be tempted to abandon all obligatory study of a foreign language, postponing it to a period of his life in which he feels real needs (professional, family, cultural tourist, etc) such as were analysed in the early work of the Council of Europe, which was - as we know - originally orientated on an adult population. Such a point of view is sometimes expressed, but more rarely acted upon - which is very fortunate, since there is no reason why the same argument should not be applied to all obligatory school subjects, so that history, geography, mathematics and science would be studied only when we felt a need for them!

Foreign languages are an integral part of the basic education of twentieth-century man and, even more so, of those whom we are today training to live - we hope happily - in the twenty-first.

Moreover, if we look closely we may conclude that the period preceding the end of infancy is in many ways the best in which to enter the new world of a foreign language: certain characteristics of natural acquisition are still present and may be exploited; certain favourable conditions in the chain of schooling and mental and physical development are apparent and can be made use of:

- even if the foreign language is not ordinarily spoken in the child's natural milieu, television, radio, cinema, popular songs, international tourism and exchanges have made the child aware in a concrete sense of a state of multilingualism even inside national frontiers, favouring - it is true - one language or another by virtue of its wider diffusion as an international language;

- the entertainment aspect of mother-tongue acquisition has not necessarily been dissipated, or the pleasure of playing with other sounds, rhythms, and music;

- what has been learned about the functioning of the first language may in some pupils give rise to a desire to make another language system work differently;

- the widespread children's taste for secret languages made by deliberate distortion of the mother tongue can lead them to seek the same advantages in a foreign language as a secret code;

- the pleasure of exoticism - of going outside the bounds of one own country - is also a factor that cannot be ignored;

- communicating in a foreign language is part of make-believe ('pretending we are foreigners'), which is the motive force of many children's games based on simulation.

In enumerating these positive factors I have no desire to draw an idyllic picture of foreign language teaching/learning in secondary education - the difficulties of which I know better than most people do. I wish simply to try to explain how a significant proportion of pupils can learn to communicate, provided the teacher offers them activities which take proper account of their natural characteristics. And here it is the word 'activities' that is fundamental, and it leads us to a very illuminating comparison with natural acquisition.

If it is true that learning theories, especially concerning foreign language learning, do not enlighten us very much because the processes involved remain mysterious and vary considerably from one person to another, we at least know from Piaget, Montessori, Frein and many others that the child learns above all by doing and not by listening in a well-behaved manner to the teacher's lessons. Here we touch upon the basic problem of learning to communicate, that of the respective places and the roles of knowledge and skills. Does one learn to communicate orally by learning the words, grammatical structures, functions and notions that linguistic communication brings into play in a given situation? Or does one learn to communicate by communicating, as one might learn to be a blacksmith in a forge? Positive responses to these questions define two extreme attitudes encountered nowadays among language teachers: a 'cognitivist' or 'mentalist' attitude and, on the other extreme, one that might be called 'communicationist' - the one based on knowledge and the other on skills. Protagonists of the first approach rightly value the fact that we are now better informed (through linguistics and sociolinguistics) about the functioning of language than we were in the heyday of traditional methods, when we knew that theoretical and abstract teaching did not really enable anyone to learn to communicate. For those on the communicationist extreme, partisans of a natural method, everything that is not communication is banished from the language class, as if the pupil were still in the privileged situation of natural acquisition of his mother tongue and of language that I have described.

It is more reasonable to consider that in reality the foreign language learner is going to need both theory and practice to learn to communicate in the language. It is in a mixture of different kinds of activity appropriate to age and stage of learning that the real answer will be found.

First let us imagine ourselves in the position of the eleven-year-old child who is experiencing a course in French as a foreign language for the first time. He knows by instinct and from his experience of his mother tongue that the prime function of a living language in everyday life is to communicate orally with other members of the same linguistic community. In the artificial atmosphere of the classroom, the francophone (or, at least, French-speaking) community is more often than not limited to the one teacher, eventually backed up by the **assistant**. The (real) situation of encounters - salutation, exchange of information on identity - between teacher and pupils offers an occasion which does indeed correspond to the pupil's own expectations: 'Bonjour!', 'Bonjour,

Monsieur..., Madame...', 'Je m'appelle...', 'Et toi, comment t'appelles-tu?' This is the best way to make pupils immediately aware of the specific nature of the foreign language class as opposed to the mathematics or geography class that precedes or follows it in the timetable. The prime object is not to strike up acquaintances but to teach mastery of another tool of communication; does this mean that all activities will be of this type and that one will learn to communicate only by imitating the speech-acts of the teacher-interlocutor? Certainly not, for from the very first, most elementary language exchanges of the sort quoted above, there are problems of a phonological, lexico-morpho-syntactic and semantic order - sources of difficulty, confusion and interference from the mother tongue. Most pupils need explanations (even if only brief ones); they want to know the reasons for the phenomena they observe and which intrigue them by differing from those they have internalised from their mother tongue and from which they have unconsciously drawn universal laws of language. Such explanations (or at least, clarifications) must not be refused so long as they do not encroach too much on the always insufficient time available for training in communication.

The number of natural classroom communicative situations is limited. The most common, apart from those already described, concern the conduct of activities, with explanations and requests for precision, and metalinguistic type exchanges ('Comment dit..?, 'Que veut dire..?', 'Pourquoi met-on un 's' à..?'). The pupil willingly learns to communicate in these situations, appreciating the freedom and initiative granted to him.

The essential thing is that the pupil is placed in situations of simulated communication, beginning with those common in the real world (house, street, sport, shows, shops, travel). The danger is that of making of a distinction between two quite separate phrases - oral comprehension (listening to a recording of a conversation, illustrated with a series of pictures), on the one hand, and oral production, in which pupils are prompted by various stimuli to draw upon their newly acquired language and that previously acquired to communicate in simulated situations on the other. The point is not that training in aural comprehension is not an indispensible element in the process of learning to communicate, but that it must be accompanied as often as possible by participation by the pupils, who therefore take control of the linguistic and language elements themselves. Take, for example, an extract from a dialogue with the postman taken from an audio-lingual or audio-visual course:

Le paquet de Londres

Le facteur: Monsieur Dubois habite ici?
Mme Dubois: Oui, pourquoi?
Le facteur: J'ai un paquet pour lui.

           Mme Dubois: Merci bien.
           Mme Dubois: Jean! Viens vite.
           M. Dubois :   Qu'est-ce que tu veux?
           M. Dubois :   Il y a un paquet pour toi.
                         Il vient de Londres.
                                    (G Capelle, La France en direct I,
                                                         Paris Hachette)

In audio-visual methodology, the 'presentation' phase of a new dialogue relied entirely on a listening task, with repetition, explanation and phonetic precision tightly controlled by the teacher, using a tape recorder and film strip projector. No initiative was given to the pupil. It should come as no surprise that only a part of the class succeeded in communicating orally in the 'exploitation' phase that followed.

In ideal learning of communication, the teacher first invites the class to talk quite freely during the first viewing of the silent pictures from the sketch. Talking among themselves, even with the very limited linguistic means of beginners, the pupils are immediately in a real situation of information exchange.

           'Qui est-ce?'

           'C'est le facteur'.

           'Et la dame?'

           'C'est Mme Dubois.'

It goes without saying that the pupils do not possess all the information they want or which they need to express themselves or to understand the situation or the development of the sketch. The teacher is there to give it to them, either himself or by having them listen to fragments of the recorded dialogue, which can fill out the lacunae in the available information (the famous 'information gap') - which is the most important factor in the whole of language learning. Thus the pupil is no longer in such a poorly motivated situation as when he has to learn to say things that he has no natural wish to express. He participates freely because he wants to know more and for the pleasure of formulating a hypothesis or even a point of view or a judgement. I was once present in a class of English as a foreign language for twelve-year-olds in the beginning of the second year who had been accustomed by their teacher to interrupt in order to pass an opinion about the new lesson (after just one run-through of the tape and visuals) - how difficult it was, its relative degree of interest, the behaviour of the characters (sometimes thought to be absurd or ridiculous!). There was already real communication, not the pseudo-communication analysed by Wilga Rivers (Rivers 1968).

It would certainly be useful at this point in our discussion to pause for a moment on what we might understand by 'real communication'. 'Pseudo-communication' may take two principal forms in a language class: one is the precise reproduction of a dialogue or fragment of a dialogue learnt by heart; the other is the false dialogue between teacher and class in which – according to Sophie Moirand's splendid analysis – the teacher 'always puts questions, even on authentic dialogues or texts, which are not really requests for information but aim rather to make the student talk in order to make sure that he has understood or that he is able to say in the foreign language what he can already say in his mother tongue (i.e. it is a check of his linguistic competence): '<u>Que demande le client? Qu'est-ce qu'il veut faire? Quelle est son intention?</u>' etc, or perhaps '<u>Qu'est-ce que c'est qui est écrit en gros en haut?</u>' – '<u>Le titre</u>'. – '<u>Très bien. De quoi parle le titre?</u>' etc. The teacher thinks he is practising communication, because the document is authentic, whereas in fact all he is doing is conducting exercises to consolidate and heighten the awareness of the learners in order to develop their comprehension.' (Moirand 1982)

Does this mean that this type of pseudo-communication should be abolished? Certainly not. It does, after all, constitute what one might call 'pedagogic communication', which has a perfectly obvious usefulness. But what is most necessary is that the teacher should be aware of his limitations and know how to offer – as often as possible – opportunities for real communication, in which the pupil is not fixed in the role of 'questioned' in confrontation with the 'teacher-interrogator' – a situation which in real life exists only in a police station or court of law!

It is notably in oral exchanges with his peers, the other pupils in the class, in pairs or small groups, i.e. in the new linguistic community which is enlarged day by day, that the pupil is in a communicative context closest to most actual situations. We now know a whole range of activities that encourage real oral communication in a way that is more motivating – because less false and more natural – whether role-play, searching for information that only one pupil or a small group of pupils possesses (a written document or visual), a language game or discussion of a topic. It is really a matter of degrees of artificiality or naturalness, for it need hardly be said that the school is a sphere of life and communication that has its own laws.

These activities are clearly not the only ones if, in the sort of 'learning to communicate' under discussion, there are, as I have suggested, learning times and communicating times, though certain classroom activities are directed toward both these objectives. The idea of banning everything that is not communication is unrealistic. The teacher must plan his programme so that there is a reasonable proportion of classroom activities that take account of the pupil's various needs. What must at all costs be avoided is preceding each stage of a lesson with a long theoretical and abstract learning phase, under the illusion that if pupils have all the elements, then the ability to communicate will automatically emerge. From the very outset, the teacher must arrange an alternation of phases, amongst which a significant place should be given to training in oral communication based on the introduction and development of linguistic autonomy.[1] It is the proportion and relative weight of each kind of activity that provides the flexibility required to enable the teacher to adapt his lessons to the needs of different categories of learner.

Another important factor is that learning to communicate orally will take on a different aspect as the content of the communication is developed and enriched. At its worst, to communicate without having something to say or simply in order to exchange banalities, without taking into account the level and age, let alone the interests of the pupils, is a pointless and extremely demotivating activity. It is by no means certain that this danger is always perceived by those whom I have called 'communication extremists'.

The contents of authentic documents of various kinds (oral, written, visual and audio-visual) will continue to play an increasing part and it is now time to reflect in particular on what I refer to as 'communication with a written text'.

Learning to communicate with a written text

Here we must acknowledge the various authors who for several years have been arguing that communication may take place even without the face to face encounter of 'transmitter' and 'receiver' that characterises oral communication, with its interactions in words, gesture and body movement, and with immediate reaction by the interlocutor.

Writing is not simply a one-way linguistic activity; in a real, if not always obvious sense, it is a form of interaction. This is evident in an exchange of correspondence, when the writer of a letter knows the person it is to be sent to and takes maximum account of that person's desired, expected or predictable reactions. It is less evident in the case of the printed word (whether journalese or literary), when the author has no first-hand knowledge of his readers (how many, from what socio-cultural background, with what attitudes, tastes and preferences). Nevertheless, it is still probable that the author of a written text will have some idea of the predictable reactions of his readers and will have responded to them in advance, creating what Widdowson calls 'interactional procedures' identical with those typical of spoken conversation. But the absence of immediate interreaction necessitates a different mode of exploitation (Widdowson 1984).

The mode of exploitation analysed by Widdowson illustrates the relatively new concept of 'negotiation' in order to take into account all types of communication - oral and written.

In the case of the 'written', the author proceeds by **expansion** : he deliberately adds to the conceptual content of his text (the ideas and facts that he wants to convey to his readers) whatever arguments and reasoning are required to assure credibility and to retain the interest of his readers. This argumentation is only in part retained from the text that results: the reader himself proceeds by **reduction** to extract from the author's discursive text that conceptual content which corresponds to his own level of knowledge or to what he wants or expects from his reading. So learning to read and to become a competent reader means learning to communicate with a written text.

Everything we have been doing for years to help pupils to become independent readers ('reading techniques') has in fact been directed to this end. I mean such procedures as:

- paying attention to the title (of the book, article, chapter) and illustrations to get a preliminary idea of what the author is trying to say;

- rapid reading in order to check the accuracy of this conclusion;

- closer and more precise reading in order: to reveal the links between the different concepts; to apply the process of **reduction**, which facilitates retention of the essence but not of extraneous details of an argument intended to convince the reader or to retain his attention; to learn to deduce the meaning of unclear words by studying the context, or from their resemblance to other words in the foreign language or in the mother tongue, if there are features in common.

This can be illustrated by an article from a magazine:

La France pour une poignée de dollars

2,200.00 Americains vont silloner la France cet été. Les poches pleines de billets verts, ils auront de quoi s'offrir de belles vacances.

<u>(This headline is followed by a photograph occupying one third of the page)</u>

Par Boeing entiers, les poches pleines de dollars, ils débarquent en terre française, citadins branchés de New York, hommes d'affaires du Texas, planteurs de Virginie, sportifs de Los

Angeles. L'invasion pacifique des touristes américains va connaître, cet été, un record absolu: 6 millions sont attendus en Europe, dont 2,2 millions en France, deuxième destination européenne après la Grande-Bretagne. Vive le dollar roi! L'envolée du billet vert par rapport aux monnaies européennes explique cette vague déferlante venue d'outre- Atlantique: il ya quatre ans, un dollar permettait d'acheter 5 Francs. Aujourd'hui, il vaut près du double.

De quoi s'offrir à bon compte des séjours quatre-étoiles dans la capitale, des virées culturelles et gastronomiques en Bourgogne ou dans la vallée de la Loire, du shopping 'made in France' et griffé haute couture. Cet été, les grands hôtels parisiens et les palaces de la Côte d'Azur affichent complet; les réservations des agences de l'American Express pour l'Hexagone sont en hausse de 30% par rapport à l'an dernier.

(L'Express, 21-27 June 1985)

To communicate with this text (or its author), the pupil must first of all look at the title - which is made very clear by the two summarising sentences and by the photograph illustrating the article. He must then isolate the three basic points of the extract expressed in the two key sentences in the first paragraph and one in he second:

- 'L'invasion pacifique des tourists américains va connaître cet été un record absolu...'

- 'L'envolée du billet vert ...explique cette vague déferlante...'

- 'De quoi s'offrir à bon compte des séjours quatre-étoiles...'

These contain the essence of what the journalist wished to communicate to his readers. The 'expansions' that he has added are intended to take the place of the means available in oral communication to convince, persuade, contradict or confirm by word or gesture. For instance:

- The idea of 'invasion pacifique' is foreshadowed by stylistic features expressing profusion ('par Boeing entiers' and the list of types of people), and the echo of another 'débarquement' on 'terre française' in the Liberation.

- The figures and percentages quoted are intended to show that the journalist has done his research and deserves to be believed.

- The second paragraph develops the idea of 'belles vacances', mentioned in the summary, with a wish to evoke both desire and jealousy in the French reader, together with a consoling thought (a collapse of the dollar would have only negative effects on the French economy, since a strong dollar brings an exceptional influx of tourists: <u>Vive le dollar roi!</u>).

Learning to communicate with the author of such a text, the foreign student of French language and culture is not obliged to appreciate all its nuances. His comprehension will depend on the level of his knowledge of French and of French culture. It may well be that the force of the expressions 'séjours quatre-étoiles' and 'griffé haute couture' will escape him. Even if the context does not clarify them sufficiently, this will not prevent him from understanding the essence and receiving the message. If the reading is to be done outside the class, a reading grid supplied by the teacher or the textbook writer will help. If the reading is done in class in order to study specific reading strategies, the teacher's assistance will naturally be requested, together with that of the other pupils in a study-group.

On this subject I must point out that I have deliberately been treating the study of communication with a written text separately simply for the sake of convenience and because of the specific problems afforded by each type of communication. In classroom practice the two may legitimately be related; it may not be satisfying (in silent reading) simply to communicate with the author of a text, because it may be more interesting – as so often in real life – to communicate orally in order to comment on the content of the text (about which little or nothing may be known by one's interlocutor – a very simple exercise to imagine) or to critise it. The article I have cited as an example, which deals with a typical phenomenon of the modern world – international tourism – lends itself very easily to detailed analysis, it may lead to discussion of the advantages (financial and economic) of that phenomenon and of the inconvenience it causes (the disturbance to the indigenous inhabitants caused by the seasonal 'invasions', even if they are 'peaceful'). It provides the teacher with an opportunity to give immediate satisfaction to pupil's needs for self-expression (of agreement/disagreement, approval/disapproval, personal tastes in questions of travel and tourism, etc).

The fact that the text I have chosen is from a journal is of no significance; it could equally well have been scientific, informational, publicistic or literary. Literature, so a number of recent publications tell us, is making a well-deserved comeback in the language class. The professional writer is more than anyone else a 'communicator', as may be illustrated by even the simplest little poem, such as the pretty little verse by Francis Bebey suggested by René Richterich and Brigitte Suter, which seems to have inspired the song written by Claude Nougaro in honour of Louis Armstrong:

> Un jour, tu apprendras
> Que tu as la peau noire, et les dents blanches,
> Et des mains à la paume blanche,
> Et la langue rose
> Et les cheveux aussi crépus
> Que les lianes de la forêt vierge.
> Ne dis rien.
> Mais si jamais tu apprends
> Que tu as du sang rouge dans les veines,
> Alors, éclate de rire,
> Frappe tes mains l'une contre l'autre,
> Alors, éclate de rire,
> Frappe tes mains l'une contre l'autre,
> Montre-toi fou de joie
> A cette nouvelle inattendue.
>
> Francis Bebey (in <u>Cartes sur table 2</u>, Hachette)

What an inexhaustible source of oral and written communication - both expressed and implied - the contents of this unpretentious little piece provides! And this applies even more to more ambitious works, when the pupils are ready to receive them and profit from them.

What teaching is required for each type of learning?

You will not have failed to notice that in treating these two forms of learning communication - oral and written - I have not been able to avoid commentary on teaching them together. This is inevitable, since the two sides involved in the pedagogical situation are intimately related (teacher and learners - the former being above all the indispensible enabler of learning).

For the teacher, the first requirement is a clear vision (constantly being revised as research advances) of the nature of language in its 'essential function' of communication. He must also adhere to the spirit of the fundamental objectives of foreign language study in school. This is difficult to generalise about, because it touches upon national policies toward foreign language learning. I hope, therefore, that you will forgive me if I take as my point of reference the consensus that has been established for some time in my own country, France.

For more than a century now the teaching of foreign languages has been an integral part of our school curriculum for all pupils from eleven-sixteen years, (new programmes are currently being elaborated which will stipulate **two** foreign languages for all), because this accords particularly closely with the final objectives of our education system, in that:

- it develops the means of expression and communication, with a significant effect on mastery of the mother tongue;

- it raises the general cultural level by revealing other ways of life and other cultural values through the mediation of languages, which are both their support and their chief manifestation;

- on the moral and humane level, it creates and develops a spirit of tolerance and openness to others, an urgent need for which is demonstrated many times over in our daily lives.

To meet these final objectives, all levels of foreign language teaching should have the following triple aim:

- **a communicative objective** (already discussed);

- **a linguistic objective:** consideration of the language in which one is learning to communicate, as well as comparison with some other language, especially with the mother tongue, which is the best way to make us truly aware of the God-given gift of language;

- **a cultural objective**, without which the new ability to communicate runs a serious risk of being worthless.

In this paper I have purposely chosen to limit myself to the first of these objectives. As Chairman of the 'Living Language' group of the Council of Europe project, I attach particular importance to what has been done during the last fifteen years to help foreign language teachers to achieve the communicative objective. We are continuing to work to this end, trying to clarify the very confused concept of communication. (This was the subject of an original work for which Professor Henry Widdowson was commissioned by the Council of Europe.) We should also like to dispel some misconceptions: the idea that one should no longer teach any grammar but only a series of functions and notions; the no less noxious and dangerous idea that communication is limited to oral communication in the most elementary forms of the language occurring in everyday life; the idea that the modern language class should be devoted entirely to communication activities.

Conscious of the three basic objectives that I have pointed out, the foreign language teacher must work out strategies most likely to assist different types of pupils to reach those objectives. He will at once realise, if he is at all well informed, that progressive mastery of an effective means of communication is a prime source of motivation and the best guarantee of success. Hence my emphasis on learning to communicate. Certainly the pupil must have confidence in his ability to acquire competence in the foreign language if he is to make any progress, and this confidence can only be born of an awareness that the objective of communicative competence is not beyond attainment. By learning to communicate orally from the very first lesson, becoming more and more independent in this fundamental activity and then learning to become an independent reader, too, he cannot help feeling confident.

But does this mean that the foreign language class should consist only of communication activities? Not in my opinion, for I think there must also be time for information-giving by the teacher (concerning both the language and the culture). It is equally necessary for most pupils to devote themselves to activities which constitute training for communication but are not of the same type, just as the scales that a young pianist practises are not music but preparation for musical expression. To continue this analogy, just as it is realised that motivating a pupil in a music lesson is an essential factor for success, and that this motivation is difficult to sustain by long and painstaking hours of theoretical study and lessons in sol-fa but requires the pleasure of very soon being able to produce music of a modest kind, so with a foreign language the pupil must very quickly have the pleasure of communicating with other speakers or with authors.

Such is the firm but subtle position that I have tried to express in these reflections on learning to communicate. Obviously I have not been able to cover the whole of this difficult and complex subject, to which a whole range of publications have been and will continue to be devoted. I may perhaps be reproached for gaps and omissions: some of these are deliberate, such as the fact that I have intentionally refrained from dealing with written production as a component of 'learning to communicate'. Among the four skills that make up oral and written communication, I consider it to be by far the least important in the everyday use of language by common mortals. This clearly does not mean that learning to express oneself in writing should not figure among the objectives of the language class, if only because it consolidates the other skills and, above all, it plays another role as a means of developing creativity and structuring personal expression.

A question that arises concerning the whole matter of the learning (and therefore teaching) of communicative competence in a foreign language is one posed by Widdowson in one of the final chapters of his most recent work, mentioned above:

> Our teaching must aim to create in the pupils the capacity to achieve their learning objectives, and these objectives must relate directly to the use of the language for effective communication. The problem of knowing if we must teach the language only as a means of communication can be solved only by reference to the teaching aim defined above.

Later, he adds:

> One way or another, we must elaborate a methodology which will lead the pupil to make use of the language as a dynamic, problem-solving activity within the limited framework of the classroom.

And we shall conclude, with him, that the responsibility for success or failure 'rests, as always, with the teacher ... and this responsibility is always the same; how to create conditions which will enable pupils to use what they already know in order some day to become independent of the teaching they are given' (Widdowson 1984).

Notes

1 Don Byrne (1984) offers a clear and convincing model for the organisation of classroom activities, with two parameters – teacher/pupil initiative and correction/accuracy. This interactive model was intended to refer especially to beginners and semi-beginners, but it is also useful with reference to more advanced levels and to adults.

References

AUSTIN, J L. How to do things with words. Oxford: Oxford University Press (1962).

BYRNE, D. A process model for classroom interaction. IATEFL Newsletter, no. 84, August 1984.

CAPELLE, G. La France en direct I. Paris: Hachette (1969).

COSTE, D et al. Un niveau-seuil. Strasbourg: Council of Europe; Paris: Hatier (1976).

GUMPERTZ, J J and D Hymes. Directions in Sociolinguistics. New York: Holt, Rinehart & Winston (1972).

JAKOBSON, R. Essais de linguistique générale. Paris: Editions de Minuit (1963).

KRASHEN, S D. Second language acquisition and second language learning. Oxford: Pergamon (1981).

MARTINET, A. Eléments de linguistique générale. Paris: A Colin (1960).

MOIRAND, S. Enseigner à communiquer en langue étrangére. Paris: Hachette (1982).

RICHTERICH, R and B Suter. Cartes sur table 2. Paris: Hachette (1983).

RIVERS, W. Teaching foreign-language skills. Chicago: The University of Chicago Press (1968).

SEARLE, J R. Speech acts. Cambridge: Cambridge University Press (1969).

TRIM, J et al. Systems development in adult language learning. Strasbourg: Council of Europe (1973).

VAN EK, J. The threshold level. Strasbourg: Council of Europe; Oxford: Pergamon (1975).

WIDDOWSON, H G. Explorations in applied linguistics 2. Oxford: Oxford University Press (1984).

The teacher's role in communicative teaching

Christopher Brumfit
*University of Southampton,
United Kingdom*

Introduction

Five years ago, in an article on the current state of EFL teaching, I listed eight demands that we were making of our teachers. I also commented that these demands were not substantially different from those which we might have demanded ten years before. However, it seems worth isolating the main needs of the profession in general terms before considering the demands of communicative teaching specifically. The eight points were:

1. Teachers should like their students, and if they do not, they should disguise it so well that no-one else realises;
2. They should be as clear as possible about why their students are learning English;
3. They should be clear to themselves about their beliefs on the nature of language learning and teaching;
4. They should always be open and free in discussion and help to their colleagues, senior and junior;
5. They should be professionally well-informed;
6. Their approach to teaching should be principled without being dogmatic, flexible without being merely fashionable;
7. They should be constantly trying to improve;
8. They should be humble, willing to recognise the merits of the past as well as the present, and the wisdom of the outside critic as well as the professional. (Brumfit, 1980)

Perhaps this is a rather sententious list, but I think many teachers would agree that they try to aspire to something like this. In this article, I hope to gloss these ideas and expand them to make them specific to teachers operating within the communicative tradition. At the same time I wish to isolate some problems for teachers in the communicative movement that are not touched upon here.

1. Teachers' attitudes to students

Of course, it has always been desirable for teachers to behave as though they liked their students, and all methodologies aimed at teachers in conventional education have demanded a positive relationship between teachers and students. This has been seen as a prime source of motivation. But in communicative language teaching this becomes even more important than in other methodologies because of the emphasis on realistic communication and the demand that students should participate as naturally as possible, without feeling ashamed about risk-taking. Some currently influential approaches (e.g. Moskowitz, 1978) demand a stronger commitment for affective learning, with implications for teacher attitudes, but it is difficult to conceive of a satisfactory communicative procedure which does not demand a high degree of positive support from the teacher. Since successful language learning requires a mature capacity to cope with the affective challenge of working with a new cultural and linguistic persona (Naiman **et al.**, 1978), support from the teacher is a crucial element.

2. Needs analysis

Experience with sophisticated needs analysis procedures (e.g. Munby, 1978) suggests that there is a risk of overkill in formal activity in this area. However, one very positive result of the communicative approach has been the serious consideration of the relationship between student needs and pedagogical practice. For most general language teachers, precise specifications may be inappropriate, but a general awareness of suitable and unsuitable needs of students is an essential part of the teacher's background knowledge. There have been many areas (for example literature teaching) where irrelevant needs have been identified for many learners. Paradoxically, it may be within the same area of literature teaching that needs are currently being neglected. There is a much stronger case than is currently being allowed for many language students being exposed to literature as part of communicative procedures. For many learners, academic needs are as important as those of casual tourist-type communication.

3. Beliefs about language learning and teaching

Within communicative teaching there is a wide range of possible beliefs: it is not a cult with a fixed framework, so much as a general orientation to language use and language learning. What are the fundamental views that are essential to communicative teaching?

One crucial factor is very simple: a belief that the process of second language learning necessarily involves genuine language use through the medium of the second language. There is considerable debate about whether this is best achieved through reorganisation of syllabus categories or whether a methodological reorientation is adequate to achieve it, but the belief itself is an essential element.

Now there has in practice been a tendency in communicative language teaching to interpret language as predominantly simply a vehicle for communication. Transmision of messages is not only the use to which language is put, and it does not only have a sociological and conventional dimension. Just as important is the use of language to assist the individual, often in isolation from others, to conceptualise, to sort out ideas, to clarify thinking, and to develop creatively. The communicative approach has neglected this dimension in theory, though sometimes it has been seen as significant in practice (see, for example, some of the materials produced by Maley and Duff, e.g. 1978; Moskowitz, 1978; and discussion in Stevick, 1980).

The effect of this sort of belief about the nature of language and language learning is to lead teachers to emphasise certain procedures in the classroom more heavily than in the past. The development of creative role plays and stimulations, the use of materials which encourage students to express themselves in the target language in relation to realistic topics and life-like activities, and extensive use of pair and groupwork, together with a commitment to individualised approaches where possible, are all developments in classroom practice arising out of this kind of belief. So, too, is a commitment to encouraging students to participate not just as cognitive learners but as people with opinions, feelings and interests of their own, even through the medium of a foreign language. Above all, in the effort to make language use as natural as possible in the clasroom, communicative teachers will allow a large proportion of their time to be spent in fluency activities in which learners may make mistakes, but are encouraged to try to understand or communicate in the same way as they would in a natural environment in a foreign country. For much of the time, the teacher's role becomes that of a communicator rather than a judge.

At the same time, the role of accuracy work will still be significant in most teaching situations. There will still be a place for formal teaching and learning work in which correction is offered and conscious effort to learn rather than use is made by the students. The point is that this type of activity should not occupy most of the class time, and its status should be clearly defined, so that students know exactly when they are supposed to be developing fluency, by acting naturally in class, and when they are supposed to be learning the tokens of the language and can expect to be drilled, to receive formal correction, and so on.

The result of this set of views is that language is seen as a complex system of human behaviour, interacting with other communication systems, and reflecting the cultural attitudes of those who use it. Language acquisition is seen partly as a process of socialisation into an existing culture, but partly as a contribution to that culture. Language users make the culture they live in, they do not just receive it passively - and this applies as much to non-native speakers as to native-speakers. So language acquisition is learning to participate in a culture to which you are inevitably going to contribute. And the result of this view is that language teaching must be seen as a process of facilitation. Teachers help students to do something in which they will actively have to be involved as participants in conversation and argument, as readers and writers, listeners and public speakers. If students are not moving in this direction, then it is not language learning but language imitation that is the goal. And that will defeat the communicative purpose of language altogether, as well as being an ideological limitation on the access to power and autonomy of minority groups, or of foreigners.

4. Openness in discussion

Particular types of relations with colleagues may not seem to be an essential part of a particular method. But if the communicative approach can be characterised in the way outlined above, there is value in insisting on certain effects for colleague-colleague relationships. This is not only because the demands made on teachers are potentially very great, and support and co-operation becomes therefore very important. It is also because the communicative approach demands a commitment to systems of communication with an emphasis on flexibility, freedom for variation and creativity within socially constrained limits, and the uniqueness of the individual's contribution, which can be exemplified in social relations between teachers as much as in language teaching itself. Communicative teachers are committed to the value of communication as a way of easing tensions, clarifying confusions and identifying areas of potential difficulty. These considerations apply in all social relations, not just in language teaching itself.

None of this is to deny that there are problems that are too fundamental to be resolved simply by a commitment to clarity and public expressions of belief. But the need for these is still great if we are to approach solutions to such problems, and we do not want to appear to support an unecessary conflict between our language teaching beliefs and our out-of-class behaviour.

5. Being professionally well-informed

This is not, of course, a characteristic to be claimed uniquely by communicative teachers. The main source of support here are the various language teaching publications and professional associations, together with official support for in-service work and initial training for language teaching. It is probably fortunate that there is no organisation (as far as I know) explicitly dedicated to the furtherance of 'communicative' language teaching. What we should be committed to is 'good and effective' language teaching, whatever our circumstances. Conditions vary in different countries, and the communicative approach has no monopoly of truth. Indeed, I have already indicated at least one area, that of personal creativity and concept-development, where communicative ideas seem to have been inadequate. But clearly the requirement to be professionally well-informed applies to any teacher who desires to be as competent as possible.

6. Principled but flexible approach

Remarks made under the previous heading lead on directly to this one. Teaching is about people, and emerges from the relationship between teachers, students and the classroom settings in which they find themselves. Of course, there are general principles that we must subscribe to, and of course we cannot responsibly set ourselves totally against the social values that surround us. But, at the same time, we have to be responsive to changing situations, and to our students as individuals with needs that cannot be entirely predicted and desires to communicate that cannot be constrained by advance syllabus specifications. In many ways this requirement is the hardest to maintain, for teachers are constantly having to reassess their contribution to the class, and the dangers of simply trying to survive from one crisis to the next, particularly in these difficult financial times, are very great. Nonetheless, this does seem to be a principle worth stating, for language teaching, particularly English teaching - for which an apparently insatiable market has developed - is all too prone to fashion. There is a con tant risk of being thought out of date simply because one is loyal to successful and well-tried procedures; equally, there is a constant risk of closing one's eyes to valuable innovation simply because of the wealth of new ideas with which we are constantly being bombarded. Laziness and trendiness are our two greatest enemies, but the path between them is narrow and perilous.

7. Constantly trying to improve

Again, this will no doubt be universally accepted as a counsel of perfection. Certainly, again, this is no monopoly of communicative teachers. But there are certain difficulties for teachers in this recent tradition which were not encountered by those working with some earlier methods. The lack of dogmatism that I raised earlier as a principle makes it harder to be sure what exactly we mean by improvement. This applies both in language competence and in methodology. If the prime purpose of language work is grammatical accuracy, non-native-speaking teachers can consult reference books to find out how their students should perform and what sort of model to provide. If the aims are appropriate language and realistic communication, this task becomes much harder. Similarly, in class it is possible to interpret the demand for fluency work as a call for any activity using language, and the distrust of correction as a demand that any language whatsoever is as good as any other. Thus it is hard to determine criteria for improvement in a communicative classroom compared with one based on a more rigid set of beliefs about language and language teaching.

The key factor here, surely, is our belief about the nature of language. If we do not believe that language is actually a tidy, defined system, then we can defend our communicative position as being closer to the truth about the nature of language. In that case we can tolerate some degree of uncertainty because it offers us increased realism. But we have to accept that such a view places greater responsibility on us to clarify exactly what we are doing in class, so that we do have principles with which to operate, even if they are not the same principles as in the past. In the last resort, with any method of teaching, the responsibility must lie with teachers themselves to determine whether or not they are trying to improve. No system of bureaucracy can overcome the individual responsibility. But we all need to try to obtain clarification where we can, and to identify areas where clarification is inappropriate or impossible to achieve.

8. Being humble

We do not often refer to this need, for it appears somewhat sanctimonious, but it does need to be said, I feel, for two reasons. One is that language teaching has been going on for a very long time (see Kelly, 1969; Howatt, 1984 for overviews). It is very easy for us to claim that we are coming in with a new idea, a new method, or a radical new approach to materials and classroom relationships. The problem is partly that people can make money out of language teaching, so that there is a temptation to claim that things are new simply to market them successfully. Much more, though, the problem is plain ignorance. It is very unlikely that we shall ever discover anything substantially new about how to teach languages. Teachers have been working on this for thousands of years, and people have not changed substantially in that period. Books written two thousand years ago are still important to us now, and the languages of that period are still living languages for many readers. Of course, the conditions in the world outside change, and minor modifications are needed in our practices and attitudes. Of course, one area of science, psychology, does develop incrementally, so that we shall benefit from insights about the nature of language learning as general understanding of human learning processes improves. But it is unlikely that we shall discover - from the practical activity of working with other people to assist them to learn - some amazing insight that has never previously been apparent. We have to look to the past for ideas, metaphors and insights, and bear in mind that - while we may like to feel that we are taking part in a new and revolutionary change - this is not going to be very significant or new in the total history of language teaching. Indeed, the reactionary teachers that we are secretly despising may well hold some wisdom, from their years of experience, that we have failed to recognise.

It is easy to overstate this, but we do need to accept that when we become language teachers we are joining a profession with its own history and traditions, not overturning the whole of the past. Of course we improve by recognising the defects of what is currently going on and trying to correct these. But we cannot do this usefully, or indeed effectively, by repudiating everything. To do that we have to say either that language teaching changes fundamentally as the world changes, or that generations of older teachers have been wantonly distorting the profession. Neither of these seems to be an acceptable position.

At the same time, we also have to acknowledge the limitations of our own understanding. Accountability is something of a dirty word in many educational circles, but we do have to be accountable to outsiders, for we have no justification for our activity except insofar as we serve the outside, genuinely language-using world. Our professional expertise should not prevent us from hearing comments and complaints about what we do from those whom we may hold to be ignorant, for we must not become a self-serving profession looking only to our own interests. And this applies equally to the activities of language teachers from outside the formally certified ranks of the profession. What has been learnt about ideas for language teaching from 'outsiders' such as Gattegno, Lozanov or Curran has been acknowledged by many teachers (see Stevick, 1980, for example). To say that we are unlikely to find fundamental new shifts is not to deny that minor reorientations in our approaches may appear very revolutionary when seen from a local perspective. Our individual lives as language teachers are short when set against the total length of time of the profession, and our own experience is always local compared with that of other practitioners.

And finally, of course, we have to recognise that our students know more about themselves than we do. We can bring an expertise that is genuinely useful to them, for we shall know more about the varieties of materials, the varied approaches to language learning, and the possible options available, than any one student. But we cannot know that one student. It may be rather idealistic to expect us to respond to individual students in typical classes and conditions, but most teachers have discovered that their expectations about particular students were totally falsified at one time or another. And none of us achieves the responsiveness that we would like to have all the time to all students.

Conclusion

The discussion here has concentrated on the general characteristics of good language teachers, with particular reference to communicative teaching. I would like finally to make one comment on the need for non-native-speaking teachers. There is one demand of the communicative movement that is extremely difficult for them, yet which is extremely important also.

Effective communicative teaching requires a relaxed attitude to language in conversation, in which fluency is more important than accuracy. By this I mean, not that accuracy is unimportant, but that we have to accept the same degree of variation from foreign conversation as we do from native-speaker conversation. Native speakers constantly make small performance errors in casual discussion. Their pronunciation, syntax, use of words, even appropriateness, varies and is corrected as they go along. The prime purpose of the conversation is to communicate and express ideas. Now, if students are to experience this kind of natural language use in class, teachers must accept that their own partial understanding (for all teachers' understanding of the target language is more or less partial) can be used fluently and naturally, even if that means making errors. This is, for many people, a very difficult position to accept, and a difficult step to take. Yet we need to help in the development of teaching fluency in the target language, through our initial and in-service teacher training course, and by other means. Without help in building up teacher confidence in this way, learner confidence is unlikely to develop.

References

BRUMFIT, C J. EFL teaching - where are we now? Practical English Teacher vol 1, no. 1, 1980.
KELLY, L G. 25 centuries of language teaching. Rowley, Mass: Newbury House (1969).
MALEY, A and A Duff. Drama techniques in language learning. Cambridge: Cambridge University Press (1978).
MOSKOWITZ, G. Caring and sharing in the foreign language class. Rowley, Mass: Newbury House (1978).
MOWATT, A P R. A history of English language teaching. Oxford: Oxford University Press (1984).
MUNBY, J. Communicative syllabus design. Cambridge: Cambridge University Press (1978).
NAIMAN, N et al. The good language learner. Toronto: Ontario Institute for Studies in Education (1978).
STEVICK, Earl W. Teaching languages: a way and ways. Rowley, Mass: Newbury House (1980).

Tailoring teaching to the pupils

Christoph Edelhoff
Hessen Institute of Teacher Training
Federal Republic of Germany

Introduction

It sounds like a truism when one speaks of basing the lesson around the pupil: what else are lessons for?

However, there is a Latin proverb which says <u>Non scholae, sed vitae discimus</u> - 'We are learning not for school but for life'. There is a tendency at school for the subject to become an end in itself - analysis and knowledge of the written language are considered to be more important than communication.

Tailoring the lesson to the pupil means adapting it to the interest, learning potential, needs and future prospects of the person being taught. This method is based on an age-old pedagogical fact - that people only learn when they want to. They have to be interested or motivated to be so. The impetus to learn must come from the pupils themselves, otherwise they will be unwilling to learn and will rapidly forget.

Who are these pupils? Each group is different. Whether child or adolescent, young adult or adult, no pupil has to know a lot about the prerequisites of learning and how to comply with these if the lesson is planned and given effectively. We have to make assumptions about the pupils since we cannot give them individual tuition. We teach in groups where all members are different but are nevertheless taught together.

There is a good reason for giving group tuition: as teachers we wish the pupils to learn, to learn together and from one another, to learn the social code, to communicate and to use this language as a means of understanding.

Tailoring the lesson to the pupil would accordingly take into account the aims and behaviour of the group as well as being geared towards each individual pupil. However, the reality is very different, as we all know.

It is impossible to get to know every pupil. They are constantly changing, in sometimes quite unexpected ways. They do not develop according to the book. They have a culture of their own; they seem to be getting younger and younger, though it is we who are growing older: pupils stay young forever. They are unpredictable, even though I know that at nine they become interested in the opposite sex - every year it's the same. So why not base the expectations around the pupils? What does tailoring the lesson to the pupil mean then? Is it a fad which will fade as quickly as it has appeared?

Autonomy and communication

The term 'autonomy' has cropped up in conjunction with 'self directed learning' in numerous discussions of teaching and foreign language teaching over the last few years. What does autonomy mean? During one workshop with Scandinavian foreign language teachers not very long ago I received the following answers:

- co-operation between pupil and teacher;
- the pupil assumes responsibility for his/her own learning process;
- teamwork;
- the person being taught is free to use technical aids on his own;
- the teachers help the pupils so they are better able to help themselves;
- the person being taught is made aware of his/her own learning requirements, e.g. social or economic; and learns how these can be influenced;
- the pupils expect the teacher to advise them; if he does not do this, they regard him as weak and unprofessional;
- autonomy is not obvious but must be constantly shown and proven.

The popular understanding of autonomy is inaccurate and relates to all types of independence; however, the sense is clear - that school and lesson should enable the pupil to learn to be independent and learn how to learn.

The Hessen 1980 <u>Guidelines for the Teaching of Languages at Secondary School Level</u>, contain the terms 'self-determination' and 'participation', i.e. all teaching should qualify a person to become aware of his individual and social rights and responsibilities in the democratic community. Can this be realised in practice through teaching? What do English or French lessons have to do with it?

The idea of autonomy plays a large role, too, in the development of the Council of Europe Modern Languages Project. Henri Holec summarised pedagogical research in a report, listing the following demands:

To take charge of one's own learning is to have, and to hold, the responsibility for all the decisions concerning all aspects of this learning, i.e.

- determining the objectives
- defining the contents and progressions
- selecting methods and techniques to be used
- monitoring the procedure of acquisition properly speaking (rhythm, time, place, etc.)
- evaluating what has been acquired.

The autonomous learner is himself capable of making all these decisions concerning the learning with which he is or wishes to be involved. (p 4)

These definitions are utopian even to the adult pupil for whom they were originally formulated. Holec therefore adds that the capacity to learn independently is not inherent but is acquired – be it in natural learning processes or in formal, i.e. systematic, planned arrangements.

Discussion about autonomy in foreign language learning leads into the didactics of communication. The student is acting as himself when he speaks and not in some foreign role, imitating a more or less plausible dialogue from his text book. He should **use** language instead of merely accumulating knowledge about it. He should express his own thoughts, opinions, desires, intentions, etc in the foreign language and be able to understand foreigners. The motto is 'speak for yourself'.

That is why autonomous, self-determined learning is involved with the capacity to communicate.

Theory and reality

Much has been written and said about the ability to communicate. There are, of course, many new guidelines and books. Many teachers have established new methods and changed the way in which they teach. But there is always another way of teaching. I found an example in an English textbook:

Good morning, everybody. Listen to me, please.
I am your teacher. You are my pupils. I teach you every day. Yes, this is what I do. I teach you English. Everyday you learn English from me. You come here, you sit down at your desks, you listen to me, and you speak English to me. You all learn English. You all like the English language. This pupil learns English, everybody learns English. And everybody likes English. English is a beautiful language.

Please notice:

I you we they	speak learn teach	English
he she	speaks learns teaches	Portugese

Here, the pupils listen to the teacher. They are, so to speak, his property. He gives, they take. He shapes them into his own image.

They sit on benches and listen and, miracle of miracles, they can suddenly speak the foreign language. Yes, they even learn to love the language in this wonderful way. The role of the teacher is to instruct his pupils. He stands there and quotes grammar at them - it is always like that; hence the 'present simple'. To be able to speak a foreign language means that you must always use an 's' in the singular. There is none in the plural. The teacher says something first, and the pupils repeat after him.

It appears that it may still be the same in some classrooms today. Perhaps not quite so drastic, but along these lines. The teacher is regarded as the focal point of the lesson, everything emanates from him; he directs and commands, makes judgments, praises and comments. He is 'all-knowing'. The pupils are more like empty containers who are bestowed the gift of foreign speech by their teacher (and textbook). Unfortunately, we often receive little thanks! Is not talk of 'pupil-oriented' lessons absurd in the face of accounts such as these? How can it be possible? Before we reply, a few other things need to be explained.

Pupils as personalities

Whatever we care to know of the species 'pupil' from the psychological, sociological and anthropological viewpoint, each one is an individual with his/her own interests, motivations, socio-cultural background and character. Each has had different experiences as regards language. They use their mother-tongue each day and have had experiences (mostly sub-conscious) in the learning of foreign languages. Many speak several languages: with children their own age at school or at home, with parents at home, or perhaps a different language - technical terminology - in a special youth group, e.g. the Red Cross, where everything is described in its proper connection. At the main station in Rome they speak 'pidgin English' with two Finnish girls.

In society they are distinguished by their age and the role they play. They still have a long way to go, but what does the future hold? As children they were still uninhibited, as adolescents they learn of the opportunities and perils of our life. They band together into groups of their own age with a culture all their own. They want to be independent in thought, word and deed, and are often poor copies of the consumer society, used and led astray, but letting themselves be led astray.

Teaching autonomy in these circumstances means showing them how to participate, be self-determined, have the courage to stand up for their beliefs and behave well socially. As far as humans who speak another language are concerned, this means training in another language to show willingness and ability to understand.

How pupils learn

How do pupils learn to put themselves in a frame of mind to communicate in a foreign language? Nobody can acquire the ability to learn from somebody else. Learning is an extremely individual thing. Even if in order to communicate a partner is needed, even if group tuition and communication situations in the class are there to express and simulate relationships in the language, each act and process of learning is a creative activity of each individual. We do not need to enumerate the different types of learners and ways of learning here, they vary according to age anyway; it is sufficient if we make clear that orientating the lessons to the pupil always takes these differences into account and includes different methods and procedures.

From the psychology of learning we also know that self-confidence and the need to be independent are prerequisites. This comes back to the discussion on 'self-directed learning', where each pupil is his own 'director of studies', so to speak. One can refer in this context to 'self-access' and individualised classes. These often take place outside school in an adult environment; however, it is the task of schools to lay the foundations, even if the focus is on personal interaction with others, by teaching communicative study skills.

Interaction and learning

Pupils are not isolated beings. They live together and learn together in groups (family, school, peer groups) - and a twelve-year-old can start to feel apprehensive if expected to spend his/her whole time in the semi-dark in front of a micro-computer. Individual autonomy stops short where social commitment starts, even if it is a question of social learning. The group must advance together in the classroom; not only is interaction the method, but it constitutes the content of the lesson in communication: questions and answers, giving reasons and agreeing, making suggestions and quoting conditions, giving references and discussing, testing the foreign language in the class. All these things require that the pupil has a partner with whom to communicate and observe the rules of interactive communication.

What applies to the individual applies also to the autonomous group and their relationship with the teaching plan or curriculum. Autonomy does not mean learning in a disjointed manner. To those being taught, the teacher is the representative of the requirements of group and society, teaching plan and curriculum. Interaction with him therefore means negotiating one's own curriculum with the set curriculum taught by the teacher.

Institutional conditions of learning

We shall now address the institutional framework which restricts self-determination and tailoring the lesson to the needs of the pupil. School is a framework for everyone. The freedom of the individual is restricted by the freedom of others. Everyone in a school should receive the same opportunities. The teacher is required to be a counsellor, not an instructer, to the pupils. Is 'pupil autonomy' conceivable within the framework of schools? Can it in fact be taught? Or does autonomy not belong to the area of adult education? Are not the terms 'institution' and 'autonomy' contradictory concepts?

The curriculum and the pupils

The lesson plan and the actual curriculum embody the pupils' requirements, which demand the development of certain skills according to a set of official criteria. Materials design and textbooks determine the linguistic phenomena, in theme and content, as well as the form of the exercises by which these skills should be assessed. Running counter to the often advanced lesson-plans, framework and instruction materials, the old, stealthy, curricula frequently dominate in foreign-language instruction: the teacher talks, the pupils listen; the teacher dictates, the pupils write; the teacher asks questions, knowing the answer in advance: the pupils answer; stories and texts, which interest no one, are read and 'prepared'; grammar is quoted and the permanent mistakes are counted. How could autonomy be learnt in this way?

Michael Legutke describes this situation in his introduction to the 'Airport' project as follows:

> Even if the term communicative has become increasingly popular, often very little is actually communicated in the language classroom. Fenced in by syllabus demands often represented by the total dominance of a textbook, the learner does not find room to speak up as her/himself, to use the language in order

to express himself, to create texts, to simulate interaction in real classroom situations with fellow learners or the teacher. Under the overpowering impact of future-orientated qualifications and school exams, the pleasure of attempting and enjoying meaningful discourse is eliminated from the classroom. Its potential for exploiting and exploring the here and now are removed to an indefinite future - a trip to England, or a job situation. (Legutke, 1984)

Since the early 1970s attempts have been made to achieve pupil orientation in the selection of themes and content. Numerous teaching materials have appeared in the past few years for teaching different foreign languages:

> Orientation to a subject as the main criterion for the development of teaching material is based on the need to derive the themes of the lesson from the experiences of the pupils. Experiences does not mean the current main interests of the pupils, but a planned interaction between the individual and social learning of each pupil in the school and in the other relationships in which he finds himself daily, e.g. the family or 'peer group'. The themes broached during the lesson should therefore be linked to the pupil's experiences, and enable him to make new ones. (Edelhoff in BAG, 1978)

In addition to gearing the themes to the pupil's experiences, a recent development, already quoted by Legutke, is to use the actual classroom as a laboratory for exploring and experimenting with the forms being taught. The question on the curriculum is therefore: What language tasks can the pupils solve that they can relate to directly? How can they learn the foreign language and culture by relating these to their own needs and requirements? In short, how can **natural** language acquisition (with which they can identify) be reproduced or initiated in the classroom?

Need and requirement

Is it really possible to relate what is taught in the foreign language to the pupil and his changing requirements? 'Communicative needs' have been thoroughly researched in the Council of Europe Modern Languages Project which has already been mentioned (Richterich, Porcher). The thresholds of who-needs-what in a foreign language need to be stated in the language curriculum. The catchphrase is 'serviceable words'. What foreign language knowledge do tourists need when they travel abroad? What elements of the foreign language need to be mastered for business and commerce? What are the minimum requirements for making oneself understood - for 'survival'?

The English word 'needs' can be translated by two terms in German with similar meaning. Whereas Bedarf emphasises more the intersubjective aspect (what is needed?), Bedürfnis is associated with the individual, subjective side (What do I need/want?). The following diagram gives a breakdown:

Communicative needs

Objective	Subjective
Bedarf	Bedürfnis(se)
Pedagogical task of the school	Curiosity (information)
Requirement by society:	Learning (knowledge)
Knowledge	Conversation
Information	Contact/exchange
Ability to speak	To translate into action
	Participation in collective knowledge and culture

Both sides, the objective and the subjective, are closely related. The needs of the individual (right-hand column) should alternate with those of society (left-hand column); however, what is needed objectively should not totally belie the subjective needs of the individual. Neither side is completely static; objective need can be simulated and met; subjective need can be aroused and satisfied.

Experiences of self and others

If pupil-orientation, as here, is not understood in the subjective sense, it is because references to experience constantly relate to experience had by **others** as well as oneself. On the one hand there is the pupil with his interests, knowledge, talents, abilities, personal needs, socio-cultural requirements, experiences: in short, his culture. And on the other, he is confronted with the experiences of others, which he has picked up himself or which have been imparted to him through the lesson or through another impetus: foreign experiences cloaked in a foreign language presenting the same, similar, or different concepts to his own. In this connection, pupil-orientation means ensuring that there is understanding between the pupil's own culture and the alien culture; in other words, inter-cultural learning.

The English-speaking world uses the term 'negotiation' here —

negotiation in its widest sense. Negotiation calls for communicative expression and communication, speech and writing, since understanding will only come about once there has been inter-cultural exchange via discourse.

Pupil-orientated foreign language teaching: practical consequences

How can such high demands be realised? Before quoting some practical examples, I shall list the features of pupil-orientated foreign language teaching which we have become acquainted with so far:

- Process-orientation ('negotiation').
- Building the lesson around the pupil's own knowledge and experiences.
- Creating possibilities for applying the language in realistic (or real) situations inside and outside the classroom. The role of the teacher is to ensure that the promise of actually applying the foreign language is kept.
- Ensuring that the pupils feel they can solve language tasks competently (The 'I have achieved something' effect).
- Enabling the pupils to become committed so that they participate fully (and can identify with the tasks). (This will only be possible if the teacher himself participates fully)
- Ensuring that the pupils receive direct feedback when they use the language experimentally. (Communication is more or less successful).
- Ensuring that the pupils have the opportunity to test their linguistic abilities (in contrast to the drill), so that they can relate to the real situation.

Real language tasks

Together with the group of Dutch and German teachers of English who have held workshop seminars over several years, we have drawn up a list of real and realistic foreign language tasks. These can be added to as you wish:

- Draw up a magazine/illustrated report/picture collage, etc. on your own town, region, local events, etc.
- Go into the local tourist office and offer your language services.
- Prepare a plan/tour of your own town (the sights), which foreign visitors can use or which can be sent abroad.
- Make a video of your own school and send it abroad to an exchange school (or a slide show with captions, pamphlets, inflight magazine).
- Make a documentary on a visit abroad (with the aid of a diary).
- Prepare a puppet (or muppet) show.
- Make short sketches (in the style of the street theatre).

- Prepare a short radio play.
- Do a survey on a topic related to your own area (e.g. the local disco, a bar).
- Cook a foreign dish, using a recipe, and eat it together.

It is important, too, that the results of the work be used; here are some clues as to how they can be used:

- sending them abroad;
- printing them in a foreign school newspaper;
- in the language club of one's own school;
- for practical use (e.g. town map or tour);
- at classroom festivals.

We thought of places and occasions (in Holland and West Germany) where the foreign language (English) can be used for concrete tasks:

- international airports;
- travelling pop groups;
- a forces station;
- radio station;
- bilingual family;
- large railway station;
- international congress or exhibition;
- embassy or consulate;
- foreign religious institutions (e.g. Church of England in Holland);
- places where foreigners meet (e.g. ticket office);
- international sporting events;
- 'twinning' events;
- international hotels;
- international training institutes;
- youth hostels;
- camping sites;
- a large travel agency;
- banks;
- car rental
- multinational companies;
- international relief organisations.

The intention behind all these is to make use of the foreign language, be it through comprehension or communication, to see whether one can establish a link with the pupils' own experiences and knowledge. Apart from the actual language-linguistic tasks, they also require the attitude and conduct which signify intercultural teaching.

Foreign language tasks abroad are not excluded but these are increasingly being prepared for by use of the foreign language in one's own country. Experiences by the pupil should be constantly related back to those of the foreigner.

The 'Airport' project as an application

What concrete language tasks can German pupils aged 11-12 years old be set in English in their own country? Their experiences of life are still developing; their knowledge of English is still very slight.

This gave no cause for frustration to Wolfgang Thiel and Michael Legutke from the Federal Association for English at Comprehensive Schools (Bundesarbeitsgemeinschaft Englisch an Gesamtschulen). The large international airport at Frankfurt, where it is possible to meet and use the language every day, was just on the doorstep. Pupils of this age are, moreover, extremely fascinated with the world of aviation, as indeed are many grown-ups.

A comprehensive plan was therefore drawn up for the pupils to visit the airport, and interviews were prepared: they had to collect material relating to the airport (pamphlets, flight timetables, stickers, etc; interviews with passengers, pilots, air-stewardesses, etc.); information about flights to New York, London, etc; collect and de-code sign-language. The most substantial preparatory work proved to be the preparation of interviews, from a linguistic as well as a technical viewpoint (using a tape-recorder). In the classes leading up to the trip interviews were simulated, question cards written and check lists drawn up. The highlight of the whole project was the trip to the airport. One pupil did not sleep at all the previous night because he was terrified he would be unable to speak to anyone.

The pupils went in search of their interviewees armed with polaroid camera, cassette recorders, pens and paper, protocol lists and cue cards. One group of girls eventually managed to record the singer of a pop group on tape (and video camera):

    Petra: Why are you in Germany?
    Star: I sing. I'm with a group called the Hornettes. I'm in show-business.
    Petra: And where in Germany do you sing?
    Star: All over, everywhere.
    Stella: And what are your hobbies?
    Star: I've got a pet snake and I like to ride.
                (pause)
    Jessica: Have you got horses?
    Star: No ...

The girls obviously did not understand what a 'pet snake' was but Jessica kept the interview going by asking about horses. When listening back to the interview on tape (still at the airport) the pupils squatted or lay on the floor, their heads close together, desperately trying to hear what they had said in the heat of the moment and realising there were some questions they had asked too mechanically, were unsure of, or to which they had demanded no explanation.

The class returned home armed with lots of information. Their results were examined and processed in the follow-up period in project books, notice boards, illustrated reports. Each group drew up a comprehensive report about the best interview they had done and the notice boards, project books, etc were displayed at the school parents' evening.

The project described was filmed by the West German Broadcasting Company (Cologne) and edited to produce a 30- minute video documentary. This can be obtained from the Institute for Scientific and Educational Material (Institut für Film und Bild in Wissenschaft und Unterricht, FWU, Grünwald, München). The video film gives a more vivid and comprehensive impression than this written report will allow. In addition, the authors have given a detailed account of the project both in German and in English. It is a perfect example to use for teacher training.

Conclusion

Foreign language classes cannot always be held at airports. Language teaching cannot always take place outside the classroom. There are times when formal language training is more important. Nevertheless, it remains an essential task of foreign language teaching to include references to real life and concrete examples of how language can be used. Spatial and idealistic differences must be bridged so that the prerequisites can be created for trust, from which linguistic competence grows.

References

BAG, 1978. Bundesarbeitsgemeinschaft Englisch an Gesamtschulen: Kommunikativer Englischunterricht, Prinzipien und Übungstypologie. München: Langenscheidt-Longman (1978).
COUNCIL OF EUROPE (ed). Modern languages 1971-1981. Strasbourg (1982).
EDELHOFF, Christoph. Real language activities and projects, example Airport. Sproglaereren, Journal of the Association of Language Teachers in Denmark, no.1, Feb 1983, p 16-31.
EDELHOFF, Christoph. Internationalität und interkulturelle Ziele des Fremdsprachenunterrichts in Europa, Verstehen und Verständigung. In Lothar Arabin, Volker Kilian (Hrsg). Deutsch in der Weiterbildung, orientieren - verstehen - verständigen. München: Max Hueber Verlag, p 75ff (1983).
Der Hessische Kultusminister (Hrsg), Rahmenrichtlinien Neue Sprachen Sekundarstufe I. Frankfurt, Wiesbaden: Verlag Diesterweg (1980).

HOLEC, Henri, 1979. Autonomy and foreign language learning. Strasbourg: Council of Europe (1980).
LEGUTKE, Michael. Project Airport, Part 1. Modern English Teacher, vol 11, no. 4, 1984, p 10-14; Part 2. Modern English Teacher, vol 12, no. 1, 1984, p 28-31.
LEGUTKE, Michael and Wolfgang Thiel. 'Airport', Unterrichtsdokumentation, Film des Westdeutschen Rundfunks Köln (30 Minuten) (1982). Grünwald: Institut für Film und Bild in Wissenschaft und Unterricht (FWU), (1984).
LEGUTKE, Michael and Wolfgang Thiel. 'Airport', Bericht über ein Projekt im Englischunterricht in Klasse 6. Westermann's Pädagogische Beiträge, 34, vol 7/1982, p 288-99.
LEGUTKE, Michael, Wolfgang Thiel. 'Airport', ein Projekt für den Englischunterricht in der Jahrgangsstufe 6. Hessisches Institut für Bildungsplanung und Schulentwicklung, Materialien zum Unterricht, Sekundarstufe I, Heft 40, Neue Sprachen - Englisch Heft 3. Frankfurt, Wiesbaden: Verlag Diesterweg (1983).

Negotiating language in foreign language classrooms

Claus Faerch
University of Copenhagen, Denmark

1. Introduction

Foreign language teaching has turned **communicative**. There is **interaction** between learners, between learners and computers, between computers and video machines. **Negotiation** takes place in the classroom between teachers and learners and among the learners themselves. These terms, which have become very popular, represent an important new orientation likely to exert a lasting influence on the way foreign languages are taught.

The three terms are all process terms: **communicate, interact, negotiate**. Process-orientation is possibly the one aspect to be singled out as most characteristic of foreign language teaching today. The terms also imply **agents** – subjects who act. Unfortunately, this is not always taken into consideration by researchers, methodologists, materials designers, etc, even if the significance of process is recognised. As I shall demonstrate, it is possible to deal with processes – both from a research and a pedagogical point of view – without paying any attention to the fact that processes are often, though not always, initiated by individuals in order to reach certain goals, that processes are aimed at individuals who through their reactions shape the further direction of the process. The concept of negotiation better than any other concept captures this subjective aspect of the learning-teaching process.

I use the term 'negotiation' in its everyday sense, referring to a process in which two or more individuals attempt to come to an agreement. To anyone primarily involved in practical foreign language teaching, the notion of 'negotiating learning' immediately evokes an association of two parties, the teacher and his or her students. I shall address this aspect of 'negotiating learning' in section 2. But there is also a different aspect of the negotiating process, viz. the negotiation between those who investigate foreign language learning – language learning researchers, and those actively involved in the process itself – language teachers and language learners. I would like to suggest that the two types of negotiation bear a good deal of resemblance to each other, and that a discussion of the researcher – teacher type of negotiation may shed an interesting light on the negotiation between teachers and learners. This is the topic of sections 3 and 4.

2. Negotiating learning - teachers and learners

Teachers and learners interact in a process of negotiation, the visible outcome of which is classroom discourse. The task of the language learning researcher is to get beyond the surface level of observable classroom phenomena in order to establish the nature of the language learning processes, the invisible outcome of the negotiation process. One trend in language learning research has been to describe the surface level of classroom discourse according to previously established systems of description, such as systems based on Sinclair and Coulthard (1975). One rationale behind this approach is that the structural properties of discourse will have some conditioning effect on learning processes. Consequently, by detecting structural patterns one obtains information, albeit indirectly, about language learning processes.

In the following, I shall explore this assumption in an exemplary manner, choosing as an example the area of repair work. This subfield within discourse analysis has been fairly well cultivated: native language discourse, in the pioneering study of Schegloff, Jefferson and Sacks (1977); interactions involving non-native speakers, in studies by Gaskill (1980), Schwarz (1980), Lauerbach (1982) and Faerch and Kasper (1982); and finally foreign language classroom discourse, in contributions by Rehbein (1984), Kasper (in press) and Madsen and Petersen (1983).

As a point of departure, let us look at a fragment of a transcript from an English lesson in the German Federal Republic:

(1) (1) T: Hm. Had you a nice/did you have a nice day yesterday?
    (2) Ll: (laughter)
    (3) Ll: Haven't
    (4) L2: Didn't
    (5) L3: Didn't
    (6) T: Judith!
    (7) Lj: Yes, I have
    (8) T: Did you have?
    (9) Lj: Yes, I do.
    (10) T: No!
    (11) Lj: I did.
    (12) T: No!
    (13) Lj: I had
    (14) Lx: No, I didn't?
    (15) T: Yes. (laughter)
    (16) Lj: Yes, I had!
    (17) T: Yes. Okay.
    (Rehbein, 1984, 26; L = learner, T = teacher)

Between the teacher's initial and final turns we find a sequence in which he corrects Judith's contribution. This sequence begins with turn number (7) and is only completed with turn number (17). We can identify the following characteristic elements of the correction sequence:

> a **trouble source:** what needs to be corrected (turn number (7))
> a **repair initiator:** a signal to the effect that a trouble source is acknowledged and the repair is needed (turn number (8))
> a number of attempted **repairs:** (turns (9), (11), (13), (14), (16))
> a **confirmation:** (turn number (17))

These four elements provide the basis for establishing the categorisation framework illustrated by Figure 1 (cf Rehbein 1984, Kasper in press).

Type number	Trouble source	Initiation	Correction	Confirmation
1	L	L	L	T
2	L	T	L	T
3	L	L	T	
4	L	T	T	
5	T	L	L	T
6	T	T	L	T
7	T	L	T	
8	T	T	T	

Fig. 1: Repair in foreign language classrooms

Example (1) can be categorised as belonging to repair type (2): the trouble source is in the learner's turn, the teacher initiates a repair sequence, the learner - together with other learners - suggests repairs, and finally the teacher provides feedback, confirming the repair.

A trouble source need not be something which needs correction because it is considered wrong, it may also be something which, in a given situation, turns out not to work and thus needs to be improved upon. This is often the case when the teacher is responsible for a trouble source. Although trouble sources located in the teacher's turns may exemplify corrections in the narrow sense of the term, they are more likely to be examples of 'repair work' in general. The following is a typical instance of a teacher self-repairing, i.e. using category number (8):

(2) T: they are all sort of projections from his mind or his brain -

> fantasy is perhaps – you can use this word fantasy – but remember <u>at det netop ikke betyder altsa det samme som det danske fantasi normalt ikke altsa</u> it is not the same as imagination all right but <u>et</u> ... ('remember that it does not mean the same as Danish 'fantasi' normally not') (Faerch, forthcoming)

Although such instances of repair work are interesting from the point of view of reception (cf. the discussion of this in Faerch and Kasper, in press a), I shall leave them out of consideration in the following. Let us briefly consider examples of the remaining three categories of learner-caused repair:

(3) T: What happened a week later?
    Ll: (bidding)
    T: Ahmmm Petra!
    Lp: A week later Dan and, öh äh/ A week later Dan's wallet –
    T: was stolen!
    Lp: was stolen?
    T: Right.
    (Rehbein 1984, 10)

(4) L: eer, I think she is very – – <u>hvordan siger man popular</u> – ['pju:pulə] ('how do you say "popular"')
    T: – popular
    L: popular – because er – many boys want to marry her
    (Faerch, forthcoming)

(5) L: I prefer classical music and I prefer to listen to it myself, because my friends don't like this music ... mmm ... they prefer pop or jazz
    T: They prefer pop <u>to</u> jazz
    L: Pop to jazz ... but I think it's noisy
    (Grandcolas 1981)

In (3), the learner interrrupts his own speech and self-repairs from 'Dan and' to 'Dan's wallet (was stolen)'. The teacher provides affirmative feedback ('Right!'). This is an example of repair type number (1).

In (4) we have repair type number (3): the learner identifies a problem in his own turn and appeals to the teacher for assistance; the teacher provides the missing word and the learner completes the utterance he had already begun to produce.

Example (5) illustrates repair type number (4): the teacher identifies a problem in the learner's turn ('pop or jazz') and corrects it ('pop to jazz'). The learner repeats the teacher's correction.

I have deliberately restricted my comments to the type of descriptive statements that can be made by applying the discourse categorisation grid to verbal performance data. There is obviously a good deal more to be said about the five examples than that they represent different structural types. I shall explore this in a moment. But first let us consider what type of information we do obtain by classifying repairs into a number of structural categories.

It can be seen directly from Fig. 1 that **a repair sequence is always completed by the teacher**, either by providing the actual repair or by providing feedback on a learner's repair. We might now want to find out whether repair sequences affect the normal pattern of classroom discourse, as this has been established in several studies (see e.g. the description in Sinclair and Brazil 1982, 48ff). This pattern can be represented as in Figure 2.

T(initiate) ⟶ L(respond) ⟶ T(follow-up)

T(initiate) ⟵ ...

Fig. 2: Basic type of interaction in teacher-centred discourse

As an illustration, consider the following example:

T: What is the capital ⟶ L: Oslo ⟶ T: No, not really of Finland?

T: Where is Oslo? ⟵

The three-phase structure provides some explanation for the fact that teachers, in teacher-centred phases of classroom discourse, typically speak more than two thirds of the time. As observed by Sinclair and Brazil (1982, 58): 'The teacher speaks most of the time. Estimates vary ... But the range of variation is between most of the time and all of the time.'

Let us now try to relate the eight repair types to this very simple basic structure of classroom discourse. The result is represented in Figure 3.

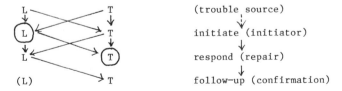

(trouble source)
↓
initiate (initiator)
↓
respond (repair)
↓
follow-up (confirmation)

Fig. 3: Repair types analysed in terms of discourse moves

There are precisely eight ways of getting from the top to the bottom of the network - representing the eight repair types. The discourse units of Initiate, Respond and Follow-up thus suffice for the description of repair types. There is a difference, however, in terms of who performs the moves: we find both the learner initiating and the teacher responding (encircled in Fig.3).

It would be interesting to know whether any of the eight repair types are more frequent than others in classroom discourse; or hether repair work in non-educational types of communication resembles what we have here. Let me just quote one investigation as an exemplification of the types of results we might obtain.

Kasper (in press) analysed repair sequences in two phases of an English lesson: a translation-type of exercise, the teacher reading aloud Danish sentences one at a time and the learners translating; and a teacher-steered discussion of a literary text. A clear difference could be established between the two phases in terms of preferences for repair types. In the translation phase, most repair sequences were initiated by the teacher and completed by the learners, i.e. they followed the typical structure of classroom discourse. In the discussion phase, on the other hand, there was a marked preference for self-initiated and self-completed repair types, both when the trouble source was located in the teacher's and in a learner's turn. This preference for self-repair corresponds to what has been found in analyses of native speaker discourse in non-educational situations, where for reasons of face-saving the person who is responsible for a trouble source is generally given the opportunity to initiate - and certainly to complete - the repair himself.

Kasper's investigation illustrates the type of information one may obtain from a purely structural analysis of discourse: it has often been demonstrated that teacher-centred discourse differs structurally from symmetric, non-educational native speaker discourse. But a careful analysis of repair types reveals that there are different discourse types represented within the classroom: 'language-centred' and 'content-centred' phases exhibit different structural properties in terms of repair types, content- centred phases resembling non-educational discourse most.

This is as far as we get with a purely structural analysis. We now have to take into consideration that discourse processes are brought about by individuals in order to reach certain goals. Unless we try to get below the surface of discourse we are unlikely to obtain really significant information. This distinction - between discourse as 'product' and discourse as 'process' - is discussed in Brown and Yule (1983, 23ff), who characterise the 'discourse-as-process' approach in the following way:

> We shall consider words, phrases and sentences which appear in

the textual record of a discourse to be evidence of an attempt by a producer (speaker/writer) to communicate his message to a recipient (hearer/reader). We shall be particularly interested in discussing how a recipient might come to comprehend the producer's intended message on a particular occasion, and how the requirements of the particular recipient(s), in definable circumstances, influence the organisation of the producer's discourse.

It is only fair to point out that none of the researchers analysing repairs is satisfied with purely structural analysis, describing what can be observed on the surface. They all supplement with interpretations of the data. Let us therefore return to our examples of repair work and attempt to interpret these.

EXAMPLE 1:
The learner has a double problem: the selection of the right auxiliary verb and the selection of the right tense. The auxiliary problem seems to be imposed by the teacher's self-repair: '...had you a nice - did you have a nice'. When the teacher initiates the repair, he does so without indicating to the learner whether the error has to do with the selection of the verb or the tense. The learner then tries out a number of hypotheses:

1. AUX have ⟶ do (do)
2. tense present ⟶ past (did)
3. AUX do ⟶ have + tense past (had)

The interpretation of the data brings to light an entirely different type of process, occurring below the surface: the teacher and the learner are negotiating learning by means of a guessing game: the learner's goal is to find the right wording of her - perfectly intelligible - reply to the teacher's initial question. She does so by trying out a number of hypotheses and by monitoring the reaction of the teacher - and possibly that of her fellow learners as well. The resulting discourse is markedly different from non-educational discourse: the overall purpose is not for the learner to express whether or not she had a nice day yesterday but whether or not to use **do** or **have** in the present or in the past tense. Unless we realise that this is the superordinate objective of the communicative interaction we are unlikely to interpret it in a meaningful way.

EXAMPLE 2:
What is most remarkable about this example of a teacher self-repairing is the surprising amount of code-shifting between English and Danish that takes place. We might formulate two hypotheses as to the cause of this: (1) the teacher code-switches because of the Danish word he discusses; (2) the teacher's code-switching reflects a shift from one level of discourse, where the literary content is

in focus, to a different level of talking about language. If one looks at more examples from the lesson from which (2) is taken one finds a good deal of evidence for the last-mentioned hypothesis. This is something that I shall return to.

EXAMPLE 3:
In this example, Petra self-repairs from 'Dan and' to 'Dan's wallet'. On the basis of the performance data alone, it is difficult to decide what she was originally going to say, and why she decided to change her plan. One possibility is that she had originally planned to say more than 'A week later Dan's wallet was stolen' but decides to reduce on the content (cf. the discussion of 'functional reduction' in Faerch and Kasper 1983, 43ff). If so, she is herself responsible for bringing about the repair. But it may also be a frown from the teacher or an elbow from her fellow student that brings about the repair.

EXAMPLE 4:
This example resembles example 2: the learner code-shifts to Danish as he starts talking **about** the language by appealing to the teacher.

EXAMPLE 5:
This is the most difficult example to interpret on the basis of the available evidence. The learner is fairly proficient, and it seems unlikely that she should confuse 'prefer pop **or** jazz' with 'prefer pop **to** jazz'. The learner, however, accepts the teacher's repair. A tentative interpretation could be as follows: The teacher personally distinguishes categorically between pop and jazz. Also, she knows that the idiomatic expression 'prefer something to something else' often causes difficulty. When the learner produces her initial turn, the teacher does not really take in what the learner is trying to say but activates her own relevant frames, triggered by the two above-mentioned factors, and initiates the repair. The learner may or may not grasp the significance of the change in content imposed by the teacher's repair; if she does, she decides to ignore the content and accept the repair as a formally well-structured phrase. According to this interpretation, there are various important factors involved in the negotiation process below the surface: the teacher's value system, assigning relevance to learner contributions without necessarily adjusting for learners' - possibly differing - value systems; the teacher's knowledge of what is normally a learning problem; and finally the learner's acceptance of the fact that form is more important than content.

These interpretations are all tentative and inconclusive. To obtain more final results, it would be necessary to supplement performance analysis with data of an entirely different type: interpretations made by the very teachers and learners who participated in the interaction. Tentative and inconclusive, however, does not mean the

same as unprincipled. Let me finish off this section by describing
the underlying assumptions about classroom discourse on which I have
based my interpretations. This will bring the notion of negotiating
learning to the fore.

Analyses of discourse into categories like Initiate - Respond -
Follow-up reflect the dimension of time. There is no difference in
principle between an analysis of this type and a syntactic analysis
of a sentence into constituents, e.g. NP(1) - V - NP(2) - AVP: just
like NP(1) precedes the verb, which again precedes NP(2) and AVP,
Initiate precedes Respond and Follow-up.

There is, however, a different dimension of classroom discourse: the
functional level at which discourse takes place, reflecting differences in terms of what the individuals have in focus and what they
want to achieve. If we consider example (1) again, we could say that
the teacher's initial question and the learner's initial reply
operate at the level of 'content': we assume that the teacher is
referring to the learner's experiences outside school, to something
he does not know about already. The teacher's question could therefore be interpreted as a genuine question. As soon as the teacher
rejects the learner's reply, however, there is a change of level to
the 'meta-level': the teacher's No no longer refers to the learner's
experiences but to the way the learner expressed these, there is now
a focus on the linguistic code. The relationship between the dimension of discourse units and that of levels can be represented as in
Figure 4.

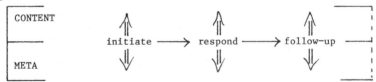

Fig. 4: Dimension of time and dimension of level

The notion of 'level' in Fig. 4 corresponds to the notion of 'plane'
in Sinclair and Brazil 1982, 32ff, of which Sinclair and Brazil
mention four types: content, organisation, discipline and discourse.
I have left out of consideration the three last-mentioned types.
Instead, content has been divided into content in a narrow sense of
the word, incorporating reference to the outside world, to teachers'
and learners' experiences, to studied texts, etc; and the communicative content, the 'meta content', of learning a foreign language,
i.e. learning **about** a language and learning **about** language
learning.

There is probably one very good reason for Sinclair and Brazil not
to mention the meta level as a distinct plane level: their description is not specifically geared towards foreign language classrooms

but towards teaching in general. Unfortunately, this results in their ignoring what in my opinion is precisely what makes foreign language teaching look different from most other types of teaching: that there is a constant change between content and meta level. It is this change, rather than any differences in terms of discourse categories along the time dimension, that gives to foreign language teaching its most distinctive flavour.

I would like to claim that the most important negotiation processes in terms of foreign language learning take place along the meta-content level, rather than along the surface structure dimension of discourse units. The teacher and the learners do not need to negotiate very much along the surface structure dimension as the rules of interaction are by and large very clear and stable. But there is a need for a constant negotiation between content and meta levels, and this negotiation has direct implications for foreign language learning.

Examples (1) - (5) also provide information about the way teacher and learners negotiate at which level interaction takes place. Examples (1) and (5) supplement each other: in (1), there is an obvious change from content to meta level, although there is no overt verbal indication of such a change. In (5), we can only assume that the learner's acceptance of the teacher's - mistaken - correction represents a similar change. Again, the change takes place with no overt verbal indication.

Examples (2) and (4) illustrate another important aspect of level shifts: that very often, a change from content to meta level is accompanied by a shift from the foreign to the native language. Although this is undoubtedly a culture-specific phenomenon, it is noticeable that one can find mention of it in descriptions of different teaching situations: Kasper 1981, 432: Sinclair and Brazil 1982, 23. In Denmark, such shifts seem to be the rule rather than the opposite. If we now relate the combination of code-shifting to the native language and a shift from content to meta level to the fact that a similar code-switching often takes place when language is used for classroom management purposes, we may get closer to an explanation of the phenomenon: when communication becomes real, serious, authentic, when what matters is how to say something in the foreign language or what to prepare for next lesson, then the native language may be preferred. When communication serves the purpose of make-believe, pretending to talk about content when the primary reason for doing so is to learn the foreign language, then the foreign language can be used without difficulty. To put it quite crudely: using the foreign language implies that communication is in fact inauthentic.

It might be objected that I have turned 'authenticity' upside down, compared to the way we normally talk about it in the foreign language classroom: that communication is **maximally** authentic when its use corresponds precisely to the way communication takes place outside the classroom. What is overlooked, unfortunately, is the fact that the social reality of the classroom differs in **significant** respects from the social reality - or realities - of non-classroom discourse: the only raison d'être for the foreign language classroom is that it is a place for learning a foreign language - in the broad sense of the term, including learning about culture and society. As seen from this point of view, authentic foreign language classroom communication takes place when there is a focus on learning the language - and not on 'how did you spend your last weekend?'.

Let me summarise some of the points I have been trying to make in this section.

1. Classroom discourse can be viewed as a process, and this process can be analysed on the basis of its surface structure phenomena (e.g. repair types; discourse units).

2. Such analysis is unlikely to capture the underlying process of language learning. In order to fully understand what goes on, we need to consider the objectives pursued by teacher and learners as well as the value systems and expectancy patterns that determine their contribution to the discourse (e.g. correction of form, not content).

3. The temporal dimension of discourse units provides the framework for a different dimension to operate: that of shifts between content and meta level. The negotiation of learning takes place along this dimension, rather than along the sequential dimension of discourse units.

4. Interaction at the meta level represents authentic foreign language classroom communication, and is often accompanied by code-switching to the native language.

5. Shifts between content and meta level typically take place without any overt verbal indication - yet teacher and learners alike in most cases seem to know which level they operate on at a given time.

3. Negotiating learning - teachers and researchers

Language learning researchers depend on foreign language teachers in a number of ways. First, without getting access to teaching situations it is limited what the language learning researcher can achieve. The rather meagre results obtained by contrastive linguistics is indicative of this - in this case self-imposed - limitation, as is borne out by the following quotation from Corder (1967):

> Teachers have not always been very impressed by this contribu-

tion from the linguist for the reason that their practical experience has usually already shown them where these difficulties lie...

Second, as could be seen from the interpretation of several examples in section 2, the language learning researcher often needs to rely on the teacher, as well as on the learners, to make sense of the recorded data. As expressed by Breen (in press): 'A researcher's interpretation of the "text" of classroom discourse has to be derived through the participants' interpretations of that discourse'. A clear indication of this is the extended use of introspective techniques in current research projects, not least in Europe (see e.g. the presentation of West German projects contained in Bausch, Christ, Hüllen and Krumm 1984; further the contributions to Faerch and Kasper in preparation). Thirdly, when language learning researchers have obtained their final results, these have to be converted into pedagogic practice. To the extent this is assumed to fall within the researchers' domain, they would be at a loss if the process were to be conducted without the co-operation of experienced teachers.

The asymmetric dependency relationship between researcher and teacher may to some extent be counterbalanced by a difference in status: being a researcher - often associated with having a university post - is generally considered more prestigious than being a foreign language teacher. The net result of these differences in dependency and status may be **polite interaction without negotiation**. On the one hand, teachers accept the researchers' expertise and willingly - though passively - receive what is being passed on to them. On the other hand, teachers feel that what the researchers talk about is only of marginal interest, that the analyses are lacking in understanding of several relevant factors, and that the researchers are hopelessly unable to demonstrate what practical teaching implications their research could have.

One reason for this sad state of affairs is the way some researchers conduct research into foreign language learning. It is perhaps not surprising that **if** the foreign language classroom is primarily seen as a treasure chest containing precious data for the researcher to describe, then it is rather difficult to imagine that the results from this research will lead to anything but polite interaction without negotiation. If the process of foreign language teaching and learning is only conceived of as an object, to be described in terms of its surface structure characteristics, then it may be more than difficult for teachers and learners to find themselves in the description as individuals who act in a goal-oriented way, rather than as producers of data for consumption by researchers.

Fortunately, many language learning researchers would be unhappy with the situation as I have just described it. They like to believe that their research does not serve theoretical objectives only but that results have implications for the way languages are taught. As a result, these researchers have either adopted quite different research paradigms, borrowed from sociology and cultural anthropology, or at least modified traditional descriptive methods in a significant way. Let me outline two important trends in language learning research which transcend traditional research methods.

A radical solution is to adopt participant observation, coupled with action research. With **participant observation** (see e.g. Ackroyd and Hughes 1981:98ff), the researcher – 'the observer' – adopts a role within the social situation of investigation. When the method is adhered to rigidly, the researcher's role has to be 'natural' relative to the situation. Thus a sociologist interested in describing the workings of a youth gang would have to join the group as a full-fledged member and conceal his or her research purpose, as did Thrasher in one of the first sociological studies to make use of participant observation in the early 1920's (Thrasher 1963, quoted from Ackroyd and Hughes 1981:102). Relative to the foreign language classroom, two roles seem particularly realistic: the role of the teacher and the role of the learner. Both roles have been adopted in language learning research. In a number of diary studies (see e.g. Bailey and Ochsner 1983), researchers have reported their experience from the viewpoint of the foreign language learner, e.g. after having enrolled in a Spanish evening class in California. The other possibility, the merging of the role of researcher and the role of teacher, is more difficult to bring about. What usually happens is that teachers become researchers, by engaging in pedagogic projects. Those who have experienced this can testify that the method of participant observation is not without problems: one and the same person has to perform a certain social role like being a teacher **simultaneously** with observing this and taking mental notes, to be written down at some later time.

There is no direct connection between the method of participant observation and doing **action research** (for the latter, see e.g. Friedrichs 1982:370ff), although the two tend to go together. For the action researcher, there is a focus on a problem to be solved rather than an object to be described. Thus an action researcher interested in the social conditions of immigrant workers will typically focus on how to improve their situation and try to do so. In this way, the distinction between social researcher and social worker becomes blurred. This is precisely how participant observation and action research come together: in order to secure change the action researcher often has to join the situation, rather than stand outside it.

Transferred to language learning research, this means that the distinction between researcher and teacher is reduced – the researcher becomes associated with the teaching role or the teacher becomes researcher. Bolte and Herrlitz (in press) advocate a research process which is close to this. The process consists of two components, **reconstructing** the underlying learning and communication processes, with a view to making the learners and teacher conscious about these, and an **intervention** process in which change is brought about in the classroom. The research process is thus closely interwoven with the teaching process itself. As a result, it makes little sense to talk about an object of investigation, as is the case with more traditional research paradigms – focus is on the process itself, on creating a better learning environment for the learners. Consequently, results obtained from participant observation and action research differ from results obtained by other methods of investigation. Action researchers will describe how they influenced the learning and teaching process and possibly assess the outcome of this, whereas they will have little to say in terms of explanation. Action research is a powerful way of securing change, but neither action research nor participant observation is ideal for obtaining detailed information about the way underlying factors interact to condition the learning process (see also Faerch and Kasper in press b).

A less radical solution is to maintain the distinctive roles of teacher and researcher, but secure a maximum of negotiation between the two all the way through the research process, from the initial formulation of research questions to the final implementation of results. Such **negotiated research** could have the following steps:

(1) there are two parties involved, the researcher and the teacher, each serving a distinctive role;

(2) the two parties negotiate the content of the investigation, establishing goals to be reached;

(3) the two parties negotiate the methods to be used in order to reach these goals;

(4) both the teacher and the learners are drawn upon for the interpretation of the data;

(5) results are discussed with the teacher and the learners and put into proper perspective by relating them to relevant factors;

(6) pedagogical implications are negotiated and possibly tried out by the teacher, the researcher functioning as consultant and/or evaluator.

In this type of research, the researcher is either visibly or invisibly present in the classroom. This presence will have some effect on the way teaching and learning are conducted, and hence reduce the validity of the data (cf the 'observer's paradox' in sociological research). The effect may be reduced in various ways but can hardly be done away with entirely. The researcher therefore needs to try to control this effect, for instance by taking the teacher's and the learners' assessments of how the researcher's presence affected the situation into consideration when analysing the data.

What, then, are the advantages of keeping the role of teacher and the role of researcher separate? Let me finish off this section by enumerating some of theses:

(1) the researcher can **compare different learning and teaching situations**, something which most teachers rarely do (in Denmark there is a joke that teachers generally know much more about their colleagues' private lives than about the way they teach!).

(2) the researcher has **distance** to what goes on, can make observations of both teacher and students. The teacher, having to teach, cannot possibly focus on observation at the same time.

(3) the researcher can make **systematic observations**, relative to explicitly formulated models of description.

(4) the researcher is not caught in the net of **tradition** to the same extent as teachers tend to be. Hence the researcher may observe phenomena which are unnoticed by the teacher and make novel interpretations.

Arguing for the need to keep the role of language learning researcher apart from the role of foreign language teacher does not imply that I would like to reserve the fields of language learning research for professional researchers: a lot of language learning research can be, and is in fact, done by teachers. What I do want to emphasise is that **when** teachers engage in research, they need to dissociate themselves from their role as teacher. This is difficult. Working in groups, making audio- or video-recordings of lessons, analysing each other's data (for an example, see Sauerberg 1985) are ways of creating the distance necessary if what teachers engage in is to be characterised as doing research - and not 'just' doing good teaching! But the line between the two is very difficult to draw and, actually, not always worth the drawing.

4. Negotiated research and negotiated learning

In both the classroom foreign language learning situation, discussed in section 2, and in the research situation discussed in section 3, we are dealing with processes at different levels. The **language learning researcher** needs to get below the surface of discourse processes to capture the much more significant learning processes. In order to achieve this, the researcher needs to negotiate with the teacher and the learners, to secure their full co-operation in the reconstruction of underlying processes. The **foreign language teacher** can manipulate surface structure discourse, e.g. by changing the typical teaching sequence of T(initiate) - L(respond) - T(follow-up) towards something closer to non-educational discourse. However, such changes are relatively uninteresting if they are not accompanied by changes in language learning processes. To explore this issue, teachers need to negotiate with their learners **about** foreign language learning. The resulting 'meta talk' - talking about learning and talking about communication - constitutes the authentic element in foreign language classrooms (cf Trévise 1979, Breen in press).

Let us now return to the description of negotiated research and apply the separate points to foreign language learning and teaching.

(1) **Keeping the role of teacher and that of learner distinct**
The ideal learning situation is **not** one of reducing the teacher to a communicator on a par with the learners. The teacher's primary function is to assist learners in learning, for instance by providing both positive and negative feedback. The 'art of teaching' is to do so without ruining the learners' willingness to learn.

(2) **Agreeing on learning objectives**
All too often, this is reduced to going through examination requirements - which (at least in Denmark) are usually notoriously vague. The learners should learn about communicative competence so that they have the conceptual framework for talking about learning objectives. Teaching materials are more than scarce in this area. Except for a couple of North American learner guides (Pimsleur 1980, Rubin 1982) I know of no descriptions of communicative competence in the foreign language which address themselves to learners.

(3) **Agreeing on methods**
This is usually reduced to discussions of what texts are to be read, or for and against group work. What I have in mind is a qualified discussion of means of reaching particular learning goals or, put differently, a discussion of learning strategies. Again, we have to point out that a prerequisite for this is that teacher and learners share some conceptual framework. Although research into learning strategies has expanded rapidly over the last few years (see Rubin 1984), we still don't have good descriptions which can be given to learners.

(4) **Interpreting the learning process**
Too often, this interpretation is done by the teacher exclusively,

as when he or she corrects learners' errors. It is essential that learners' interpretations are also drawn upon, as these may reveal that the learning process is in fact developing differently from what the teacher believes. As we know, errors are not just errors but the result of different hypotheses; sometimes these hypotheses are well worth supporting - even if they result in errors.

(5) **Interpreting results**
Usually, this is done by means of examination-type activities. Thus if the final examination contains a written translation task, written translation is likely to be used as one way of assessing the results of the learning process, even if translation is unlikely to be a good way of assessing whether the learning objectives have been reached. Instead, the teacher and the learners should adopt tests which relate directly to the learning process and to the defined objectives.

(6) **Negotiating implications**
In many respects, this is the most important aspect of the negotiation process. As foreign language learners need to go on learning languages after they have left school, we need to make sure that they are well equipped to do so. For this reason, the concept of **learner-driven learning** is essential: learners need to learn how to learn (cf Knapp's (1980) concept of 'Weiterlernen'). The notion of **strategic competence**, as regards both learning and communication, is crucial here.

To summarise, negotiating learning primarily takes place at the meta level of classroom discourse. Learners need to be made conscious of learning processes and of the way these interact with and depend upon communication processes. To achieve this, good descriptions for both teachers and learners are required. Unfortunately, such descriptions are scarce today. Producing such descriptions is one obvious task for language learning researchers and teachers to collaborate on. A rather different task is to investigate more ways for the negotiation of learning to take place within the totality of foreign language learning and teaching. This, too, calls for close co-operation between teachers, learners and researchers.

PART THREE: INNOVATION AND LANGUAGE TEACHING

In this section we have a plea for innovative methods by an American and an account of a long-running experiment in perhaps the most innovative of them all by a European.

A great deal has been heard in recent years about the so-called innovative or 'humanistic' methods of language teaching/learning - the Silent Way, Counseling Learning, Comprehension Training, Total Physical Response (TPR`, Suggestopaedia/Accelerated Learning, etc - each of which goes outside the conventional boundaries of linguistics to find its rationale. In most cases the impetus has come from North America, and in Europe the methods have frequently been greeted with sceptical suspicion as having connotations of gimmickry and commercialism. In particular, they tend also to demand rather more of the teacher than can, in a crowded classroom, be given. For this reason they may perhaps seem peripheral and irrelevant, requiring the establishing of special schools or institutes - or at least unconventional teaching spaces - rather than being absorbed into everyday teaching practices. Paradoxically, on the other hand, they may also be perceived simply as glossy packaging of familiar (and sometimes discarded) practices, with perhaps a subtle new twist. Recently, interest in these methods has been reawakened for many teachers by the appearance of a comprehensive theory of language acquisition, incorporating elements of several of them, exemplified in Krashen and Terrell's Natural Approach. It is therefore timely that a new look be cast at them, and this is the tenor of our first article.

Parish organises his discussion around a response to Jack Richards' plea for a rigorous examination of the claims made by protagonists of innovative methods, citing Michael Long on the difficulties of in fact conducting such research and his comments on the relative efficacy of exposure to language as against instruction, and making a 'timid plea' also for the place of intuition and common sense. While not disputing the possible usefulness of scientific research into innovative methods, Parish asks for a clear definition of the researchers' aims and assumptions, and for proper control. Citing Chomsky on the tenuous relationship of linguistic theory to classroom practice, he warns against the potential 'tyranny' of science. He disputes Richards' belittling of the founders of innovative methods as outsiders with 'personal philosophies' without demonstrable theoretical bases; offering generalisations about the way people learn may be a genuine service, and more is implicit than may be spelled out. It is not helpful to polarise teaching and research, leaving no room for pragmatism. Parish looks further afield for expert opinions and finds that others are less dismissive of the sensitivity of the teacher, which is not susceptible of scientific validation. The infinite variety of individual learners and language activities throws doubt on the validity of any one set of findings. In particular, the affective role of innovative methods is difficult to measure. Parish examines this topic in some detail and reviews relevant aspects of the methods in question. Teachers should not accept claims at face value, he concludes, but neither should they be warned off.

In the second article, Schiffler takes up a European stance and looks at the main European 'innovative' method, which originates from the perhaps unlikely setting of Bulgaria - Lozanov's <u>Suggestopaedia</u>. He poses the age-old question of seduction versus coercion: will a student learn more effectively via induced relaxation or as a response to gentle pressure? Suggestopaedia relies heavily on the relaxing effect of baroque music as conducive to rote learning of vocabulary, claiming miraculous results, which, however, have not been subjected to rigorous validation. Research experiments in Eastern Europe and Canada had serious procedural defects; Schiffler describes a more carefully controlled project being carried out with a group of native French teachers and some 72 students, mainly of science subjects. First results are encouraging but firm conclusions cannot yet be drawn.

The combined message of these two papers is an argument for a restrained but open-minded approach to new and - at first blush - perhaps outlandish ideas. Avoidance of the 'panacea fallacy' combined with flexibility and a willingness to experiment with new ideas, allowing a proper role, within current demands for scientific validation, for the teacher's own intutition and experience is the most potentially rewarding course.

In defense of innovative methods

Charles Parish
University of Illinois, USA

Introduction

There is a growing assumption that the theories and approaches of the Silent Way, Counseling-Learning, Total Physical Response (TPR), Comprehension Training and Suggestopaedia deal with trivial issues rather than with the primary substance of language teaching and learning. A denial not of seriousness but of validity is increasingly being heard. Richards has called for 'accountability and evaluation' through rigorous scientific experimentation, seen as the only alternative to the 'unsubstantiated and often irrelevant claims' of supporters of these approaches to syllabus and instruction. Scovel, Maley, Richards, and others express serious reservations about these methods and approaches, citing lack of universal applicability, of data-based evidence of gain, and of reasonableness. This paper discusses the question of experimentation with methods and the limitations of certain types of experiment; the importance of the uniform emphasis on the affective component; the issue of additudinal problems as separate from cognitive tactics in learning; and the accepted validity of the psycho- and sociolinguistic premises underlying these methods. The recognition of and compensation for the failure-orientation of language students may logically precede concern with the more currently respectable issues of curriculum development and language program design. The attention given to overcoming negative attitudes and experiences is seen as an essential, basic and non-trivial component of the entire language pedagogy gestalt, vital to the teaching profession.

The defense

Describing the language learner in a 'new perspective', Muneo Yoshikawa says in a recent article that 'without understanding this assumption of the holistic individual as essentially an active, voluntary, responsible, self-motivating, relational, autonomous, and free being, mere methodologies or techniques are reduced to artificial and mechanical schemes that fail to be meaningful' (1982: 394). There are many facets to Yoshikawa's holistic individual. One wonders whether science can deal with such a completed creature?

The fact is that science has lately become an important issue vis-à-vis the instructional theories and teaching approaches of the group of methodologies called Silent Way, Counseling Learning, Suggestopedia, Total Physical Response, and Comprehension Training. Increasingly, they are being interpreted as removed from the larger concerns of language teaching, as procedures dealing with trivial issues and not with the critical substance of language teaching and learning. Whatever their contributions, Professor Jack Richards says that they are founded on a 'weak empirical basis', and he has emphasised - in 'The secret life of methods', a plenary address at TESOL-Ontario, later published in the TESOL Quarterly - the need for 'accountability and evaluation' through rigorous scientific experimentation to replace what he sees as the 'unsubstantiated and often irrelevant claims of methods promoters' (1984:21).

I am sure that we can all agree with Richards about the desirability of both accountability and evaluation, but I do not believe that we can arrive at those ends via the route he recommends, primarily, a 'true experimental design'. He points out (relative to communicative language teaching) that as yet 'no studies have been undertaken ... to demonstrate that classrooms [using the target language] ... are indeed more conducive to successful language learning than classrooms in which the teacher dominates much of the teaching time or where the primary focus of activities is on more controlled and less creative uses of language' (1984:19). He admits but rejects the 'intuitive appeal of claims for the value of natural communication' because they are supported merely by 'anecdotal evidence'. Richards points to the recent articles of Michael Long as an example of 'carefully designed research', and we can easily agree. Long does us a great service in an article which points out the importance of classroom-centered research as the basis for analysis of 'process' and 'product' in ESL program evaluation, as well as in a second one, analysing the research done in assessing the role of language instruction in language achievement. In the first article, 'Process and product in ESL program evaluation', he goes into meticulous detail to demonstrate why 'an exclusively product-oriented evaluation ... is inadequate' for evaluating language programs: 'Product evaluations cannot distinguish among the many possible **explanations** for the results they obtain because they focus on the product of a program while ignoring the process by which that product came about' (1984:413). Later, however, in analysing **process**, he cites the work of Swaffar et al., who conclude in disappointment about their research: '... Defining methodologies in terms of the characteristic activities has led to distinctions which are ... not confirmable in classroom practice'. He says also that 'similarly depressing results have been obtained in two classroom-centered studies of the effects on classroom language use of ... (supposedly) different types of teaching materials' (1984:421). Thus, although the 'depressing' results are traced and attributed to insufficient understanding on the part of the personnel conducting the classes, the results are still depressing; that is, the studies do not provide the results hoped for.

In Long's second article, on the question of whether second-language instruction makes a difference in language learning, there is the same close analysis of the various studies he is reviewing; for example, the absence of 'inferential statistics' in the Hale and Budar study and other 'flaws' are sufficient 'to invalidate any claims they might wish to make' (1983:364). Their claim, incidentally, was that 'exposure only' (that is, 'immersion') students did better than 'ESL-instructed' students (1970). In Long's study, all the results that support the view that exposure is as powerful a factor as, if not more powerful than, instruction are subjected to a scrutiny and analysis which makes them seem vague and inconclusive. There is no suggestion here that Long distorts the results of those studies; apparently no study has been carefully enough designed so that the results **can** be conclusive. One may suggest, however, that possibly no study can ever be that carefully designed, if the subjects are humans behaving in individually normal ways. Overall, his attempt to analyse the relationship between and the priority of importance of instruction and exposure goes as far as it can. His criteria for admissibility of results are linked tightly to accuracy of design and of statistical procedure; he therefore finds various instances of unsupported or dubiously interpreted results. One cannot argue with the legitimacy of Long's approach or of any other similar approach without rejecting careful scientific scrutiny, but one can offer a timid plea that common sense occasionally justifies our intuitions: while the method of analysis may be reasonable, the data cannot be complete. The data are selected always on the basis of their being familiar, recognisable, quantifiable factors. But we know also - even if intuitively - that there are many other factors, in every situation that we analyse: vague, individual, random, capricious, and unstable. We cannot pretend they do not exist just because we cannot label, define, and hold them constant. One can react very positively to this reasonable, although not scientific, comment near the end of Long's meticulously-reasoned article: 'Put rather crudely, instruction is good for you, regardless of your 96 proficiency level, of the wider linguistic environment in which you receive it, and of the type of test you are going to perform on' (1983:379). His final paragraph expresses a pervasive and perhaps permanent problem: '... Even if, as I hope, the data on instruction have been correctly interpreted here, they're obviously not as clear-cut or as 'positive' as most TESOL professionals would like' (1983:380). And while he points out that 'there is obviously a genuine need for further research' on his basic point and related points, we may feel, without being anti-intellectual and anti-scientific, that this further research may never produce the kind of ideal findings that some continue to wish for. It is even possible that the need for those findings really is not so crucial.

If, however, one insists that such information is indeed crucial, that methods or sub-routines of methods must prove themselves empirically, then we can in turn insist that the following criteria be met:

1. A consensus must be reached on what the constructs or traits of competence of any kind are. They must be identified and described fully.

2. A consensus must be reached on what elicitation procedures are to be used to elicit test data.

3. Tests must be given to a randomly selected pool of subjects who have been taught ESL (in this case) by a specific method and to a similar pool who have been taught by other contrasting methods, the two pools being absolutely identical except for teaching method.

4. Data must be elicited from both groups in accordance with steps 1 and 2.

5. The data must be analysed by statistical procedures and these data must meet all the assumptions of the statistics.

Steps 1 and 2 - basic to a design - have not been done, and step 3 may be impossible. The studies which have been done cannot be truly compared because they have tested 'language-like' behavior only, and the designs of the experiments are so divergent that the crucial variables cannot be isolated. The findings of Long's studies cited above are at best working hypotheses for further **truly** experimental research. In short, one may contend that no-one has done any definitive empirical research yet on the efficiency of language-teaching methods.

Still, it is certainly true that studies like Long's, based on classroom-centered research, are miles ahead of the vast projects conducted fifteen and twenty years ago, projects like the Scherer-Wertheimer Colorado study, comparing the Grammar-Translation method and the ALM, and the Pennsylvania project supervised by Phillip Smith, comparing the ALM and the 'cognitive' approach. But all too often, in spite of attempts at careful research design and a principled attempt to control both process and product, the results are more often disappointing than cheering. Just as Long is justified in using factors he considers valid to cast doubt on the accuracy of the results of the relative importance of 'instruction' versus 'exposure to language', so may we insist that all the indefinite, vague, idiosyncratic, hitherto unquantified factors whose existence we know of although we cannot specify their precise shapes - all of these may invalidate the neat outcomes of 'careful experimental designs' which by choice or by default tend to ignore their existence. Long says 'the answer is not as convincing as we could wish', while Mark Clarke says 'the teacher should pay attention to what works and what doesn't', (implying that 'scientific studies' may or may not be valid for the teacher) (1982:448). So we are not being too audacious in saying that we believe an approach or method is productive if our intuitions and experiences as teachers tell us it is productive. (In fairness to Long, it should be pointed out that he does not claim success in using such verification procedures, only faith in the **eventual** success of such analysis.)

At this juncture, we may become aware of a genuine dilemma that our profession is faced with. In 1966 Chomsky offered the well-quoted opinion that 'there is very little in psychology or linguistics that [the language teacher] ... can accept on faith'. 'Teachers, in particular, have a responsibility to make sure that ideas and proposals are evaluated on their merits, and not passively accepted on grounds of authority, real or presumed. ... It is the language teacher himself who must validate or refute any specific proposal' (1966:45). In response to this, we have as a profession encouraged and succeeded in generating our own cadre of researchers and analysts in language-related issues, linguistic, psycholinguistic, and pedagogical. An excellent summary of this development is given by Krahnke and Christison in a recent TESOL Quarterly article (1983). Richards' contribution to methods analysis and Long's to classroom- centered research are both soundly motivated and they provide clear stimuli for continuing self-examination within our profession. This self-examination will eventually lead to believable and applicable findings, we can be certain, but it may be some time before results yield solid bases to which teachers can relate their overall approach, their specific methods, and precise techniques in language teaching. And there is a danger that 'scientific' positions insufficiently substantiated by our own researchers and analysts will be as tyrannical as those positions that Chomsky warned against.

A further aspect of this dilemma is the role and function of people like Charles Curran, Caleb Gattegno, Georgi Lozanov, James Asher, and Harris Winitz. All of them are outsiders to the language- teaching profession, but since they have all dedicated an important part of their professional lives to the concerns of teaching language, they ought certainly to be considered at least **honorary** members of our profession. Their attempts to extract valid psychological and procedural premises for the population of language learners surely entitles them to that. We might even feel gratitude that psychologists, educationists, and counselors have been willing to break into our relatively closed ranks. Richards contends that Asher, Curran, and Gattegno 'were prompted not by reactions to linguistic or sociolinguistic theories but rather by their personal philosophies of how an individual's learning potential can be maximised' (1984:11). Considering that at least Asher and Curran, as well as Lozanov, clearly enunciate what seem to be obvious sociolinguistic dicta about the handicap of the average language student - stress, insecurity, fear of involvement in class, and fear of failure - one may be puzzled by what a 'reaction to a sociolinguistic theory' has to be. Does the fact that they do not quote Douglas Brown or John Schumann - both of whom they all precede - invalidate their ideas? And are not Gattegno's and Lozanov's ideas about learning potential worth a somewhat more dignified label than 'personal philosophies'?

It may also be true that none of these innovators reacted to linguistic theory per se. So much the better, perhaps. A reliance upon linguistic theory is too easily equated with the unacceptable position that the linguist is the source of all useful information about what and how people learn. Counseling-Learning is flawed, Richards implies, because, like TPR, it is 'predicated upon assumptions about how people best learn rather than on theories about the nature of languages' (1984:12). Actually, this may be a rather good idea: there are certainly many people who think that theories about the nature of language are relatively useless in offering generalisations about how people learn, and too often these theories simply provoke sub-theories, variable and capricious, about the rule-content and the sequencing of rules in a pedagogical grammar.

The last point one might make about these 'outsiders' is in connection with Richard's observation that these innovative methods 'operate without an explicit syllabus model' (1984:11). A model is at least implicit in the 159-hour lessons that Asher offers in his Learning another language through actions (1982), in the 150 half-hour lessons of Gattegno for his English-through-videotape series, in the 120-hour course with dialogues in Suggestopedia (described in Bancroft, 1975), and in the four-book series called the Learnables for Harris Winitz's Comprehension Training (1981). Even in Counseling-Learning, with its student-generated dialogues, the moderately skilled counselor-teacher can easily organise those materials into a grammar-plus-practice-plus-activity text - not a pre-shaped syllabus, admittedly, but still a syllabus in an important intrinsic sense.

A discussion of syllabus and text calls to mind Peter Strevens' idealist view: 'The very best teachers rely rather little upon materials prepared by other people, often making their own improvements or replacements and using the prescribed textbooks only as a general guide. The poorest teachers, on the other hand, rely totally on the teaching materials and are only as effective as the textbooks permit them to be' (1977:31).

Another part of the dilemma mentioned earlier is the polarity of the scientist-methodologist and the classroom teacher. On the one hand we have Richards' statement of the maximum obligation of the supporter of a method - 'Once an instructional theory takes the form of a method, with theoretical bases in language and learning theory and operationalised practices in syllabus design and teaching procedures, claims made at each level of method organisation must be regarded as hypotheses awaiting verification or falsification' (1984:20) - on the other hand we have a less stringent, more moderate view like that expressed by Mark Clarke, who after warning us about bandwagons and the 'gurus who come and ago', concludes that 'as ESL teachers, as professionals, we should look to our own experiences in the classroom and measure our own successes and failures for evidence of what works and [what] doesn't work' (1982:- 447-448). From this one concludes that Clarke would accept ideas- that-work, regardless of whether they come from gurus or from eminent and established members within the profession.

Do others believe that we can verify or falsify the claims of new methods as rigorously as Richards says we must do? Here are comments by other members of our profession on that topic. Alan Maley, in his witty and incisive paper at the Honolulu TESOL, '"I got religion!": evangelism in TEFL', says (specifically about Silent Way, Counseling-Learning and Suggestopedia, but also about teaching methods and approaches generally), 'Like any teaching/learning theory, they are not open to the principle of verification because the number of variables is too large to be held constant. Likewise they are not open to ... [Popper's] criterion of falsifiability since they are not framed in such a way as to be tested. They are, scientifically speaking, neither true nor false, since no [truly] adequate tests can be performed upon them' (1983:81). In spite of his distrust of slogans and aphorisms about the sensitivity and delicacy of the language learner, Maley doesn't believe that the scientific procedures espoused by Richards are possible.

It is clearly undesirable, not to say dangerous, to take a position against 'true experimental design' and 'carefully designed re- search'; in our field we have as much obligation to careful analysis and evaluation of our procedures and our products as in any other field. But it is realistic and not anti-scientific to conclude, how- ever reluctantly, as does Peter Strevens, that 'twenty-five years of [critical, evaluative] experiments reveal only the multiplicity of confounding variables and the astonishing particularity of [each] separate school, class, teacher, and learner. The lessons to be learned from research are clear and repeated: first, it is extremely difficult to design experiments in comparative methodology that are not falsified by unforeseen or fortuitous circumstances, and second, the great variability of learning-teaching situations may render the results of any single valid experiment only partially applicable to the precise conditions in which particular learners are working elsewhere' (1977:4). We can continue to search for a metric by which to evaluate the impact of instruction, gains, and second-language maturation in the student, but if we believe at all that learning and not teaching is what ultimately accounts for control of another language, we have to temper our faith in teacher, syllabus, and cur- riculum and increase our respect for the learners, who are almost always a frustratingly unquantifiable complex in their totality.

Other members of our profession comment on the product of their careful analyses and research and the confounding factors. One admires the concluding remarks of Savile-Troike in her 'retrospective analysis' of research into the ESL achievement of a group of children as much as the research itself. She points out that 'no cause and effect relationships can be claimed' about their 'very different levels of achievement in English-medium instruction at the end of that year' (1984:200), and she says that 'perhaps the most important point to be made from the analyses ... is the extent to which there were individual differences among the subjects. Statistics for groups of students too often can mask what is actually happening to individuals as they succeed or fail in learning English ...' (1984:215). (Her conclusions are actually broader and involve the relationship between ESL and academic achievement.)

Considering what is required of the language learner, the complexity of activity required for organisation of input and intake, we can easily agree with Savile-Troike about the difficulty of establishing cause-effect relationships and about the magnitude of the individual differences among students.

The complex of language processing is not just another scientific abstraction subject to scientific analysis. Henry Widdowson's interpretation of reading, which is 'not a reaction to a text [and therefore teachable] but an **interaction** between writer and reader mediated through the text' (1979:174), points to this complexity. And so does Malcolm Coulthard when he says of 'discoursal meaning' that 'the language teacher cannot hope to explain ... [it] in the traditionally regarded 'cut-and-dried' way of teaching grammatical rules', that 'ways of teaching should shift from teacher-telling to learner-interpreting ... Learners need to become analysts of discourse themselves' (1977-xii-xiii). My points are first, that any attempt at **measuring** such personal interaction by rigorous means will be extremely difficult to manage, and second, that the importance of the learner's responsibility cannot be overemphasised. The teacher can describe the geography and explain where the road is supposed to go; after that the student sets out relatively alone. Often the teacher can only observe the student's progress and report on it - anecdotally.

Certain reservations having been established, one may agree more easily that the innovative approaches should provide evaluative studies (although one can continue to believe that language teaching methodologists are not required to test their methods the way the American Environmental Protection Agency tests cars for pollution). Ultimately, these studies should be forthcoming either from the practitioners themselves or from others. But one may continue to insist on the difficulty of securing true empirical data, as well as to maintain the validity of these methods founded in the complex affective domain of the language learner. The primary obstacle is trying to find a measuring system for what Kenneth Chastain calls 'the hesitation and misgivings many people have about treading new waters as they move into a different linguistic and cultural world' (1976:282). Chastain expresses a familiar but important fact about the affective domain: the 'problem in dealing with attitudes and feelings is the multitude of intangibles involved. This lack of specificity causes some educators to shy away from a serious consideration of [it]' (1976:177). He points out the appropriateness of phenomenological studies of these factors. The problem is how many phenomenologists do we have in our profession? (And how welcome would they be these days?)

Regardless of how successful we are in measuring or even in specifying the effective component, it is pretty much taken for granted that we are dealing with something of great importance. Chastain emphasises that 'some psychologists [maintain] that the influence of attitudes and feelings is a greater contributing factor in determining student achievement and success than the cognitive' (1976:176). Tracy Terrell makes the truly sweeping statement that 'the evidence at this point [i.e. 1977] indicates that the primary factors which influence L2 acquisition are affective, not cognitive' (1977:328). In 1982, he said, 'I am even more convinced that the lowering of affective barriers must be the overriding concern in classroom activities if acquisition is to be achieved' (1982:124). In their review of current research, Krahnke and Christison say that 'there is general agreement within the field that social and affective factors have a major effect on who learns languages and how well they learn them. ... For all language learners, affective factors influence the ability to use new languages spontaneously and effectively' (1983:639).

(These views are probably all based on what Richards would call anecdotal evidence. Surprisingly or not, very little research has been applied to affective components. John Oller's attempt to quantify motivation, in his article 'Can affect be measured?' (1981), showed that adequate measuring instruments are lacking. Although, of course, there were the Guiora et al experiments to determine how many cocktails facilitated student success in pronouncing Thai words (1972). The jury is still out deciding the relationship between ego-permeability and pronunciation and language-acquisition in general [e.g. Schumann, 1975].)

This absence of specific application of studies of the affective factors and their impact on the language-teaching classroom may not be too surprising if we realise that the history of our awareness is not very long. When Douglas Brown began writing about 'affective factors' in 1973, he was not exactly a lone voice crying in the wilderness, but there were not many people echoing (but see Schumann 1975 and 1978). Rigorous analyses are few, and the application of research procedures to those factors has been meager. Psycholinguistic and sociolinguistic premises and hypotheses figure strongly in our discussions of teaching and learning procedures, but it may not be unfair to say that except possibly for a few areas of recent intense research - schema theory, for instance - they have not arrived at the status of hard sciences: demonstration, proof, replicability. To look at it a different way, if affect cannot be measured successfully, why should we bother trying to construct rigorous experiments? Still, we are aware beyond argument of its existence, and we acknowledge its importance, so is it reasonable that out of frustration with its tenuousness we challenge or reject it? If affective factors are very important - or even 'most important', as some of our colleagues say - perhaps we should simply accept them, together with our ignorance about their specific workings, until there is some breakthrough thanks to as yet unknown measuring instruments. It may be more reasonable to accept what Richards calls 'the sanction of [Earl] Stevick's uncritical treatment' (1984:15) of what he found in the Silent Way and Counseling-Learning than to reject them because their claims could not be verified by means of 'true experimental design'. And yet Richards concludes that 'the field of methods in language teaching has been revitalised by different theories concerning the nature of language, by new theories concerning the central process of language acquisition, by innovative proposals for syllabus development and the design of instructional systems, ... [and] the use of a variety of novel practices, techniques, and procedures in the language classroom' (1984:21). And Alan Maley, after poking fun at the evangelism of these innovative methods and their 'ritual set of procedures, a priesthood, ... and a body of holy writ and commentary', points with fairness to the 'positive insights' they have provided: 'the independent and individual role and status of the learner', 'the importance of group supportiveness ... [as a] security system for learning', 'the importance of relaxation and the reduction of threat', 'the hidden capacity of the human brain ... and the important role of peripheral and subconscious learning', 'the role of **play**', 'the view of error and its correction', 'the importance of building inner criteria', and 'creative silence'. He adds that the 'list is not complete', and 'we owe [these innovators] ... collectively an enormous debt' (1983:81-82). Maley also provides us with a reasonable basis for suspicion about the methodologies he discusses (i.e. Silent Way, Counseling-Learning, and Suggestopedia) - a reservation shared in part by Richards, Clarke, and Scovel in their comments. 'We can believe', he says, in 'their value as language learning paradigms ... so long ... as no **one** of them lays claim to total truth' (1983:83). We can certainly consider that a fair enough reservation.

Still, the appropriate proportion of sensitivity to the personal qualities and needs of the individual learner is by no means a universally-accepted premise. Tom Scovel, also speaking at the Honolulu TESOL Convention, concedes that the innovative methods, together with the Notional-Functional syllabus, have indeed made a 'positive contribution to language pedagogy', but he considers the American humanistic approach to pedagogy to be the 'typically American worship of individualism', especially as advocated by Earl Stevick (1983:90). And the priority of importance conceded to the affective domain is not always the highest. Francine M Schumann and John H Schumann discuss in interesting detail some of their personal problems - preferences, fixations, resentments, withdrawal - in their 'Diary of a language learner', emphasising various affective elements and their importance. They caution, however, that ' as the profession comes to recognise more and more the importance of affective factors in SLL, there is the danger that language teachers will assume the roles of pseudo-psychologists and language classes will become group therapy sessions'. They point out the essential importance of 'an awareness of the affective nature of SLL', but they also say that 'we must be careful not to neglect the importance of grammar, drill, and the other traditional components of language instruction' (1977:248). Considering the record of success of 'grammar, drill, and the other traditional components of language instruction', perhaps we ought not to hesitate too much about the teacher's intervention in learners' problems; those problems - Terrell's 'affective barriers' - are not going anywhere if teacher and students both do not make some attempt to solve them. 'Pseudo-psychology' and 'group therapy sessions' are unsympathetic labels for attitudes and procedures that may be far more productive than grammar and drills.

Let us take for granted, then, a general belief in the existence of and importance of Affect. By **affect**, let us understand everything that is not obviously a part of the cognitive-intellectual complex, lumping together social factors, affective factors, and personal factors - specifically attitudes, language and culture shock, motivation and the lack of it, self-image, self-esteem, anxiety, withdrawal, discouragement, loss of interest and involvement, rejection, alienation, lack of confidence, fear of failure. Whether these factors exist before or develop during contact with language learning is not important, except perhaps to the sociolinguist. Through observation we can be sure of the existence of various components of this conglomerate, even if we are not sure how to identify them specifically; after all, we are language teachers, not psychologists, and precise identification is not our goal.

It is also reasonable to suggest that we dignify the observation that we are all capable of - or at least of becoming capable of through sensitization - as just that: observational analysis. There is a tendency in those who believe only in empirical data to reject such observation, to cheapen it with the label of 'anecdotal'. This is not a necessary position: many observations and retrospective analyses have eventually produced more respected empirically-based evidence and conclusion.

Many people have contributed to our understanding of the affective side of our students, and we have been brought to awareness not so very long ago from a position that can be called unawareness of and insensitivity to the affective life within those students. Among these people are the innovators of the methods under discussion, and their contribution as a group has been a massive and powerful one. They have been practising on the fringes while our profession slowly grew into awareness - in large measure because of Earl Stevik, who has a singularly open mind.

Perhaps we can even concede that larger curricular concerns per se are not dealt with significantly beyond the initiation and induction of the student into the domain of the foreign language. But these reassuring, calming, gentling, and mind-awakening procedures have turned out to be far from trivial and irrelevant to learning. Let us call those methods 'approaches' if we feel that curriculum and syllabus and precise techniques are not sufficiently stabilised yet to earn them the title of true method. But even as approaches, Silent Way, Counseling-Learning, Total Physical Response, Suggestopedia, and Comprehension Training provide an impressive entrée to a foreign language. They usually create an awareness among learners that the cultural, psychological, and social barriers which have practically become part of the psyche of modern language students can be overcome. In their varied ways and through different channels, they give the learner the security and confidence that most teachers find lacking in most learners. Perhaps once the learners find that learning actually occurs, it does not matter very much how a curriculum unfolds afterwards. After all, Gattegno calls teacher silence just a **tool** which makes the mind of the student work harder, Curran and Rardin consider the counselor's function to be the **facilitation** of the learner's capability rather than 'language teaching', Asher and Winitz have shown that the learner's silent physical response (and the silent response to Winitz's picture stories) solidifies comprehension - that often-neglected skill - and triggers other language-skill development, and Lozanov's complex and unconventional rituals are in the service of overcoming the 'anti-suggestive barriers', which he sees as a powerful educational principle, allowing the mind to become engaged more profoundly and more efficiently in learning.

It is obvious, and therefore not necessary to confess, that much of the preceding is, as Richards says, 'promoting and justifying these methods through reference to intuitively appealing assertions and theories' (1984:19). Nonetheless, that stance is appropriate in supporting the idea that the **approach**, that is, the underlying principles, of these methods is at least as important as the techniques themselves.

At this point it is necessary to retract some of the concessions made about the simple entrée into the language provided by these innovators, and their lack of concern with 'larger curricular matters'. That statement is unfair to those people who have continued to construct what we could call 'intermediate levels' for these methods, materials we have seen in print by Asher (1982), La Forge (1982), Contee Seelye (1982), Bertha Segal (1981), Harris Winitz ((1981), and others. And on the subject of empirical research, we should also note James Asher's numerous well-designed experiments aimed at defining the parameters of achievement in learning and retention by various groups in various activities related to Total Physical Response (e.g. Asher 1969a, 1969b, 1977; Asher and Price 1967; Asher, Kusudo, and de la Torre 1974; Kunihira and Asher 1965).

The conclusion of this paper will be anecdotal, summarising how these methods - or approaches - deal with the rights and obligations of the learners. The innovators have recognised the power of negative thinking in learning, and they have incorporated procedures and constructed environments intended to overcome, correct, and manipulate these negative factors, either nullifying them, thwarting them, correcting them, or making useful positive qualities of them. Teachers of these methods remain sensitive to the impulses of the learners, they monitor their activities and responses in a different way from the usual 'teacher will fix' way, they foster the students' desire to learn, they allow them to be excited by new things, they heighten the emotional comfort of the learner - they do lots of unusually nice things to and for the learner. Attention is paid to soothing the learner and minimising anxiety: new identities and biographies are given out in Suggestopedic sessions (and the student's view is that 'It's Monsieur Duval from Marseilles who just said that awkward sentence, not me'); there is no pressure to answer at once in Silent Way (and the student feels 'I am entitled to take my time or even pass if I don't want my turn'); the teacher does not want the learner to talk in TPR and in Comprehension Training (but the student may say 'If I can't resist the urge, I can talk under my breath'); and there is no obligation to participate in a conversation in a Counseling-Learning session (and the student may say, 'The rest of the group don't mind if I don't grab the microphone; there's that much more time for the others who do want to talk').

Asher, Winitz (e.g. 1981), the late Valerian Postovsky (1974, 1981), and the late Judy Olmsted Gary (1975) accept the premise (after demonstrating its validity) that the delay of speaking minimises stress in the learner, and they see the benefits of saving the learner from that stress while studying a language. In spite of the irregular fact that no one is talking as in the usual language class, measurable learning is going on without anyone suffering from the usual stress, anxiety, and discouragement. The sense of achievement at being able to follow commands precisely or being able to follow picture stories with full understanding substitutes confidence and pride for the other, commonly occurring, negative feelings. The achievement is measured, of course, by successful response to the commands and successful results in the half-hourly quizzes of Winitz's program (1981:<u>passim</u>).

The Silent Way teacher helps, forces, allows the independence of the learners, who slowly become aware of their capabilities. **They** do all the work, take the responsibility for what they do, and they get the credit for what they learn. Each member of the group being in the same boat, struggling with the same problems, they quickly learn to accept each other, help each other, and learn from each other. Discovering that they can actually figure out what they are supposed to learn, they begin to take pride in their abilities, and not having the constant mirror of what they have done in the teacher's modeling, they see their individual achievement and feel proud of it. Shaping and reshaping their own product, they do not need the artificial support of the 'real' form that is usually provided by the teacher - along with the inevitable invidious comparison that it provokes.

Counseling-Learning allows the student to be cautious and non-receptive until he or she believes it appropriate, desirable, and safe to be receptive; no time limit is placed on the attitude of self-defense. The Counselor-teacher demands nothing, having the role of a willing implement in the hands of the learners. What the learners want to learn makes up the lesson, the pace they want to go at establishes the pace. They learn - faster or slower - the role of co-operation, interdependence, and trust in themselves, their companions, and the instructor/counselor; this acceptance teaches them to take chances in learning and in expressing themselves; and the language becomes a meaningful part of their lives, at least within their 'community'.

Suggestopedia allows the student to relax totally, to be unstressed in the face of masses of language material, to be as cuddled as a child by pleasant surroundings and by invitations to remember only happy times, to stretch and get the kinks out of the adult body by exercising as preparation for learning, to have a strong and reliable authority figure of a teacher whose power is only positive, to be led to believe that their mental capability is far greater than anyone else has told them it was.

The common denominators among these approaches are simple and even banal: they focus in a very determined way on the individual learners, and they provide a lot of nurture for the learners. At first, it often seems that each of these methods is doing something different from the others - until we look at the learners. If they can be satisfied, working contentedly with a sense of achievement and confidence in their linguistic future, whether they are talking or being silent, whether they are guessing wildly or assembling their structures methodically and painstakingly, whether they are following or leading, then we can believe that the product will be a lot more learning, proportionate with the individual's overall capabilities, naturally. In short, learning will be optimised. The one thing we cannot afford is to get fed up and impatient with these affective needs: we have to cater to them, and each of these approaches does that according to its best interpretation. If they contradict each other in some point of handling the overall task, that is probably all right: after all, we are dealing with a species that is capable of being happy one day, sad the next, tolerant one hour, impatient the next, cheerful one minute, surly the next.

We must avoid the temptation to be too scientific about the entity under discussion, the language student. And while we may continue to desire and aim for careful studies of the processes and results of these methods, we should also continue to respect their intentions and their successes. The 'multitude of intangibles' will always be there. It is reasonable to invite teachers to examine these methods before accepting them, but it is unreasonable to warn them away from them.

References

ASHER, James J. The Total Physical Response technique of learning. Journal of Special Education, vol 3, no. 3, 1969, p 253-62.

ASHER, James J. The Total Physical Response approach to second language learning. Modern Language Journal, vol 53, no. 1, 1969, p 3-17.

ASHER, James J. Children learning another language: a developmental hypothesis. Child Development, vol 48, 1977, p 1040-48.

ASHER, James J. Learning another language through actions: the complete teacher's guidebook. Expanded 2nd edn. Los Gatos, California: Sky Oaks Productions, Inc (1982).

ASHER, James J, Jo Anne Kusuda and Rita de la Torre. Learning a second language through commands: the second field test. Modern Language Journal, vol 58, 1974, p 24-32.

ASHER, James J and Ben S Price. The learning strategy of the Total Physical Response: some age differences. Child Development, vol 38, no. 4, 1967, p 1219-27.

BANCROFT, W Jane. The Lozanov language class. Toronto, Ontario: Educational Courier (1975).

BROWN, H Douglas. Affective variables in second language acquisition. Language Learning, vol 23, no. 2, 1973, p 231-44.

CHASTAIN, Kenneth. Developing second-language skills (2nd edn). Chicago, Illinois: Rand McNally (1976).

CHOMSKY, Noam. Linguistic theory. In Language teaching: broader contents, Robert G Mead, Jr (ed), p 43-49. [No place of publicn]. Northeast Conference on the Teaching of Foreign Languages.

CLARKE, Mark A. On bandwagons, tyranny, and commonsense. TESOL Quarterly, vol 16, no. 4, 1972, p 437-49.

COULTHARD, Malcolm. An introduction to discourse analysis. London: Longman (1977). [Cited in Krahnke and Christison, p 633.]

GARY, Judith Olmsted. Delayed oral practice in initial stages of second language learning. In On TESOL '75, Marina K Burt and Heidi C Dulay (eds), p 89-96. Washington, DC: TESOL (1975).

GUIORA, A Z, B Beit-Hallahmi, R C L Brannon, C Y Dull and T Scovel. The effects of experimentally induced changes in ego states on pronunciation ability in a second language: an exploratory study. Comprehensive Psychiatry, vol 13, 1972, p 421-28.

HALE, Thomas and Eva Budar. Are TESOL classes the only answer? Modern Language Journal, vol 54, 1970, p 487-92.

KRAHNKE, Karl J and Mary Ann Christison. Recent language research and some language teaching principles. TESOL Quarterly, vol 17, no. 4, 1983, p 625-50.

KUNIHIRA, Shirou and James J Asher. The strategy of the Total Physical Response: an application to learning Japanese. IRAL, vol 3, no. 4, 1965, p 1219-27.

LA FORGE, Paul. Interviewing with community language learning. Cross Currents (LIOJ), vol 9, no. 2, 1982, p 1-15.

LONG, Michael. Does second language instruction make a difference? A review of the research. TESOL Quarterly, vol 17, no. 3, 1983, p 359-380.

LONG, Michael. Process and product in ESL program evaluation. TESOL Quarterly, vol 18, no. 3, 1984, p 409-27.

MALEY, Alan. 'I got religion!': evangelism in TEFL. On TESOL '82: Pacific perspectives on language learning and teaching, Mark A Clarke and Jean Handscombe (eds), p 77-83. Washington, D.C.: TESOL (1983).

NATTINGER, James R. Communicative language teaching: a new metaphor. TESOL Quarterly, vol 18, no. 3, 1984, p 391-407.

OLLER, John. Can affect be measured? IRAL, vol 19, no. 3, 1981, p 227-35. [Cited in Krahnke and Christison, p 639.]

POSTOVSKY, Valerian A. Effects of delay in oral practice at the beginning of second language learning. Modern Language Journal, vol 58, no. 5-6, 1974, p 229-239.

POSTOVSKY, Valerian A. The priority of aural comprehension in the language acquisition process. The comprehension approach to foreign language instruction, Harris Winitz (ed), p 170-87 (1981). [Originally presented at the Fourth International Congress of Applied Linguistics, Stuttgart, Germany, 1975.]

RICHARDS, Jack C. The secret life of methods. TESOL Quarterly, vol 18, no. 1, 1984, p 7-23. [Revised version of a plenary address at TESOL- Toronto, March 19, 1983.]

SAVILE-TROIKE, Muriel. What really matters in second language learning for academic achievement? TESOL Quarterly, vol 18, no. 2, 1984, p 199-219.

SCHUMANN, Francine M and John H Schumann. Diary of a language learner. In On TESOL '77, H Douglas Brown, Carlos Yorio, and Ruth Crymes (eds), p 241-250. Washington, DC: TESOL (1978).

SCHUMANN, John J. Affective factors and the problem of age in second language acquisition. Language Learning, vol 25, 1975, p 209-35. Reprinted in Readings on English as a second language (2nd edn), Kenneth Croft (ed), p 222-247. Cambridge: Massachusetts: Winthrop Publishers, Inc, 1980. [Same edn later published by Little, Brown and Company, Boston, Massachusetts.]

SCHUMANN, John H. The acculturation model for second-language acquisition. In Second-language acquisition and foreign language teaching, Rosario C Gingras (ed), p 27-51. Washington, DC: Center for Applied Linguistics (1978).

Music in teaching French by suggestopaedia

Ludger Schiffler
*Free University, Berlin,
Federal Republic of Germany*

The theory of learning

The theory behind the suggestopaedic method says that the pupil will be more successful in a relaxed and anxiety-free situation than in a strained and tense learning environment. This theory has been recognised for a long time, and has been supported by psychological and educational scientific research (Singer, 1981) as well as biological research (Vester, 1975). However, there is still uncertainty about the effectiveness of methods advocating relaxation in the individual fields of learning. For it has also been proved that it is possible to increase performance by applying a certain amount of pressure, e.g. through the authority of the teacher or use of a marking system.

Without going back to the research carried out in the West, the doctor and psychiatrist Lozanov (1978) has been trying since 1955 to prove the theory that in a relaxed situation most effectively brought about by baroque music, the ability to retain things in general, but in particular to remember the significance of foreign words, could be dramatically increased.

He is referring here to 896 'suggestopaedic sessions' of up to three hours, where up to 1000 words were presented with music to volunteers. On average, they were able to retain between 92.2% and 96.1% (166) of these words. Such phenomenal feats of memory exceed all previous knowledge of the human capacity for learning and retention.

The results obtained after a longer, intensive, foreign-language training course, where the volunteers learnt at least 80 words of vocabulary each day, had an equally high retention-rate of 92.9 - 99.7%. These could even be described as 'miraculous'. It should, however, be pointed out that the Bulgarian school system from the outset puts great emphasis on learning things by heart, e.g. from literary texts. In spite of this, these abnormal results can only be considered valid if they are confirmed by repeating the experiments.

However, it is difficult to repeat these experiments because, although Lozanov mentions a large number of experiments, he does not describe any in such detail that they can be accurately understood.

Moreover, the raw data of his experiments have not been jointly published anywhere, so it is not possible to check them by computer. In addition, Lozanov makes no hypotheses, nor does he give details about statistical methods, as is usual in the West when scientific empirical investigations are carried out. Details of the comparability of experiment and control groups are also missing. However, allowances can be made in the case of Lozanov in that this scientific attention to detail is not usual in the majority of corresponding publications in Eastern European literature.

Since, on the one hand, Lozanov's learning hypothesis is supported by the research mentioned above but, on the other, his empirical investigations can have no general validity in their present form, more detailed investigation is required.

Although Lozanov's investigations have been repeated and confirmed in Eastern Europe (cf. Schiffler 1980 and 1983), the same criticism can be made of the way they have been depicted.

The most thorough investigation which has also been described in full is that carried out in Canada by Racle, using two experimental and two control groups (Commission, 1975). The results agree with the majority of investigations carried out in the West, i.e. that although the 'miraculous results' of Lozanov could not be confirmed, the suggestopaedic method of teaching proved slightly superior. In Racle's investigation, this was true of oral communication.

It is regrettable, however, that this extensive investigation shows serious procedural errors of a similar nature to those found in the numerous other smaller experiments, which we have no time to elaborate on at this point. In the Canadian investigation, the participants of the suggestopaedic experimental group were exceptional in that they were allowed to choose which group they went into, something which has never before been allowed in the history of empirical science. No doubt these were the enthusiasts; moreover, they were aware of the special status they held. Different teaching material was used in the experimental and control groups, and different teachers taught in these groups. The results obtained were therefore due to the teaching material as well as to the ability of the teachers.

The aim of the present study was to avoid all these mistakes and to carry out a perfect experiment which would examine the genuinely new elements of suggestopaedic foreign language teaching.

What elements of suggestopaedic foreign language teaching are actually new? Here is a brief account of the essential features.

The characteristics of suggestopaedic foreign-language teaching and an outline of the investigation

THE TEACHER

Suggestopaedia tries to promote in the learner a conviction of his learning success in both a conscious, verbal and a sub-conscious, non-verbal way. Moreover, it should create a pleasant, anxiety-free interaction between the learner and the group, so that there is a good atmosphere for the promotion of learning

The positive effects of a teacher's behaviour on learning success is doubtless not a new discovery and will therefore not form the subject of the present investigation.

The task of the present study was to find four teachers and a reserve teacher of the same sex, similar age and background, equal length of teaching experience and similar knowledge of the foreign language (as mother tongue), and with similar interest in the suggestopaedic method, for the four groups, and to train them together in the suggestopaedic method of foreign language teaching. Since, as we have already mentioned, the effect created by a suggestopaedic foreign language teacher is not what we are interested in here, the fundamental influence through the behaviour and qualifications of the individual teacher should, if possible, be excluded by each teacher, teaching each of the four groups for an equal length of time.

TEACHING MATERIAL

Three or four times the scope

The teaching material should contain three to four times as much information as the normal textbook, and correspondingly more new vocabulary (approximately 200 words). The learner should have been told that he will be able to learn correspondingly more at a greater rate in the suggestopaedic foreign-language course.

Texts in two languages

To help master the enormous quantities of text, all passages will be given in two languages. This is done by placing foreign language and mother tongue in two columns side by side.

The content

The passage should contain information that will motivate the pupils, and show attractive people with whom he can identify during the role-play part of the teaching. Apart from the scope and the bilingual texts, the requirements made of the teaching material are also not new. Teaching material which has proved itself in practice in adult eduation should be found, which either complies with these requirements or can be adapted accordingly.

STRUCTURE OF LESSON

Music

The reading passages are given in an active recital phase, with classical or baroque music, and in a passive recital phase with baroque music (largo). During the active recital, the teacher presents the foreign language text, adapting his voice to the music. Meanwhile, the pupils read the text and compare it with the translation next to it.

In the passive, recital phase the pupils close their eyes and listen to the teacher in as relaxed a way as possible, in repeating the text while a baroque concerto is being played.

As the only thing that is new in the suggestopaedic method is the relaxed presentation of the extensive texts due to music, the experimental and control groups should differ only as regards these variables. The experimental groups should hear all the texts in the form of the two-recital phase, while the control group should be given the passage together with slides and the original tape recordings that go with the lesson. Both groups should be given a written version of all texts in two languages.

The active speech phase

During this phase an explanation of the grammar is given in the mother tongue and the new lessons practised in as playful a way as possible. Role-play plays a large part here, but written exercises are also planned.

To ensure that the active speech phase in the experimental and control groups proceeds in a similar fashion, the teaching material should contain e.g. a French-German grammar section, and in addition grammar exercises (for completion by the pupil), detailed instructions and linguistic aids for the interaction and other language games for practising the new constructions.

Intensive form of teaching

Suggestopaedic teaching is usually intensive, comprising several hours of teaching a day. That is why all four groups should also be given four 45-minute lessons daily over a 3-week period (56 hours altogether).

If an increase in performance related to music can be determined using the intensive teaching method, after an interval of one month the investigation should be continued on the same number of students, but using the extensive form of teaching – two lessons twice weekly over three and a half months. To increase the empirical accuracy of the results, the experimental groups should become control groups, and vice versa.

Design of room

The suggestopaedic classroom should be made to look like a living room, using pictures and plants. The pupils should sit on comfortable armchairs instead of hard-backed chairs, and should sit in a circle so that language games can be played. Two of the experimental groups should be in a room like this, the other experimental group should be taught in a normal classroom. This should enable one to assess whether the design of the room has any effect on learning performance.

The research hypothesis

— Adult pupils (students) achieve a higher level of performance in intensive (four hours daily) teaching in beginner's French if they read and hear the texts in a relaxed state brought about by the playing of baroque music, than those pupils who hear and read these texts without a background of music.

— The performance of the above students is increased not only because they are in a relaxed state due to the music, but because the design of the suggestopaedic classroom enhances performance.

— Adult pupils (students with prior knowledge) achieve a higher level of performance in extensive (two hours a week) teaching of beginner's French if they read and hear the texts in a state of relaxation brought about by baroque music, than those pupils who do not read and hear the texts against a background of music.

Procedure of the investigation

In 1983 fourteen French female teachers who had replied to an advertisement and declared a personal interest in the experiment, were selected to take part in the investigation on the basis of the criteria previously mentioned. The fifth (reserve) teacher was also established at the outset. All of the teachers had had several years' experience in teaching adults. They were subjected to a 35-hour intensive training from the project leader and from Madame Vayssière-Dumas (Paris), who had been trained in Sofia by Lozanov and had been teaching for years using the suggestopaedic method.

At the same time, 128 students aged 20-24, mainly from scientific fields, enrolled for the investigation. On the basis of the language test FTE 7+ (Gerhold, 1974) and a personal survey, 72 volunteers without very much knowledge of the French language were selected, and divided up **randomly** into experimental and control groups. Also on the basis of the test results, a weaker and a stronger group were formed within each group. Care was also taken to ensure that the proportion of males and female in each group was approximately equal.

C'est le Printemps (1978)

This was the teaching material chosen, for a number of reasons:

- Owing to its content, the material had proved to be very motivating to students when used in class, although the number of monolingual texts and the amount of new words introduced in each lesson had always been a problem. It was exactly these disadvantages which made this teaching material suitable for the suggestopaedic method of foreign language teaching. All the texts were arranged side by side with a translation, and a bilingual vocabulary list was additionally drawn up for each lesson.

- The dearth of grammatical explanation in the foreign language and the complete absence of written exercises were recognised to be a weakness with this teaching material. Adapting it as described above was a necessary addition to the existing teaching material.

The following pieces of music were the main ones used in the active phase:

Beethoven : Piano Concerto, no 5, opus 61

Brahms : Violin Concerto, no 77

Mozart : Prague Symphony

              Violin Concertos, nos 5 and 7

and in the passive recital phase:

Vivaldi : Flute Concerto

              The Four Seasons

Corelli : Concerti Grossi, 2 - 12

Pergolesi : Concerto for Flutes, no 1 - Adagio

              Concerto for Flutes, no 2 - Largo

Händel : Water Music

At the start of the lesson the pupils were given a talk by the project leader, who pointed out in a convincing manner the greater learning performance achieved with music and a bilingual text.

The control groups received a corresponding talk in which the project leader, also in a convincing tone, told the pupils that the bilingual texts and the different mother-tongue speakers on the tape speaking at their original speed would improve their learning performance.

The active speech phase was set up in the same way in all groups. The project leader observed the teaching in all groups.

The intensive teaching method was carried out as planned. Only in isolated cases did the volunteers give up.

The size of the group for the extensive teaching method was much smaller, as some students were no longer able to participate because of their time-table. A few participants in each group gave up owing to pressure of work.

Although the control groups received bilingual vocabulary lists during the extensive teaching programme, all text was in the foreign language. This caused problems with some of the students, who demanded a translation from their respective teachers where they were unclear. As the teachers almost always gave in to these demands, the investigation could no longer be used to examine these variables.

Results of the investigation

This research project has not yet been finished. The preliminary study is being repeated for a third and fourth time at present. Not only are the results from the present investigation being re-examined, but also the question of the influence of the suggestopaedic teacher. In contrast to previous studies, one teacher teaches in each group. In addition, the question of whether the positive results obtained so far can be improved if the text is read in the foreign as well as the pupil's own language during the passive recital phase, in a breathing cycle of eight seconds (four seconds breathing out, four seconds breathing in), with four seconds of text while not breathing.

```
         WITH MUSIC                    WITHOUT MUSIC

                              STUDY 1

    | Group 1 - weaker pupils |      | Group 3 - weaker pupils |
                          \           /
                      Change of teacher
                      All 4 teachers
                      teach for equal
                      periods in all
                      groups
                          /           \
    | Group 2 - stronger pupils |    | Group 4 - stronger pupils |

                      After 56 lessons (3 weeks):
                      6 different final tests (level 1 and 2)
```

```
                              STUDY 2

      WITH MUSIC                      WITHOUT MUSIC

   Lesson given in                 Lesson given in
   2 languages                     1 language

   | Group 3 - weaker pupils |    | Group 1 - weaker pupils |
                          \           /
                      Change of teacher
                      (see above)
                          /           \
   | Group 4 - stronger pupils |   | Group 2 - stronger pupils |

                      After 56 lessons (3 1/2 months):
                      6 different tests (levels 3 and 4)
```

Result of significance test (study 1)
Both groups with weaker pupils
Group 1 (with music) compared with group 3 (without music)

	F	significance	s = significant ns = not significant	
Final test 7th year				
Vocabulary	0.34	0.55	ns	
Structures	0.00	0.95	ns	
Final test 8th year				
Vocabulary	0.00	0.93	ns	
Structures	0.06	0.79	ns	
C-test	7.31	0.01	vs	p < 0.01 very significant
Translation from	7.96	0.00	vs	p < 0.01 very significant
Translation into	2.56	0.11	ns	tendency
Oral communication	0.04	0.83	ns	

The null hypothesis was refuted in two examinations. In the complex test measuring rading comprehension, orthography and grammar and in examining the translation of French words, among the weaker pupils those taught with music were clearly superior to those taught without. In translation into French they tended to be superior too.

Result of significance test (study 1   Table 2
Both stronger groups
Group 2 (with music and suggestopaedic room design) compared with group 4 (without music)

	F	significance	s = significant ns = not significant	
Final test 7th year				
Vocabulary	2.75	0.10	ns	tendency
Grammar	2.82	0.10	ns	tendency
Final test 8th year				
Vocabulary	2.62	0.11	ns	tendency
Grammar	4.36	0.04	s	p < 0.05 significant
C-test	0.01	0.90	ns	
Translation from	0.79	0.38	ns	
Translation into	4.17	0.04	s	p < 0.05 significant
Oral communication	1.10	0.30	ns	

The null hypothesis was refuted in two cases. In three cases a tendency (at the 10% significance level) was detected.
Among the stronger pupils, the group with music and suggestopaedic room design was superior to the group without music in a normal classroom with regard to the mastery of grammatical structures and translation into French. They also tended to be superior as regards vocabulary.
The superiority of this music group compare with the music group in a normal classroom speaks in favour of providing pupils with special armchairs in which they can relax.
* Illegible original text here.

1st study: survey of pupils

With music Participants 37		Without music 36
Approve of music	73%	
Doubt effectiveness	27%	
(1 rejects music	3%)	
Suggestopaedic room design	30%	
Positive		
Intensive teaching	35%	32%
Teaching material	30%	22%
Interaction games	27%	11%
Teachers	19%	14%
Negative		
Change of teacher	35%	35%
Too little repetition	25%	19%

The outstanding result is that three quarters of the participants approve of the music. In addition, one third are in favour of the internsive approach to teaching.

Study 1   Table 4

The groups with music
Group 1 without suggestopaedic room design compared with
Group 2 with suggestopaedic room design

	F	significance	s = significant ns = not significant
Final test 7th school year			
Vocabulary	0.32	0.57	ns
Grammar	0.81	0.37	ns
Final test 8th year			
Vocabulary	0.31	0.71	ns
Grammar	0.82	0.37	ns
C-test	1.00	0.32	ns
Translation from	0.10	0.75	ns
Translation into	4.17	0.04	ns
Communication	0.61	0.80	ns

The null hypothesis was not refuted in a singel case.
Suggestopaedic room design was not observed to have a positive influence in this study.

Study 2 — Table 5

Both weaker groups
Group 3 with music compared with
Group 1 without music

	F	significance	s = significant ns = not significant	
Final test 8th school year				
Vocabulary	0.00	0.93	ns	
Structures	0.19	0.66	ns	
Final test 9th year				
Vocabulary	1.96	0.18	ns	
Structures	1.86	0.19	ns	
C-test	2.54	0.13	ns	
Translation from	0.16	0.69	ns	
Translation into	1.20	0.28	ns	
Communication	15.97	0.00	s	$p < 0.01$ very significant

The null hypothesis was refuted in only one case.
In extensive teaching music proved to have a positive effect only on oral communication in the weaker pupils among the advanced beginners.

Study 2 — Table 6

Both stronger groups
Group 4 with music compared with
Group 2 without music

	F	significance	s = significant ns = not significant
Final test 8th school year			
Vocabulary	0.23	0.63	ns
Structures	0.08	0.77	ns
Final test 9th year			
Vocabulary	0.51	0.48	ns
Structures	0.13	0.71	ns
C-test	2.27	0.14	ns
Translation from	0.77	0.38	ns
Translation into	1.70	0.20	ns
Communication	0.26	0.61	ns

The null hyu
      pothesis was not refuted in a single case.
No positive effect was deducted from the music in extensive teaching among the stronger advanced beginners.

Oral assessment of study 2: Illegible!

2nd study: Pupil survey   Table 7

With Music		%	Ohne Music	%
Participants	22	100	23	100
Approve of music:	13	59		
reject it:	4	18		
Positive				
Teachers:	9	40	8	34
Atmosphere enhances learning	8	36	8	34
Small group	5	22	7	30
Bilingual texts	6	27		
Teaching material	4	18	4	17
Negative				
Progress too fast	4	18	18	78
Time of lesson	8	36	9	39
Grammar not systematic enough	4	18	5	21

It is striking that almost two thirds of the participants expressed a positive opinion towards the music, but 18% a negative one.
Moreover, it seems that the music does work, that the participants are able to accept the large quantities of material, since only 18% complained about this, while 78% in the group without music complained it was too much.
The time criticised by both groups relates to the extensive teaching of 4 lessons a week <u>during</u> term time.

Final results

1. Baroque music causes better performance in adults in intensive teaching courses.

2. The positive influence of baroque music is essentially reduced in extensive teaching of 4 lessons a week, as is usual in schools.

3. Baroque music has a strong motivating effect on the majority of adult pupils of foreign languages.

4. It prevents most students from feeling 'snowed-under' despite a doubling in the learning speed.

5. Suggestopaedic room design has no or only a slight effect compared with music.

6. Intensive teaching with the teaching material available, in conjunction with suggestopaedic behaviour by the teacher, presentation of the text in two languages, and interactive speaking exercises causes at least a two-fold increase in adults in the speed of learning normal in extensive teaching in schools, even without music.

References

CESCO, C, G Gschwind-Holtzer, Ch Larenne, J Montredon. C'est le printemps, Paris (1978).

Commission de la Fonction Publique du Canada. Une expérience d'enseignement avec la méthode suggestopédique; A teaching experience with the suggestopaedic method, Ottawa.

GERHOLD, K. Fremdspracheneignungstest FTE 7+. Weinheim (1974).

LOZANOV, G. Suggestologia Sofia. (1971).

LOZANOV, G. Suggestology and outlines of suggestopedy, London. (Translation of Suggestologia, Sofia). (1978).

MINISTRY OF EDUCATION, Research Institute of Suggestology (ed), Problems of suggestology. Sofia (1973).

SCHIFFLER, L. Interaktiver Fremdsprachenunterricht. Stuttgart (1980).

SCHIFFLER, L. È opportuno introdurre l'insegnamento suggestopedico delle lingue straniere nelle nuostre scuole? G Lozanov, and E Gatera, (eds) Metodo suggestopedico per l'insegnamento delle lingue straniere, p ii - xviii, Roma: Bulzone Editore (1983).

SINGER, K. Maßstäbe für eine humane Schule. Frankfurt (1981).

VESTER, F. Denken, lernen, vergessen. Stuttgart (1975).

PART FOUR: COMPUTER-ASSISTED LANGUAGE LEARNING

Like the previous section, this one comprises two contributions with different viewpoints on a topical and controversial subject – in this case the use of high-tech equipment in language studies. From the USA we have a linguist's analysis of the role the microcomputer may play on the background of the comparative failure of two previous technological innovations, the audio-lingual method and machine translation; and from Europe – a perhaps reluctant acceptance of the fact that computers are here to stay and that the language teacher's task now is to come to terms with them.

Karttunen traces the rationale and history of the language laboratory, examining the reasons why it failed to live up to the applied linguists' expectations and stressing the part played by boredom. The underlying assumptions of the behaviourists proved unjustified. Similar assumptions when computers first appeared led to unsuccessful attempts to devise a system of automatic translation from one language to another – implying a view of the nature of language that is very much open to question. Both the language laboratory and machine translation discredited the image of the applied linguist in the actual business of language teaching. On this unpromising background, what is the likely future of the microcomputer? In what way has it more to offer than the equally discredited programmed learning of the sixties? Karttunen cautiously cites the role of the computer in motivating the learner; the increasing range of facilities it offers; its genuinely interactional nature, etc. On the debit side, the charge of irrelevance to the real world of language use still remains. But provided the limitations are recognised, there is certainly a role for the microcomputer in language learning.

Hägg, looking at the situation in Sweden as an example, takes up where Karttunen leaves off, recognising the controversial aspects of the use of computers but accepting also the inevitability of their adoption in schools. The task therefore is to look now at the practical implications and to ensure that language teachers assume control of what is to happen in their own field. He discusses practical questions of costs, ease of use by the technically inept or suspicious, types of program, classroom organisation and implications for teacher-training. Properly regarded, the computer may become a source of enrichment of teaching.

Written in refreshingly untechnical language, these two articles make a reassuring and easily comprehensive introduction for the uninitiated or review for the already informed.

A linguist looks at computer-assisted instruction

Frances Karttunen
University of Texas, USA

Introduction

In this paper I am going to discuss two instances in which technology has failed to fulfill its promises in the area of applied linguistics, and then I will go on to talk about the latest technological offering, computer-assisted language instruction. Before I begin my presentation, I wish to pose a rhetorical question to you that we will come back to later on. The question is, 'Have you ever seen anyone asleep at a computer terminal?' Now on to the substance of my talk.

Several years ago an advertisement appeared in a number of magazines that today would be styled 'Yuppie-magazines', that is, magazines that at that time had a readership of adult professional men. The advertisement consisted of a photograph of a small, dark-skinned child clutching her mother's hand and peeking shyly from behind her skirts. The advertisement proclaimed, 'If she can speak Urdu, so can you'.

Consider for a moment the implications. What made this advertisement effective in marketing a set of recorded language lessons, Urdu or one's choice from a large number of other languages, mostly less exotic to western sensibilities? First of all, the company really did not expect to sell many sets of Urdu lessons. One covert message was, 'Urdu is harder than French or German, or even Russian'. Hence, if even Urdu is within the reach of the child in the picture, then French and German and Russian are masterable. The second implication was, 'You, the reader of this advertisement, are vastly more advantaged than this child'. Hence, in anything even **she** can do, success is guaranteed. After all she is very young, timid, female, dark-skinned, and probably living among illiterates. How could she possibly master anything that would elude an educated middle-class Western man?

I think we can be confident that few if any people managed to learn Urdu from these lessons, and that the success rate for the French and German and Russian lessons was not high, either.

What does a linguist have to say about this, and what relevance has this to Computer-Assisted Language Instruction?

The language laboratory

To begin with, American structuralist linguists of the 1950's contributed to the appeal and marketability of recorded language lessons by making a strong public case against what they called the 'grammar-translation' method of classroom language instruction.

They pointed out, as a number of eminent linguists before them had, that few people learn to speak new languages by having the grammatical points of the language explained to them and being set to making translations. For centuries schoolchildren had been laboring over Latin and Greek and French and German that way, without being able to speak the languages or to retain what they had been drilled in beyond the day they left school. Everyone could see that this was true, and everyone could also see that some individuals nonetheless **did** manage to become bilingual and even polylingual. How was this accomplished?

The common-sense answer was that people acquire languages by using them, not by learning about them. Language learning must be direct, unmediated by grammar exercises and laborious word-by-word dictionary-aided translation. One would retain vocabulary if it were connected to concrete objects and real-world experiences. The most effective language-learning context would be 'total immersion', where one could only meet one's simplest needs by figuring out how to comunicate in the target language.

Total immersion, however, is prohibitively expensive for most would-be language learners. Professional diplomats and army intelligence trainees get to spend weeks in Foreign Service Institute courses, and it is almost required of graduate students in anthropology that they go off to live for a while in as unfamiliar a society as possible to try to come to terms with a new language-and-culture complex. But the majority of us do not have the leisure and the funds to do this. The efficacy of total immersion has not really been tested on masses of people. It remains a common-sense idea based on the undeniable fact that there are many languages spoken by the peoples of the world, and the ability to speak Urdu or Russian or English is not reserved for a few geniuses. Languages are clearly masterable in the proper context.

And so efforts were directed at replicating the proper context. Teachers should be native speakers of the language. Learners should listen to radio broadcasts in the target language, go to foreign-language movies and try to ignore the subtitles, have social hours with other students and with native speakers. The commercially marketed language records would give one an extra hour or as many hours a day as one could spare with the target language spoken by a cultivated native speaker. And there was a bonus; one could listen to the same section again and again until one 'got' it. Hence, one's learning became self-paced.

The advent of language laboratories was supposed to mark a revolution in language learning. Some of the earliest were hardly different from listening to radio broadcasts of language lessons; students simply sat in individual booths and all listened to the same master tape broadcast to everyone at once.

But the idea of self-paced work in the language laboratory asserted itself from the beginning almost everywhere. Each booth was to have its own tape player, and students were to check out copies of the master tape to use as long as each needed to, backing up, replaying, skipping through what was easily masterable to places that were harder and more demanding. Some students might need only a few hours a week with the tapes, while others would need many. The point was that in the language laboratory one had on tape a tireless model of the language, unfazed by endless demands for repetition. There was no division of attention, no competition with other students with other learning speeds and styles.

And what was the consequence of this revolution? Was the world flooded with successful language learners? Did the next generation become polylingual? Nothing of the sort. Students universally proclaimed the language laboratory **boring** and rebelled against using it. Even those with the best intentions were often quite unable to stay awake in the language laboratory. The soporific effect of putting on the headset was appalling.

It is not surprising that foreign-language teachers were put out with their language-laboratory resistent students. In a language classroom one is in competition with all the other students. Responce is either in unison or it comes only a few times per class hour, whereas in the language laboratory one is challenged to make a response to every single question, and one's response is either confirmed or corrected every time. Moreover, one is at all times listening to a cultivated native speaker, while one's classroom teacher may not be a native speaker or even a very confident speaker of the language being taught. How could one fail to benefit from such advantages?

Students complained that language-laboratory exercises were far removed from 'the real world' and were not likely to help them in the free and unpredictable give-and-take situations they would meet there. And even the most diligent students, the ones who really wanted to take advantage of the language laboratory, found they simply could not stay awake. The language laboratory was minimally interactive, in that the student had control over repetition and that there were spaces built into the exercises for student response followed by reinforcement - by a repetition of what the right answer should be. But this was clearly not enough of the right context to facilitate language learning.

It was time for the linguist to take another look. Unlimited access to spoken language was not sufficient. Language students were still nearly as passive as the ones involved in grammar lessons and translation exercises, and their success rate did not seem markedly better.

Underlying assumptions

What were the assumptions of the 1950s 'audio-lingual method' that proved so disappointing? It was basically behaviourist, assuming that language is a set of habits built up through repetition and reinforcement. (Some extreme proponents felt that whenever students made wrong responses, they built up habits that would prove ineradicable, so it was better that students make no response at all rather than take a chance on the wrong one.)

It also counted on very primal motivation. If it failed in the language laboratory, that was because students were insufficiently motivated. In the sink-or-swim context of true total immersion, motivation would be the need to get food, protection, information (i.e. the same needs that children must learn to meet). The scapegoat for failure with the audiolingual method was lack of motivation. Yet when people invested in recorded language lessons or enrolled in language courses, they clearly brought to the enterprise some initial motivation, at least. What factor could possibly destroy that motivation so effectively and so universally?

Let us look for a moment at how one gets from the idea 'If she can speak Urdu, so can you' to the recorded drills of the audiolingual method. Very few people try to engage their babies in pattern- practice drills, yet by the time babies are a year and a half old they begin to speak, and by the time they are five years old or so, like the little child clutching her mother's sari in the advertisement, they speak their home language as well as all but the most highly educated adults in their society. (One never gets over the sense of wonder that little children speak so clearly, especially when they are speaking a language that the listener has struggled with for years without real satisfaction.)

Children get the elements of grammar from the swirl of language about them, and if we were to take the common-sense approach that this is how we are to acquire additional languages, then total immersion or some approximation of it, with no 'grammar' or structured approach, should suffice. One would connect chunks of the swirl of language with certain things or activities; one would make a note of the predictability of these connections; one would try to make things happen by using the predictable chunks, and thereby begin to speak the language.

This approach has been tried more and less rigorously many times over, and it tends to produce students even more rebellious than the sleepy language-laboratory students. They beg for and insist on some explanation, and the temptation is to go back to the grammatical explications that had fallen into so much disrepute. In line with behaviourist principles of stimulus and response, the solution was to give minimal explanations but to place the burden of mastery on the student's participation in pattern practice drills. The student was not to sit and passively absorb grammatical information, which clearly had not benefited most students in the past, but to establish patterns of verbal behaviour from repeating the same task over and over again with minimal changes and substitutions. This was to be done in class, but the classroom with its limitations imposed by number of students and capacity of teachers could only provide a fraction of the drill needed. The rest was to be carried on in the language laboratory on the student's own initiative, and a great many strategies for maintaining and rewarding initiative were devised.

But when pattern-practice drills were devised, a tacit admission had been made that older language learners do not learn in the same manner that children do. Except in the case of severe neurological deficit or total isolation, children cannot be **kept** from learning the language or languages of their immediate environment, while older learners acquire additional languages only by the application of great effort tempered by strong self-discipline. During the 1970s this observation was seized upon by American generative linguists as a major key to understanding the nature of the human mind. People who had read the work of Piaget were already familiar with the notion that the nature of reasoning changes as people advance by stages from infancy to young adulthood, and people who work with aphasic patients were aware that children have a much better prognosis for recovery from speech impairment than adult victims of stroke and other sorts of neurological trauma. Theoretical linguists now turned on the earlier behaviourist assumptions about language learning and took the position that the adult can no longer learn languages as children do. From infancy through childhood humans have an ability to learn language from a totally unstructured and even impoverished context, until around the age of puberty, that ability shuts down. That the little girl can speak Urdu has no implications whatsoever for any adult who does not already speak Urdu.

Linguists who took this position essentially abandoned the area of applied linguistics that deals with foreign-language instruction. This abandonment was by no means necessary or inevitable, but theoreticians interested in the nature of human intelligence for the most part restricted their interest to the beginnings of that intelligence as it is manifested in child language acquisition. Few concerned themselves with what goes on in post-adolescent language learning, and I think this has been less from prejudice than from a perceived need to understand fundamental things first, before passing on to much more complex processes.

So linguists have ceased to give advice, direction, or encouragement to language teachers, and sometimes they give the very pessimistic impression that any language learning that goes on after childhood is some sort of fluke, something that really shouldn't be possible at all.

Yet people do learn languages after childhood, and many of them learn very **well**, although there is no question that mastery of a new language is very hard work and generally remains somewhat incomplete. We also know that many of the old behaviourist strategies of language teaching really **do** help, even though they are currently in theoretical disrepute. The audio-lingual method failed to live up to the high standards of success that structuralist linguists projected for it, but it **is** an improvement over grammar/translation work. To put it another way, the audiolingual method can't take the burden off the teacher or the student, but it can offer useful aids to the process of language teaching and language learning.

Automatic machine translation

Now I will move on to the second technological disappointment that I want to talk about, automatic machine translation. In the 1950s, at the height of the structuralist linguists' confidence and influence, computers first became available, and their application to translation seemed a matter of course. Basically, it was believed at the time that one could, with ingenuity, store vocabularies of two languages plus grammatical outlines of both languages in a computer and by algorithm map a text in one language onto the other. A German or Russian document could be input, and an English translation would be typed out. A great deal of time, effort, and ingenuity was invested in building such automatic translation systems, until after a decade a feasibility study was issued that declared that automatic machine translation could not be implemented and no further public funds should be invested in such projects. However, private funding has continued throughout the 1970s and 1980s with very little return on the investment. There are automatic translation systems that can make rough translations of documents on narrow topics written in highly restricted grammar with additional grammatical coding added to the text. Not only is pre--diting required, but post-editing as well, and so far there is little commercial or practical use for automatic translation. It is no wonder that people with a practical and professional interest in language feel disenchanted by the promises of technology.

I would like to point out that the failure of automatic machine translation after a decade of research and development had a great deal to do with the abandonment of linguists' behaviourist approach to language. If languages are truly built up from a finite set of patterns transmitted by stimulus and response plus a vocabulary of words of that language that can be inserted into specific positions within these patterns, then it should have been possible to build translation devices, to program a computer to recognize the patterns, map them onto the patterns of the target language, and replace the individual words with the words of the target language. But as linguists tried to define the patterns of English, German, and Russian, they found that there was simply no end to the patterns. It was not just that computers were not yet powerful enough and did not yet have sufficient memory capacity to store enough dictionary information about particular words. Some linguists, mathematicians, and logicians (Professor Jaakko Hintikka among them) became convinced that the formal nature of natural languages (as contrasted with computer programming languages) makes automatic translation impossible.

The complexity of English that revealed itself to the linguists who were trying to write a complete grammatical description of their own language hastened the abandonment of behaviourist views of language. The little girl who could speak Urdu was not to be viewed as a disadvantaged waif but as a wondrous language-acquisition device, something that could not be modeled on a computer, no matter how powerful and sophisticated. The linguists and other cognitive scientists who went on working with computers and language scaled their expectations down from working with two whole languages at a time to trying to get a computer to begin to take just a step or two in the direction of understanding sentences that most children would have no trouble with whatsoever. This is not a trivial task, but it is has nothing to offer to foreign language teaching.

Computer assisted instruction

It is really not surprising that after investing so much of themselves and their prestige in two things, the audio-lingual method and automatic translation, that are now perceived as such failures both within linguistics and by the people who hoped to make use of them, linguists have had very little to say about computer-assisted language instruction. They have left the whole matter to the educational psychologists and the software-development companies. Glossy journals such as that published by CALICO (the Computer-Aided Language Instruction Consortium) that advertise and review the latest educational software are pretty much in the hands of small computer corporations and microcomputer 'wizards', whose approach is pragmatic and not theoretical at all. These Vendors are concerned with 'user-friendliness' and attractive packaging, because, after all, they are in the business to make money. Like the school textbook industry, the educational software business stands to earn millions of dollars, and the competition is fierce.

One of the obstacles that the purveyors of computer-aided instruction must overcome is the distrust of technology that we linguists had a hand in creating. Language teachers and tax-payers do not want to be sold a bill of goods and to find themselves with a pile of expensive but obsolete hardware and floppy disks in the stockroom. They have every right to ask, 'Can you assure me that this is worth the investment?'

And now we come back to the question of whether you have ever seen anyone asleep at the terminal. I, for one, have not, in years of working in computer centres and around home terminals. I have seen people refuse to sit down for a first session 'on the computer' because they are gripped with tremendous apprehension, but anyone who begins to learn how to do things with the aid of a computer quickly gains confidence and curiosity. (I should insert here a disclaimer about computer use. I suspect that people who work in banks and travel bureaux or in secretarial pools with computers eight hours a day may indeed fall asleep over them or certainly want to, but they are involved in a sort of drudgery aside from what I am talking about.)

The computer offers frustrations in that it does not tolerate typing errors or vague instructions. Except for some experimental systems, computers are relentlessly literal-minded, but they are interactive in a way that the language laboratory could not be. They recognise the right answer. If they get anything else, they can prompt with another chance at the right answer and applaud it if it comes. After persistent wrong responses they can offer clues or explanations of the task at hand and keep on until the person working at the keyboard gets things right or deliberately ends the session. As a matter of course, computers can offer items in random order so that one does not know which of several will come next (the computational equivalent of shuffling one's vocabulary flashcards). Computers will keep score, report on one's progress, move one on through increasingly demanding exercises. (This is as true of language drills as of arcade games.)

Much of the most recent work in the field of Artificial Intelligence, as well as in commercial software development, has been concerned with creating more and more 'lifelike' or 'natural' interaction between humans and computers, to remove the constraints of the computer's literal-mindedness and earlier poor generation of sentences with even limited syntax. The result is the impression of dealing with an intelligent machine, one that can understand human beings and react in human terms. As such programming feats have been achieved, initial human frustration with dealing with computers has been replaced by fascination and a natural drive towards mastery that does not have to be prodded on with external rewards. This phenomenon among both children and adults with access to computers has recently been described compellingly by Professor Sherry Turkle at the Massachusetts Institute of Technology in her book <u>The second self: computers and the human spirit</u>. I think this book should be of enormous interest for all people interested in Computer-Assisted Instruction, because it seems to address and resolve the question of motivation. The many people that Turkle observed and interviewed, despite several distinct and identifiable learning styles, were all driven by a strong internal motivation towards mastery - mastery of tasks for which the computer served as a tool and mastery of the computer itself. Like the child who cannot be kept from learning the language of his immediate environment, Turkle's subjects - adults and children alike - could hardly be kept from involving themselves with the computers to which they had access. And as they experimented, tried to outsmart the machine, questioned what the machine was doing and how it managed to do it, her subjects seemed to develop their own cognitive capacities in ways that they would not otherwise have done. Mastery became its own reward for these people, just as language teachers would hope that ultimately the mastery of a new language would be its own reward for language students.

There are apparently two interconnected factors involved in the holding power of computers, especially as contrasted with the lack of holding power of language laboratories. These are the issues of interactivity and control. In the language laboratory, control was limited to choice of tapes and linear movement through the chosen tape, the ability to move ahead and to back up. This sort of control is expanded in computer interaction. Of course, one can turn the machine off and go away in frustration, and if one stays, one can always return to the beginning, to what is often called the 'opening menu'. But in a well designed computer tutorial the student is offered options (often called 'branches' or 'forks') and may at any time request a review of information. One may ask for 'help' or 'information' as often as one pleases. The instructional program may suggest from time to time that the student might like to see the contents of the 'help file', and the student may choose whether to do so or to try to work on without it. This choice of options and freedom to call for help at any time confers a satisfying sense of control that is lacking in the language laboratory, in classroom interactions, and especially in the unpredictable give-and-take of spontaneous language use, and this can remove a significant burden from the language learner and let him get on with some of the tasks of language learning.

In computer-assisted instruction some control is also handed over to the program. One of these is determination of order of presentation of material. In the language laboratory, after listening to a taped exercise once, one knows the order in which the stimuli will come, and in subsequent repetitions of the exercise one cannot help using cues from what went before and what went after, anticipating and remembering the frame in order. It is no wonder that students protest that language laboratory exercises are of no help to them in 'real-world' situations. On the other hand, even the most elementary computer tutorial system will randomize its order of presentation so

that the student deals with just the unit at hand and not with what
went before and after. More sophisticated programs, like computer
arcade games, take student performance into account; correct responses are tallied up, requests for help counted. The program can
gradually increase the difficulty of the tasks and in the end report
a score to the student. This is a long way indeed from the language
laboratory.

Computer tutorials for electrical engineering and for basic logic
courses have been designed and used with great success, and they
have been in a wide use for a number of years already, long enough
for cognitive scientists to concern themselves with what is going on
when students interact with these tutorials. To what extent should
the CAI program model what the student is actually doing?

Some tutorials simply provide challenges to produce factually
'right' answers, while others are very carefully designed to follow
the steps by which a learner is reasoning and to steer him or her
away from anticipated mis-steps. These programs that model what the
student is actually doing as he learns are of much greater interest
to cognitive scientists, linguists among them, than simply pragmatic
programs.

For the last two decades theoretical linguists have repeatedly
issued disclaimers that their theories about the nature of language
are not to be taken as theories about how the human mind actually
works but as hypotheses and models. Many linguists have been at
great pains to point out that their theories are not to be taken as
'psychologically real', and this is certainly very frustrating to
people trying to apply linguistic knowledge to practical tasks such
as language teaching. Now we see the issue taken up in CAI, namely
whether a tutorial program that matches student response against
some 'right' answer, without following the actual steps by which a
person (as opposed to a machine) would get to that answer, can be an
effective tutor.

Another question we must address is whether CAI can help to build
cognitive structures useful for language use. The fact that computer
tutorials have been designed that are effective in teaching skills
in engineering, mathematical reasoning, and logic does not necessarily mean that computers can take over language teaching. It is a
relatively trivial task to write a program that can automate flash-
card drills. In fact, this was my first experience with CAI, many
years ago, when a colleague of mine decided that vocabulary building
would be facilitated by having cues randomly displayed on a printing
terminal and having the student type in the correct translation or
inflected form of the word. (This was so long ago that CRT terminals
had not yet become available.) It is also a simple task to design
multiple choice 'games', in which a question is posed in the target
language, and the student indicates the number or letter of the

answer he or she chooses (e.g. the CAI program recently developed by a University of Texas graduate student in Foreign Language Education). But these are fairly 'dumb' programs (to use computer jargon for minimally interactive programs), and they do not have much holding power. The criticisms that I have heard from teachers trying to make use of computer-aided language instruction software is that it is too often of this simple-minded type and that such software is difficult to integrate into language courses. Thus increasingly sophisticated interactivity and integration into course design are two crucial goals for future development of CAI software.

Looking back to the disappointments of the audio-lingual method and of automatic translation, we see that the frustration and failure arose in part from misdirected expectations. The audiolingual method did not make polyglots of us all, and we cannot feed great works of Russian literature into a machine and get English translations out the other side. But shifting emphasis from learning **about** language to learning to **use** language was essential, as in the field of machine translation, in which the computer serves the human translator as a tool rather than taking over his or her task entirely. When we have revised our expectations, we find these things to be less disappointing than they seemed. So, too, with computer-assisted language instruction, Computers cannot reasonably be expected to take over the job of language teachers. For one thing, their interactivity is limited, and they can make no judgements whatsoever about the student's oral use of language. Synthesized speech is of little use as a model for human students, and speech recognition is still in its infancy in computer science. Thus, computers are only of use in teaching skills with written language. Nor can any computer tutorial engage in free, unconstrained conversation with a student. Hence, the old criticism of irrelevance to the 'real world' use of language remains.

Yet if we see the mastery of language as the acquisition of a set of several different skills, we can find the place for computer assistance. Recognition and production of vocabulary is one such skill, and one in which CAI can be of enormous help. For inflected languages, production and recognition of correct forms of words is another skill that can be practised with the aid of a computer. Programs for developing these skills have been devised by a number of people, among them John Higgins and Tim Johns, whose book <u>Computers and language learning</u> contains descriptions of a whole collection of computer games devised by themselves and others for these purposes. This book includes lines of programming code showing how these instructional programs have been implemented.

Conclusion

In closing, I want to make a few remarks that really have nothing to do with linguistics but everything to do with practical use of computers. The sort of intense absorption with computer interaction that Professor Turkle describes in her book depends on virtually unlimited access to a computer. The user must not have to compete for the machine or relinquish it to someone else at the end of any set time. There must be one machine for each user. When one reads books like those of Davies and Higgins, or Higgins and Johns, one sees that language teachers have to make use of one computer for several students, so that each student has only a few minutes of computer interaction per day and does indeed have to compete with others, even if the competition can be manipulated for the benefit of group interaction. Providing the sort of worthwhile computer interaction described by Turkle is currently prohibitively expensive, except in a few experimental schools. Aside from the expense, there is another factor that we must deal with, and that is the male domination of the computer subculture. Computer arcade games are almost exclusively the preserve of boys and men, and girls and women are generally driven away either by the exclusionist attitude of the males or their own disinterest in the commercial war and fantasy games. Boys who have become experts at arcade games have a strong tendency to take over school computer facilities as well, and this has very negative consequences for other students, who might well make very good use of computer facilities. Another serious dilemma is how to prevent a great gulf from opening between those students who have a personal computer at home and those whose only access to computers is in school. Just as the introduction of the snowmobile instantly polarized Lapp communities into those who could own the machines and those who could not and hence were at a severe economic disadvantage, so the availability of personal computers in the home carries the potential for polarizing us into those who are 'computer-literate' and those who are excluded. It is important that this should not happen, and so we must all come to terms with computers and help our students come to terms with them, being careful to foster confidence and interest among all equally and resisting the strong and natural tendency for the development of an elite at the expense of the rest of us.

References

BARR, Avron and Edward A Feigenbaum (ed). The handbook of artificial intelligence. Vol 1, p 223-361. Understanding Natural Language, Understanding Spoken Language. Vol 2, p 225-94. Applications-Oriented AI Research: Education (Review of 8 'intelligent' CAI systems, including SHRDLU and ELIZA). Stanford, California: HeurisTech Press (1981).

COMPUTER-ASSISTED LANGUAGE INSTRUCTION CONSORTIUM, USA: CALICO Journal.

DAVIES, Graham and John Higgins. Computers, language, and language learning. London: Centre for Information on Language Teaching and Research (1982). Using computers in language learning: a teacher's guide. Second, revised edn. London: Centre for Information on Language Teaching and Research (1985).

HIGGINS, John and Tim Johns. Computers in language learning. London and Glasgow: Collins ELT (1984).

TURKLE, Sherry. The second self: computers and the human spirit. New York: Simon and Schuster (1984).

Micro-computers in language teaching

Ake Hägg
University of Stockholm,
Sweden

Introduction

The views I will express in this article are those of a full-time language-teacher (English, Russian, German) at secondary-school level (upper forms) who has grown to become a computer amateur, especially interested in the use of micro-computers in one particular field, namely that of language-teaching.

The terms used for this - CALL (Computer-Assisted Language Learning), CAI (Computer-Aided Instruction) - I consider slightly unfortunate since it is for **practice** and **training** in particular that I can see a natural and beneficial use of micro-computers. Moreover, reinforcement and practice are two aspects very necessary when learning a language, along with many other activities. They are also the aspects we tend very much to leave to the student to do on his own, which is fine for a gifted student but rather difficult for the poor ones, who need our help and guidance.

I am perfectly aware that this is a rather controversial subject. It conjures up an image of rigid, mechanical teaching, impersonal and of rather poor quality. The objections you hear to using the computer in language-teaching are, for example, 'too expensive, too complicated mechanically, and totally lacking in communication'.

I would like to examine these points here; discuss the costs, how complicated the machine is, in its advantages and disadvantages; describe the situation in Sweden, and talk a little about teacher-training and in-service training for teachers.

The situation in Sweden for language-teachers is gradually deteriorating. We face larger classes, the gap between the best and the poorest students is growing, and on top of all that we also face a reduction in the number of periods per week. To counter this we would have to make our own teaching more efficient, but the point when this is no longer possible will come rather soon - if, indeed, we have not reached it already.

In such a situation it would be quite natural to say: I wish we had a sort of machine that could for example keep a word-list in its memory, a word-list based on texts which are fresh in the student's memory, which could pick examples at random and train the student and reinforce his basic vocabulary. Such a machine could then keep track of the student's score to show him how long he needs this kind of training. It would also keep a record of the student's mistakes, and after a suitable lapse of time let him or her try those examples again. It should be flexible enough to accept any number of synonyms and be able to distinguish between real mistakes and simple spelling mistakes. It should also make it easy for a teacher to write his own lists of words and synonyms for the student to practise.

Well, such a machine exists already. There is a rather typical drill-program for a computer which I will demonstrate. Some of you may say that this is not the type of exercise we do in the classroom. True, but this is not intended for the classroom. This type of exercise is meant for a student who wants to do it outside the classroom, in his own good time. Many students need this and have developed their own techniques for doing it. We could give them some help here, especially the weak ones.

The same is true for grammar and structure programs. A basic difference between an exercise-book and the same material in a computer program is that the computer is interactive and can keep constant track of the student's performance. But, you say, all this can be done by a teacher. Yes, but not with many different students at the same time. While we, as teachers, correct something in one corner of the classroom, other students are making mistakes that remain uncorrected elsewhere. We will later come across them, and correct them, but we cannot as easily erase from a student's mind a mistake that has been learnt. We cannot adapt ourselves to each individual student's pace, either. If we ask a question, and are perfectly willing to wait as long as is necessary for a student to answer, the very atmosphere in the classroom will act on the student, hands will go up elsewhere, and he will feel the pressure to respond as quickly as possible. The computer, an inanimate object, can 'wait patiently' and it is up to the student to set the pace. If he answers promptly, the next question will follow immediately. If he takes his time, the computer waits.

A student does not have to feel 'stupid' when he makes a mistake. Nobody else is watching. There is no teacher who makes a mental note of his weak performance. The computer can become the friend that helps the student to improve his skills, with which he can then surprise the teacher.

But it is a dead machine, you say. But if we were to make an honest comparison between a tape-recorder and a computer we must say that a student can nod off completely in front of a tape-recorder. It does not require any response from him. Moreover, it will run its course, irrespective of the student's performance. A computer constantly asks for responses from the student. Each response is then evaluated and comments are made. The same exercise will be reshuffled and changed each time it is run, and thus be different each time.

We have come to regard tape-recorders as common ingredients in our teaching. No one raises an eyebrow if he enters a classroom and sees a tape-recorder in a corner. I predict that in a few years time it will be the same for computers.

Cost

But what about the cost? Isn't this an expensive way of teaching? Well, hardly teaching; we would be doing that with the rest of the students while the computer helped us with some others. If computers were bought solely for language-training, they would indeed be expensive. However, the situation today is that schools are buying computers for quite other reasons. Our curricula demand that we prepare our students for the type of world they will live and work in, and computers form an integral part of that world.

If we walk around in our schools and open some doors in departments where we language teachers seldom go, we will find in most cases that our schools already have computers. They are used in teaching computer science and related subjects, but they are not used all the time, and this is where we come in. If we had the relevant programs, we would not have to include the cost of the computer in our budget. In fact, by using the computer when it is not reserved for other teaching, we merely justify the large sums of money that are already invested in the equipment. We only have to look at the cost of software, at how much programs cost, and we will find that they are actually cheap considering the range of students that can use the same programs. A program, for example, with which a teacher can write his own material, and thus use it in many different classes and age groups, can cost something like £75.00 – which is cheaper than the tapes with recorded texts from a certain book, which can only be used by one age group. Considering their versatility and usefulness, the programs are cheap teaching material.

I exclude programs that illustrate only one thing, a certain grammar point for example, and cannot be supplied with new material by the teacher. This type tends to become a once-only program and therefore does not give value for money.

Ease of use

Complicated, then. Isn't the computer a complicated machine? If we compare a tape-recorder and a computer we will find that they are very much the same.

1. We switch them on. Sometimes the switch is at the back of the

computer, or there's an extra switch for the disk drive, but it is still quite easy.

2. We place the cassette in the tape-recorder and we place a disk in the disk drive. The cassette can be put in back to front, and so can the disk, but it is easy to learn the right way.

3. We press PLAY on the tape-recorder, and we write RUN + the program name (or sometimes just the program name), and we're in business. The computer is as easy to handle as the tape-recorder.

A few years back computers were far more complicated to run, especially the bigger ones, but with the advent of the microcomputer, which is easy to handle, this is past history. An important point is the programs. They can be made in such a way that they are simple to run, and it is the programmer's job to do that. If you need special knowledge of how a computer works in order to run a program, the programmer has simply done a bad job. A ready-made program should start after one command has been given, usually just RUN + program name. Any student should be able to handle it, and it should offer a teacher who has previously never seen a computer no difficulty whatsoever. There are many such programs about, and if a program does not come up to this standard, it is simply not a finished product.

We language teachers should not have to become programmers to get the programs we want. Just as we normally do not produce our own textbooks, tapes, video-tapes, etc, we should not have to produce our own computer material. Publishing companies will do that for us, which will ensure the standard and availability of good programs. Until recently there was no real market for computer programs in Scandinavia. It is the old chicken and egg problem. Publishing companies did not produce computer programs before there was a demand for them, and there was no demand before there were programs to be had that could stimulate interest. Therefore the initial period has been a rather hesitant and slow process, but is now rapidly picking up and the major publishing companies in Sweden have started producing data disks based on material in their textbooks, available in the same way as tapes and other material. This has created an interest and a demand for new material, and has started the ball rolling.

Good programs

What, then, are the criteria of good programs? First and foremost a program should be easy to start: It should require just one command. It should be menu-oriented, by which I mean that the program should present a menu from which the user can choose what he wants to do. All the instructions should be on the screen, and if a user makes a mistake, the program should not crash under his hands, but simply give new instructions on how to proceed. Technically, a program should run without hitches, even if a beginner runs it for the first time. If these requirements are not fulfilled, it does not matter how good pedagogically the program or the teaching material that has gone into it are. When a program has reached this technical standard, the essential thing is, of course, its strategy and method. Here the best programs are those where teachers can write additional material, using so-called 'authoring programs', which are programs that guide a teacher who does not even know the build-up of the student program, so that the end product is a new exercise for it. By using authoring programs, the material we prepare can be our own material, adapted to our own students, and at the right level. Not all program packages contain authoring programs, since it takes a programmer an even longer time to produce than the student program, and would mean that the consumer, the teacher, would not be as dependent on the creator of the program for new material. Still, it is the only acceptable way of avoiding material not quite suited for a specific level, or too general and watered-down to be of interest to us language teachers.

Other criteria

There are certain other demands that we should make on the programs we let our students use. The programs should, for example, reflect the methods we use in the classroom. By that I mean that they should treat the student with respect, not ridicule him for mistakes but not be so exceedingly generous with praise that it appears ridiculous. When a student gives a correct response in the classroom, we go on with the next question. However, there are many computer programs where every correct response is greeted with a rewarding fanfare, a graphic symbol of some kind, or words like 'Correct, well done!'. In the long run this can become rather tiresome for a student who knows that his answer is correct, and who wants the program to proceed to the next problem. A mistake must be pointed out, but as a gentle reminder, and not over-emphasised. Many programs start with the words 'Hello. What's your name?' After the fourth or fifth attempt the student will most probably answer 'Donald Duck' or 'Superman', and it is quite depressing to watch the program treat this just as seriously. 'Well done, Donald Duck', 'your score is 70%, Donald Duck', etc is not likely to create the right attitude to a program; in fact, it can sometimes be quite harmful. Programs should be neutral and balanced in their attitude to the student.

A program should efficiently train what it sets out to train. The rest of the trimmings should only take up a minimum of time. If a student already knows the instructions, he should be able to pass them through quickly. There are programs where the start of the program with a graphic presentation of the producer's logo and the introduction of the program takes such a long time that some users lose interest. Not the first or the second time, of course, but quite soon. In some others the action around the computer exercise or the special way you enter your 'answers' in a computer game completely obscures the only relevant factor, namely what the program purports to practise. Here, I think, we language teachers will gradually weed out the worst one- and let them quietly disappear, but in the initial period we are bound to be unduly impressed and make mistakes.

Typical programs

What can a program look like, then? I will briefly describe a common type - a kind of cloze-test or text manipulation program. With an authoring program the teacher writes a text, preferably out of the student's textbook, or a text related to something the student has worked with. The text is simply typed in the computer, and the program gives all the instructions. When the text is written, the teacher gives it a name and it is stored on the disk. When the student runs the student program and names this text, it will be shown on the screen for a short time After that the program will delete some words at random, leaving only the first letter. The student then works at restoring the text again by writing suggestions, which will then appear on the screen if they are correct. There are a number of help-facilities, and the student can, for example, ask to see a certain letter or the whole text again. The program trains both structure, vocabulary, and reading comprehension like the usual cloze-test.

Another program writes a text up to a point predetermined by the teacher. It then stops and asks for a suggestion from the student. The correct answer, which can be one of many different possibilities, will produce the next part of the text and so on. The same program can be combined with a tape-recorder that plays the text, including the part missing on the screen.

There are, of course, also the bread-and-butter programs, training vocabulary and grammar structures. If these programs are flexible enough - for example, distinguishing between spelling mistakes and real mistakes - and supplied with authoring programs, so that the material trained is relevant, then even the simple drill programs can fulfil a function in the limited sphere where they are necessary, as long as they are not used alone **instead of** at the same time being used by a teacher.

Conditions of use

The situation when we let students work with the programs can vary, depending on the number of computers available and the possibility of making them available to the students without much supervision. Preferably, we leave the computer room open and let the students avail themselves of the opportunity. The computers generate enough interest to attract the students, and if the programs are of good quality, and related to the courses the students take, they will see that it is an advantage to use them. If possible, we should keep every minute of our lessons for other methods of teaching. Sometimes it is good policy to split a class up into smaller groups, working with different things. One group could then work at the computers while we, the teachers, remain in the classroom to use this opportunity to work with smaller groups.

A natural place for a micro-computer is the school library where the students can get help from the librarian in choosing the relevant material.

In general it can be said that if we can make the use of computers optional and a free choice of a student we will probably reap greater benefits than if we make it compulsory.

Teacher training

What do we do about teacher training? This is a vital question because we have to start learning to use computers before we implement them in our teaching. To our students the computer presents no problem, but to most of the language teachers they do since we belong to another generation. However, even if we language teachers have no intention of using language programs, we all should try using a word-processor. We teachers produce a lot of written material and it is quite a help to use the word-processor for that. When we are confident, we can introduce it to our students and let them write business-letters or reports or compositions or whatever. We would then simply train the student to use a method he will use later in life anyway, while at the same time reaping the benefits of a rational way of working.

Recent developments

You can hook up a tape-recorder to a micro-computer and get some interesting new combinations. There are tape-recorders, especially the Tandberg TCCR 530, which can be made to wind and rewind and find any spot on a tape with great accuracy. The readings on the counter are minutes and seconds, and it is never wrong by more than 5 seconds. A slight pause in front of a sentence is enough for the tape-recorder to find it. All kinds of listening exercises are now possible, and the most striking difference between a working station with a computer and tape-recorder, and with the traditional language laboratory, is that every station is individual and does not require a teacher to supervise the work. In a language laboratory we are mostly confined to giving all the students the same exercises, and we only monitor one student at a time. A computer-tape-recorder combination will monitor the work itself, and no teacher supervision is necessary.

To sum up

I believe that the micro-computer is a good tool in our schools, even for language teaching, provided we select the areas where it can contribute in a positive way, and avoid some areas where it does not add anything to other methods of teaching and instead only means a waste of valuable teaching time. I also believe that it will come into our schools whether we want it or not, and if we do not start studying its potential now, we will only end up having others – who are not language teachers – creating the systems for us, which will be worse. By taking an active part now we can influence its development and turn it to our advantage.

When textile workers once wanted to protest against the automatic weaving machines by throwing their clogs into them to break the machinery, they created a new word, 'sabotage', from the French word for clog, <u>sabot</u>. As we look at the industry today we can see what little effect it had, so let us not throw our clogs into the microcomputers. Let us study them, make them our friends and allies and use them the way we have enriched our teaching with other inventions.

PART FIVE: EXAMINATIONS AND TESTING

Our final thematic section deals with the topic that is a necessary concomitant of any language course - testing. In two quite lengthy articles we see the problems of testing modern languages in the context of a crowded school curriculum by a nationwide bureaucratic system and after an intensive course in a highly specialised institution. Once again, our two contributors are based in Europe and the USA respectively.

In our translation of Luukkainen's article we have adopted two terms that perhaps require glosses: for the German Sprachgefühl - as it is used in this paper - we use the modish 'language awareness' because both seem here to have the same lack of precision, encompassing both an intuitive 'feeling for language' and a certain acquaintance with a given language under discussion; and although the examination in question is a Finnish one, we have allowed "'A' level" as a rough equivalent. This, like many of the points the author makes, will no doubt strike ready chords in readers from many countries.

Luukkainen selects three topics for special attention - the range of languages offered in schools, the use of different teaching methods, and the means of evaluating results. Curriculum reforms decrease the amount of time available for language study at school, so the feasible aims must subsequently be reduced and the emphasis of teaching and testing adjusted. School language learning becomes more a basis for further learning in later life, the emphasis being thrown on performance and on quality as opposed to quantity. In the fluid state of constant reforms and revisions it is difficult to ensure congruence between what is taught in the classroom and what is tested at final examinations. Examinations should test what is taught, but the shape of an examination may in fact dictate the teaching, making the achievement of communicative teaching aims more difficult. Discussing what should in fact be tested, Luukkainen sees accuracy, appropriacy and fluency as only elements in a complex of extra-linguistic factors affecting learning; the teacher can assess these but they cannot be tested in examinations. Particularly in the context of reduced lesson time, the examination must be limited to communicative ability and awareness of language. Methods of testing these are discussed with reference to several research projects and through computer analysis of actual examination papers, with special reference to multiple-choice tests of reading-comprehension and the writing of essays.

Attacking the general theme of testing from a very different angle, our second contributor proceeds from the experience of the US Defense Language Institute at Monterey - a pioneer institution in the field. If the realistic aim in terms of language performance at schools is, in Luukkainen's view, extremely modest, the equally realistic aims of the Monterey courses in spoken language are very high indeed. Clifford nonetheless opens with a basic problem that is common to both widely-separated spheres - that of the gulf between language as a subject of study and language as used in the world at large. Proposing three main purposes of testing - individual mastery of a course of study, adequacy for performing certain tasks, and competence relative to native speakers - he discusses achievement testing, performance testing and proficiency testing, tracing the Monterey experiences with all three and their implications for course development and teaching activities. In the achievement teaching/testing phase, a tendency to regard the contents of one textbook as the whole aim only widened the gap between classroom and real life; a shift to job-related (performance) orientation also led to a shrinkage of purview; a further shift to a proficiency orientation became necessary. Clifford looks at the problem of defining language skill levels (in which the Defense Language Institute has exerted perhaps its greatest influence) and measurable standards for criterion-referenced tests; scoring techniques and the evolution of performance profiles; elicitation techniques and positive communication exchange in oral tests, etc. In his conclusion Clifford denies that you should test what you teach (since this is too limiting) but asserts that you should **teach in the way** you test.

Taken together, these two articles, though written in very different styles, illumine each other and this important topic in an enlightening and informative way.

Language awareness, communicative competence and testing

Matti Luukkainen
University of Helsinki, Finland

Introduction

Confidence, motivation and creativity - three constructive and pertinent topics - are the basis of the current debate. My first task is to discuss language tests - a task which often provokes a negative reaction. However, I am convinced that there should be no contradiction between teaching and testing, and that evaluation can be understood as a constructive and natural element in the acquisition of a foreign language. Whether we like it or not, we shall always need language tests. They are a necessary means of feedback both for the pupil and for the teacher. Moreover, a society has a right to find out about the language ability of its citizens.

When we talk about foreign language acquisition, three aspects must be taken into account: the multiplicity of foreign languages being offered, the use of successful teaching methods, and the evaluation of results. Although the theme of my talk relates to the third point, I cannot completely ignore the two other fundamental factors. They are all intertwined.

The teaching methods of the old and the new school are different in that in traditional teaching language is treated as a structure, an end in itself, whereas today language is viewed as a means to an end. We should therefore continually keep in mind that language is a means of communication, in the lesson as well as in the test.

A communication situation arises when a message is being sent from a sender to a recipient. Therefore an overriding role is always played by an idea, the intellectual content, which is sent or received, using a certain system of sign language. Two opposing methods of behaviour can be distinguished when using the language, which the Finnish lecturer in teaching methods, Viljo Kohonen, has described by the pair of terms 'language as master' and 'language as servant'. In the former, energy is directed to external form: in the latter, the focus is on content. This comparison, which on the one hand represents the development of language teaching methods, and on the other the degree of communicative competence, will be a recurring theme in my paper.

Figure 1

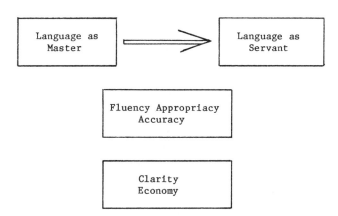

On the currently much discussed topic of foreign language policy and its consequences for foreign language teaching, I believe that almost every problem encountered in language teaching can be traced back to the unhappy situation of the range of foreign languages being offered. As a result of the numerous consecutive so-called reforms, language choice and learning time has been severely restricted in Finland over the last few years. 32% fewer students took German for 'A' level in spring 1985 than in spring 1984. There was a 22% decline in the numbers taking French, and as much as 35% in Russian.

Not only does this development contradict the vital interests of a small country, but it also contradicts the final acts of the conference on 'Safety and Co-operation in Europe', where the member states swore to 'promote the study of foreign languages and civilisations as an important tool for the expansion of communication between peoples, to improve their knowledge of the culture of each country, and to strengthen international cooperation' as well as 'to simulate the further development and diversification of the choice of language taught at different levels to this end within their jurisdiction'.

My paper today deals with German, French and Russian, i.e. with the languages chosen by us to be the third and fourth foreign languages, or as we in Finland say, the C and D languages. Since the Upper School Reform which came into force in 1982, in the last year, C and D languages are no longer obligatory to all pupils. It is in fact impossible to choose these languages with certain subject combinations, especially in the third year. Whereas before the Reform mentioned above, which has caused numerous problems in the opinion of many people, each 'A' level student studied German, French and Russian, the latest statistics show also that of the reduced number of pupils learning C or D languages in the second year, almost a half no longer choose these subjects in the third year. As a result of a new Reform introduced at the beginning of August, and the resultant increased competition between the different subject areas, it is anticipated that the study of German, French and Russian will experience even greater setbacks.

We should therefore assume when examining, that we can no longer expect all-round communicative competence as a result of school teaching. It should be seen much more that the learning of foreign languages remains a life-long process. Therefore what matters at school is creating the right motivation and developing an **awareness of language.** Creativity plays a central role as an essential factor of language competence. Instead of learning by heart, as in the old school, special value should be placed on applied knowledge, i.e. on performance. As regards the special position of German, French and Russian among the subjects, it is inevitable that the learning material will be reduced as a result of the reduction in learning time. In order that the pupils nevertheless develop a feeling of security, the automation of central studies relevant to communication and the development of strategies for comprehension should assume an important position in teaching. The aim is therefore economy, clarity, and a certain degree of fluency. Further expansion of the knowledge of a language would therefore take place if necessary at a later stage in life. Consequently, school teaching should be more concerned with quality than with quantity.

Before I begin to analyse the structure of the pupil's ability being tested, I would like to restrict my subject even further. As you may already have noticed, my remarks largely relate to the situation in Finland, where we still have a centralised 'A' level system. Every spring and every autumn the 'A' levels form a hot topic of discussion among the public. Not only are the individual tests widely discussed by the mass media, but they are also mentioned in Parliament.

The language examinations are reproached for the following reasons: they do not relate to the courses in question and make excessive demands on the competence of the 'A' level students; they do not actually measure use of language; the comprehension tests are more a question of trial and error than of language knowledge; the results do not correspond to the impressions of the teacher, since bad pupils get good marks and good pupils get bad marks; the tests are not commensurable, since more difficult tasks are set in German than in French and Russian; it is due to the testing technique of the 'A' level committee that the choice of C and D languages has decreased in such a disastrous way.

Against this background, and since justification for and the form of the 'A' level is a topical question in Finland today, I shall concentrate largely on the problem of language tests in the 'A' level examinations, not least because I was myself a member of the 'A' level Committee during the period 1977-1984. We shall come to the degree of difficulty and significance of the 'A' level test and its validity and reliability later on, when we analyse the tests of the previous spring and their statistical evaluation. As far as the decrease in numbers of pupils is concerned, we have already shown that this is related to the Upper Schools Reform and the increased competition between the different subject areas. It has already been anticipated that the tests in Russian over the last few years were among the easiest - even excessively easy from the point of view of examination technique. However, we saw above that the decrease in 'A' level students was most noticeable in Russian. The moderation in degree of difficulty therefore in no way signified an increase in motivation.

The evaluation of the 'A' level system and the structure of the Upper Schools are, of course, closely connected. We have already mentioned that there are many who question the teaching content of the 1982 Upper Schools Reform. With this Reform, which was intended to reduce the numbers of pupils at high schools and high school classes in favour of technical colleges, the learning material in each subject was divided up into very starkly separated courses, which the pupils had to complete in strict sequence. A few weeks ago, the Head of the Upper Schools Authority expressed the opinion that the 'A' level system in use today was to blame for the fact that the teaching objectives of the Upper Schools Reform were not being realised. He said that learning by heart, not applied knowledge, was what the 'A' level tested. Therefore the 'A' level should be abolished, unless it could be radically changed.

The proposal made by the Head of the Upper Schools Authority has been turned down by many, not least by the teachers, since despite all its shortcomings it is a better guarantee than the Leaving Certificate of uniformity of assessment throughout the entire country. On the basis of my experiences on the 'A' level Committee, I would like to stress that the relationship between 'A' level and the Reformed Upper School is exactly the other way round from what the Head of the Upper Schools Authority believed. In each subject in the 'A' level, tasks are set which require creative thought processes and adaptability, and where stolid learning by rote is not rewarded. This is, of course, the only possible procedure in view of the predicted function of the 'A' level. Nevertheless, some teachers' criticisms are levelled at the type of question where the 'A' level demands something which is not directly contained in the courses in question.

On the other hand, I cannot help thinking that the oppressive examination technique related to the completion of different courses at the reformed High Schools is reminiscent of the methods of the old school. These courses, which are packed with enormous amounts of material, can stifle the creativity of teachers and pupils alike and even force them to learn by heart. Moreover, the atomistic nature of the new High Schools contradicts the didactic and psychological reality of pupils of that age. This is especially true of a subject like languages, where no fragmentation is possible but where the development of a feel for languages depends on continuity. One may therefore take the view that in these changed circumstances an 'A' level exam which tests not only a certain part, but knowledge in general, is much more important than ever before. The Learning Certificate and the 'A' level Certificate therefore perform different functions.

A fair examination technique must take various things into account. There is obviously an essential difference between tests carried out during teaching and the end-of-school examination, i.e. between the tests an individual teacher carries out with his own class for teaching purposes and an examination carried out contemporaneously throughout the country via a powerful bureaucratic machine. On the whole, it should be true that the accent in teaching may be on formative or diagnostic tests, whereas the final examination should merely fulfil a summarising or predictive function. However, one thing is certain – even when examining we should ensure that the pupils are not discouraged, but encouraged. In contrast to the old school, the catch-phrase here is 'competence through confidence'.

We have shown above that motivation and easy tests do not coincide. The majority of pupils should understand that effective, creative thought is an essential factor in the learning process (Vuorinen, 1984). Motivation is first and foremost a matter between the school and the teacher. The 'A' level Committee must, however, take into account the particular psychological situation of the candidates. Any unnecessary worry for the examinee is reprehensible, even if the relative assessment usual in Finland each year yields the same distribution of marks. But it is not easy to draw up tests which function reliably with the best as well as the weaker students. Among the six grades used, for example, a reliable difference between the two upper categories would give meaningful information for the High Schools admissions procedure, but if – in the preparation of the tests – only this limit were heeded, then the population as a whole would perhaps find the tests too difficult.

Whereas the language tests used in class should in my opinion cover all areas of communicative competence and not differ essentially from the exercises used in class, so that the pupil feels secure, the language tests contained in the final examination have to satisfy quite different criteria. In particular, they must be as reliable, realistic and economical as possible. For example, they do not have to follow scrupulously all the latest fashions. Feasibility and reliability are important criteria. Validity is equally important, i.e. they must relate to the thing being tested. And here we come to the crux of the matter: What is the object being tested?

What do we want to test?

Those people who complain, for example, that genuine language use is not tested at 'A' level, probably believe that a native speaker should be present at each examination to test the communicative ability of the 'A' level student. However, such ideals can seldom be realised in real life. Any form of examination is incomplete. Each has its advantages and disadvantages. There may be an abstract, ideal version which, owing to the numerous contributory variables, is more or less not ideal in practice. Anyway, the best of methods becomes dull in use. On the other hand, test procedure will only be a compromise solution at best, since the thing being tested, ability to communicate, is a very complicated and complex concept.

The old school's idea of language ability acquired at school was simple and non-problematical. One had to work through and translate a certain number of fixed pieces. The formal side outweighed the content. Nowadays we admit that it is practically impossible to distinguish speaking ability from other human activities. Ability to communicate manifests itself in a communication situation. How effectively the message underlying the communication situation in question is passed on to the recipient, i.e. how well it succeeds, largely depends on the accuracy, appropriacy and fluency of the spoken code. However, ability to communicate depends on a whole series of other aspects not directly related to the spoken code, and which we have therefore to designate as para- or extra-linguistic factors.

My paper is a very typical example of a communication situation. How well the message is conveyed from the brain of the speaker to the brain of the listener, depends on the knowledge the speaker and the listener have of the language. In addition, there are factors on both sides which have nothing to do with ability in a language, but are connected with a person's disposition and temperament. These include intellectual capacity, ability to concentrate, emotional make-up, affective situation, etc. In particular, it depends on how well the speaker has thought out his ideas and internalised them; how clearly he has structured his material; how committed he feels to his subject; how interestingly he treats it; and whether he reacts calmly or emotionally in the given situation. Successful communication calls not least for effective use of voice, gesture and facial expression. I believe we could draw up an even longer list of factors which influence the communicative ability of speaker and listener. Anyway, it has been proved that ability in a language only forms one half of the ability to communicate. The other half is a more or less universal affair, which involves factors that play a similar role in the native language as well as the foreign language.

In this connection, I would like to refer to a diagram (Figure 2) in which Kari Sajavaara and Jaakkoo Lehtonen illustrate the process of communication (the essay from which it comes is contained in the 1980 AFinLA yearbook). It is not perhaps necessary here to explain each box in the diagram; let us merely establish that this machine, which looks very like a computer, with both INPUT and OUTPUT, is meant to represent the human brain. The three boxes at the bottom illustrate the extra-lingual factors of the personality.

Figure 2

A simplified model of message processing

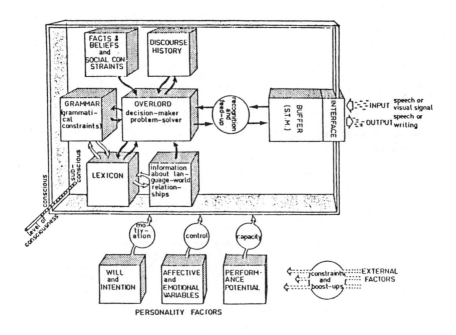

(Sajavaara & Lehtonen 1980, p 29)

There are obviously enormous differences in the way in which each individual communicates - one method of communication works better for one person, a different one for another. We have to take account of these individual differences in class, and we also have to evaluate the different means of communication in a similar way. For the same reason, oral and written ability must similarly be weighed up. This applies to the teacher's assessment - he knows the personality of the pupil and can take all aspects into account.

The 'A' level language tests are somewhat different. Since their scope is restricted, their relevance must be safeguarded using other criteria. Moreover, one should be aware that the 'A' level Certificate and the School Leaving Certificate, as I have stressed already, have different functions. For example, it is neither possible nor necessary in the 'A' level to perform a special language examination. Owing to its purely predictive function, the 'A' level must concentrate on a carefully thought out, more limited area of communicative ability, which focusses on language awareness. This limitation is all the more urgent today, since learning time at school has been cut. The communicative aspects are important even when evaluating language awareness, since a language only lives in different types of communication situations where it serves to convey a message. I cannot decide whether input and output should or can be tested at the same time. The extent to which language can be 'real' in a test situation, whatever technique is used, is a question which I have already commented on.

I would like to refer to two more studies on communicative ability which appeared in print in the publications of the Association for Applied Linguistic Knowledge in Finland. Viljo Kohonen illustrated communicative ability in the 1983 AFinLA yearbook by means of the following two diagrams. Kohonen speaks of grammatical, sociolinguistic and strategic ability. Exactness and accuracy of expression are connected with grammatical ability. Sociolinguistic ability refers to acceptability and strategic ability to comprehensibility.

Figure 3

A model of communicative competence

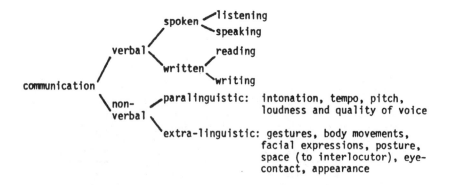

(Kohonen 1983, p 41)

Figure 4

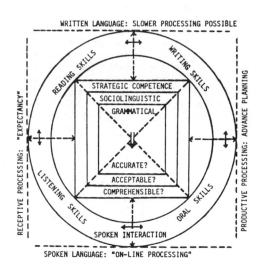

(Kohonen 1983, p 42)

In the 1980 AFinLA yearbook Norman Davies shows how, in his opinion, linguistic and communicative ability overlap (Figure 4). Besides these two terms, Davies introduces the term 'global competence' which is composed of the factors fluency, acceptability and accuracy.

Personally, I find the division into fluency, acceptability and accuracy appropriate from the linguistic point of view, and very applicable from the didactic point of view.

Figure 5

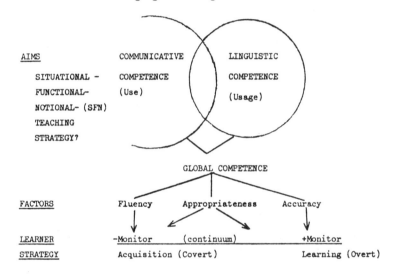

(Davies 1980, p 22)

'Language awareness' is a key term in my paper. It appears to me that the erudite term 'linguistic competence' is more or less inappropriate in the didactics of language; in this context I prefer to speak of 'language awareness' since this is a **dynamic** term and can be expounded on in class. Language awareness or - **if** we wish to keep the erudite term - linguistic competence, **is the** fundamental element of communicative ability.

Wolfgang Mueller, in his article entitled 'Language awareness on the test stand for philology' observed that linguists dislike this term and would rather avoid it, as it is not precise enough. Mueller goes on: 'as linguists they seek solid ground beneath their feet, which they believe they can find in regularities, generalisations, abstract formulae, i.e. in media far-removed from language, or mathematical logic'. Based on his studies, Mueller formulated the following definition of language awareness. Language awareness is regarded as intuition, sensitivity, instinctive feeling, even as a kind of sense and also a knowledge of norms, of possibilities for fashioning shapes and, and as a result, as an ability to apply this knowledge. Hence all spoken remarks are by implication subordinated to 'language awareness'. Language awareness is something that refers to the production of language, which puts someone in the situation of being able to use language correctly to suit the situation, and hence to evaluate speech produced differently. From the ability to convert knowledge into independent use is derived the ability to be able to decide whether something is 'right' or 'wrong'. In my opinion, these are the qualities conveyed by the linguist through the term 'linguistic competence'.

My model of communicative ability, published in the 1985 AFinLA Yearbook in an essay entitled 'Knowledge and skill in acquiring a third and fourth language', looks as follows:

Figure 6

Communicative ability

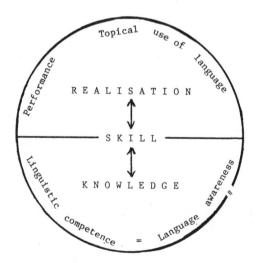

(Luukkainen 1985, p 216)

Linguistic ability and language awareness are compared here with performance or topical use of language. The relationship between knowledge and skill forms the fundamental problem of the didactics of language. Whereas knowledge is a part of linguistic ability or language awareness, skill belongs on the one hand to linguistic ability or language awareness, and on the other to performance or topical use of language, to which in turn among other things belong paralinguistic and extralinguistic methods. As a pure term for performance, realisation forms the antithesis to knowledge. Skill is the link joining the two. This is understood to mean capacity for linguistic organisation and ability to use language in the appropriate context.

The three components - knowledge, skill and realisation - are constantly interacting (expressed in the diagram by the arrows pointing in both directions). The more a language is used (language use is understood here to mean not only active, but passive use), the sounder is the skill, and the greater the linguistic ability. It can be seen from this how important presentation of the target language material is in all classroom situations. The pupils should be constantly subjected to the target language. Increased use of the mother tongue, which seems to be the order of the day with today's methods, is in my opinion very harmful to the development of language awareness.

Being able to speak a language is without doubt the aim of the learning, and it should also be what we measure in our class tests and at 'A' level. We can therefore refer to it as 'applied knowledge'. 'Skill' can be broken down further into the three elements 'accuracy', 'appropriacy' and 'fluency'. Appropriacy would then be a matter of language awareness; accuracy would belong partly to language awareness and partly to performance; and fluency would simply come under performance. All three elements are equally important to perfect communication. They are interconnected and difficult to separate. However, too much emphasis can be placed on each. In traditional teaching, too much emphasis has been placed on accuracy, causing appropriacy and fluency to suffer. We all know examples of where a linguistically correct speech act has failed to achieve the desired effect, even if today the danger is that the pragmatic viewpoints are exaggerated and the entire lesson is based on a colourful array of more or less natural 'situations'. The two criteria - ability to communicate and linguistic accuracy - are closely connected.

In our diagram (Figure 6), therefore, the lower half represents the genuinely monolingual sector; the upper half, containing realisation, which can be better evaluated at school than at 'A' level, is more or less universal. It may be that others would place more emphasis on the conventions of interaction which differ from one language to another; I am aware that they are relevant and belong within the framework of the learning. However, in view of the restriction in learning time it would be over-fastidious to exaggerate these at the expense of linguistic detail. I mean, therefore, that Finns should remain Finnish even when speaking German or French.

How do we want to test?

Until the 1970s the final examination in Finland included translation from and into the target language. However, since the 1960s it had been possible to sit an alternative examination where the translation component was smaller, and where, in addition, questions were asked on the content and vocabulary of the set text, which had to be answered in the target language. An essay was also written. However, this form of examination was soon discontinued, as the questions on content and vocabulary were not functioning properly and were difficult to evaluate. It was unclear whether receptive or productive skills should be assessed, and it is well known that the two things often contradict one another. In 1972 it became optional, and in 1977 obligatory, for all 'A' level students – in place of the translation test – to sit an aural comprehension and a reading comprehension test, and to write an essay. The essay was later supplemented by a grammatical structure test. The 'A' level in Finland today therefore comprises a total of four tests. Aural and reading comprehensions are tested by multiple-choice, whereas grammar is tested by means of a test where the pupils have to fill in the correct answers.

It is a fact that the type of 'A' level has an effect on the work done in the school. The test method must therefore be well thought out. The introduction of the aural comprehension test caused a great change in teaching methods. It was particularly fruitful, since an aural test is a very effective way of developing creative ability and hence awareness of language. Although there is no oral test at 'A' level, everyone can confirm that the students' ability to speak is better today than at the time of the translation examination, since they have a better-developed awareness of language today.

The 'A' level examination can also have a detrimental influence on teaching if the individual test forms, i.e. those intended for examination, not learning, are practised unilaterally. This applies in particular to the multiple-choice, which accounts for too large a share in today's 'A' level examination. It is therefore planned to make the 'A' level components more flexible in the foreseeable future, and to slightly vary them from one year to the next. To conclude my paper, I append samples of the examination in German as a third and fourth language from spring 1985. I shall compare a few results of this test with the results from the corresponding test in French and Russian. You will see on page 178 of the Appendix a part of the reading comprehension test; page 180 shows the corresponding statistical evaluation of the results and page 181 the essay topics; page 182 contains the grammatical structures test, followed on page 183 by three examples of essays written by 'A' level students. In addition, there was an aural comprehension test. It could be argued that working out multiple-choice tasks demands a lot of specialist knowledge and care. One needs to have a good knowledge of the intellectual and linguistic level of the target group, and at the same time to take many different factors into account. That is why there are good and bad multiple-choice tasks. The quality of the individual test can be seen in the corresponding statistical examination, which shows the percentages for correct solutions, the correlation coefficient of the individual items, and the reliability of the test as a whole. In my opinion, at 'A' level the average number of correct solutions should be two-thirds the maximum, i.e. 60-70%.

If the degree of difficulty increases or decreases, reliability can fall, thus showing how consistently the overall test is in fact measuring a certain property.

Multiple-choice tests

So long as one is unable to isolate linguistic competence from the other talents of the individual, one cannot say that multiple-choice tests comprehension of the language. It is obvious that qualities such as memory, creative ability, presupposition, and guess-work play a part in these tests, as they do in spoken communication. If the guessing component in the test is based on simple coincidence, and not on language awareness, this becomes apparent in the reduced correlation coefficients of the item in question, which shows each time how consistent the solution to this item is with the success of the pupil in the test as a whole. One can always find a technical error if there is a low coefficient of correlation.

For a test to be reliable, the original text must be relatively difficult and should also contain elements that are unknown to the pupil, who will then 'guess' by process of elimination and his awareness of language. On this assumption, 'red herrings' can be used which stand out sufficiently from one another. If competent people are unsure which alternative is the correct one, the task has been wrongly set with regard to the ability of the 'A' level students. If the original text is more difficult than for example a text destined for translation, it is possible to set questions based on linguistic, and not logical connections. Tasks which require detailed logical deduction in order to solve them should be rejected; they reduce the reliability since they are testing not awareness of language but something else. The correct solution must be able to be found fairly explicitly in the text, so that any interpretation deviating from this is excluded. The correct solution should require no real-life knowledge, but should be plausible on the basis of the linguistic information. Although the text on which the questions are assessed must be difficult, it should not be too abstract or uninteresting with regard to the level of the target group. The psychologically different situation must be taken into consideration in the reading and aural comprehension test. In the latter, the text - as well as the tape-recording - must be particul rly clear, so that the purpose of this productive form of testing is not lost.

All in all, test technique and motivation should bear equal weight when evaluating the 'A' level test. These are requirements which can scarcely be met by a single human being. That is why each test is a compromise. Fortunately, it is possible to correct the effect of the failed item afterwards by means of the statistical evaluation.

Let us turn first to page 180 of the Appendix. The middle column contains the evaluation for all 9,820 studies. The average number of correct answers is 80.9%. From the point of view of test technique, the test was apparently much too easy, and it therefore had a reliability of 0.81. The left-hand column shows the evaluation of the answers from the best third of the 'A' level students, the right-hand column that of the weaker third. Since this test was so easy, it was not capable of recording the difference in ability between the better pupils; the percentage of correct solutions is 93.8%, and consequently reliability is provided with a negative sign. In contrast, the test functioned as intended with the weaker pupils; the percentage of correct solutions here is 62.1%. This disharmony between the best and the weakest can hardly be avoided in today's heterogeneous target group consisting of pupils studying C and D languages.

Now to the individual questions. The numbers with an asterisk denote the correct alternative The number of pupils who chose A,B,C or D appears each time in the first row. The corresponding percentage appears in row 2, and in row 3 the average absolute score of the pupil in question in reading and aural comprehension tests as a whole - the maximum score is therefore 180. It can be seen from this how good or bad those pupils who chose these alternatives were in the overall test. In the middle column, on the right, is the coefficient of correlation between the item in question and the overall test. This coefficient shows whether a single item has been reliably evaluated, or whether the answers were based on chance.

We can see, for example, that question 7 was reliable, although it was too easy for the best 'A' level students ('She did not like the gossip of the old glider pilots'; in the text it says 'However, she did not enjoy the company' ... and 'There were grandads there at the bar prattling on about their flying adventures - she remarked with contempt - still today'). One third of the weakest third opted for C ('She admired the elderly glider pilots' thirst for adventure'), since they had mistakenly interpreted the strongly negative attitude in the text to be positive. Rather a lot, indeed, from the second best group in the entire population chose D, since they had identified the terms 'slow machine' and 'antiquated machine' with one another, which does not apply in this context, as it is to do with the difference between a glider and a powered plane.

By contrast, question 8 did not function properly, as only one quarter of the total population chose correctly. There is a glaring difference between the best and the worst third. The majority of the best pupils were successful here, too, and opted for C 'because they feared death', while one half of the weaker, and also over 40% of the entire population, chose the wrong alternative - A. Even among the best pupils a quarter opted for this. This is an instructive point for those responsible for test technique. If the text is completely understood, alternative C is clearly correct (cf. the text, ' ... hourly, had to consider a crash ... when you are no longer there ...'). However, the adjective **important**, which contains a value judgement, destroys the whole item in the wrong alternative - A ('since they were needed for more important tasks'). Madlene Clausen was a programmer first, then had to work exclusively in documentation. What exactly an 'important' task is seems to be a matter of interpretation for the target group. Normally questions such as this are eliminated in the final evaluation.

Question 9 is an example of an item which works excellently. Its coefficient of correlation is even 0.52. The average percentage for the correct answers is approximately 70%. The best pupils proved their ability convincingly, while the weaker ones did the exact opposite. They vacillated between the correct alternative - A, and the wrong one - B; even D attracted quite a few who did not have a good knowledge of German. Question 10 can again be said to have tested the understanding of German ideally. Two-thirds of the entire population chose correctly... . There is a clear difference between the way in which the best and the weakest behave. On this sheet of examination tasks we therefore have examples which require no real communication situation to solve, but despite this reliably bring to light gradual differences in feeling for language, which forms part of communicative ability. Unlike the previous test, the structural test on page 2 is an integral type, requiring at the same time reading comprehension and creative ability. Like the multiple-choice test, the test which involves filling in gaps is not a real communication situation. On the other hand, it effectively measures language awareness.

The essay as a test

The essay is the written part of our 'A' level, and is partly guided. Ability to communicate, and how clearly the 'A' level student can express his thoughts in the target language, are taken into consideration in the evaluation. A prerequisite of the highest, to come back to Kohonen's terms, is that language should be treated as servant, not master. Accuracy, appropriacy and fluency naturally play an important role.

In the paper written by Kohonen in 1983, to which I have several times referred, he put forward three stages in the assessment of communicative ability in a diagram which is shown as Figure 6. As we can see, the three stages can overlap, since it is well known how hard it is to delimit them. At 'A' level we have 6 grades which can perhaps be described as <u>very good</u>, <u>good</u>, <u>satisfactory</u>, <u>adequate</u>, <u>poor</u>, <u>inadequate</u>. <u>Very good</u> would be equivalent to Kohonen's grade 3, whereas <u>good</u> would be on the border between grade 2 and 3. <u>Satisfactory</u> would come under grade 2, and <u>adequate</u> between grade 1 and 2. <u>Poor</u> would come under grade 1 and <u>inadequate</u> would come bottom on Kohonen's scale. As I have already pointed out, the difference between <u>very good</u> and <u>good</u> would be particularly relevant, owing to the predictive nature of the 'A' level.

On page 183 you will find three essays. If we consider how well the 'A' level student has expressed himself, i.e. whether he has regarded the language as master or servant, it turns out that No. 1 has not proved himself. The sentences do not link up, and the thoughts are unclear. There is a lack of personal commitment. We could say that his use of language is not appropriate. The teacher would have given a <u>good</u>, while the 'A' level committee plumped for <u>satisfactory</u> (essay No. 1). The two others were given a <u>very good</u> by the teacher as well as the committee. No. 2 is an example of how simple, fluent use of language conveys a pleasant and personal impression. Readable style reveals a good feel for the language, and hence also good communicative ability. Since the courses today are so short, the concern is not for wealth of idioms. If they are not used properly, idioms can have an oppressive effect (essay No. 2). The last essay shows how important creativity is during class and during examinations. This student obviously enjoyed writing this essay, and he therefore also managed to make the reader enjoy reading it. In cases such as this, one is glad to overlook the mistakes, as they do not interfere with the communication (essay No. 3).

I think any teacher will confirm that pupils suddenly forget their fear of mistakes when they are writing about a topic they find interesting or important, or even about which they get very excited, and produce a language one would not have expected. We can therefore see how important the emotional base is to the acquisition of a foreign language. As far as examinations are concerned, pupils should be neither overestimated nor underestimated: they should be valued.

Languages compared

The above sentence can also be interpreted as follows: that our language tests should be pleasant, but effective, neither too difficult nor too easy. I said before that ideally the average score should be two thirds of the maximum, i.e. 60-70%. The following table shows the percentage for the correct solutions in all parts of the German, French and Russian examinations. The reliability of aural and reading comprehension tests is given in brackets; the effect of the poor items is corrected for by the number of right solutions, which is why the degree of difficulty is somewhat less than in the original evaluation (Figure 7).

Figure 7

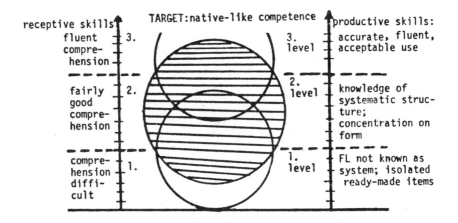

(Kohonen 1983, p 48)

	Aural comprehension	Reading comprehension	Structures	Essay
German	76.8% (.76)	81.6% (.81)	66.2%	76.5%
French	76.5% (.74)	73.7% (.84)	77.6%	76.1%
Russian	79.5% (.74)	88.0% (.69)	63.7%	73.6%

We have no space here to analyse the percentages in greater detail, but one typical characteristic should be mentioned: where there is the greatest number of correct solutions (in the Russian reading comprehension test), reliability is also very low. Such an essay test is neither effective nor meaningful.

The use of computer analysis

Computer analysis produces a lot of information each year – a treasure trove for anyone interested in this area. One statistical study which examined how the result in the reading comprehension test compared with the mark given by the teacher in school, showed that the results agree well, especially in French but also in German, while the picture is less certain with Russian as the task was too easy.

We can also show statistical studies which examine how well the different individual components in the examination correspond with one another as regards giving information about the structure of linguistic ability. It would appear that there is a high correlation between the different individual tests, and that the object being tested therefore forms a relatively uniform whole. As expected, the greatest correlation is usually either between reading and aural comprehension, which evaluate receptiveness, or between essay and structural test, which are aimed at the creative capacities. The lowest correlation is between aural comprehension and structural test, or between aural comprehension test and essay.

One could in addition investigate the different behaviour of girls and boys in the C and D languages on the basis of statistical analysis. Year after year, boys seem to be less successful in German and Russian than girls. The fact that boys frequently have the best marks in French (distinction) shows they are more strongly motivated in this language (Figure 8).

Figure 8

	Total	Boys	Girls	Distinction		
				Boys	Girls	Total
German	11176	28.4%	71.6%	22.29%	23.09%	22.86%
French	2630	12.8%	87.2%	25.82%	22.72%	23.12%
Russian	1216	15.3%	84.7%	19.89%	23.11%	22.62%

In one study which I carried out some years ago with Professor
Konrad Schroeder, it emerged that in the Federal Republic of Germany
as well as in Finland girls were generally more motivated than boys
in learning a foreign language. However, the study revealed that at
that time there was not such a significant difference between the
motivation of the Finnish school girls and school boys who studied
French as between the pupils in other countries. It also showed how
strongly motivated the boys were who chose this rarer option. This
supports the observation that motivation and success in learning a
foreign language are related.

References

DAVIES, N F. Language acquisition, language learning and the school curriculumn. AFinLA Yearbook 1980. Jyväskylä: Publications de l'association Finlandaise de linguistique appliquée 28, 1980, p 17-24.

KOHONEN, V. Learners, teachers and graded objectives in communicative language teaching. AFinLA Yearbook 1983. Oulu and Helsinki: Publications de l'association Finlandaise de linguistique appliquée 36, 1983, p 37-67.

LUUKKAINEN, M. Wissen und Können im Erwerb der dritten und vierten Fremdsprache. AFinLA Yearbook 1985. Tampere: Publications de l'association Finlandaise de linguistique appliquée 41, 1985, p 209-26.

LUUKKAINEN, M and K Schröder. Diversifikation und Motivation im Fremdsprachenunterricht. Eine vergleichende Studie zwischen Finnland und der Bundesrepublik Deutschland. Turku: Publications de l'association Finlandaise de linguistique appliquée 29 (1981).

MÜLLER, W. Das Sprachgefühl auf dem Prüfstand der Philologie. Eine Materialstudie. In: Ist Berufung auf 'Sprachgefühl' berechtigt? Antworten auf die Preisfrage der Deutschen Akademie für Sprache und Dichtung vom Jahr 1980, p 204-320. Heidelberg (1982).

SAJAVAARA, K. Kielitieto ja kielitaito kieliluokassa. AFinLA Yearbook 1984. Jyväskylä: Publications de l'association Finlandaise de linguistiqe appliquée 38, 1984, p 65-73.

SAJAVAARA, K and J Lehtonen. Language teaching and acquisition of communication. AFinLA Yearbook 1980. Jyväskylä: Publications de l'association Finlandaise de linguistique appliquée 28, 1980, p 25-35.

VUORINEN, R. Hyvä muisti saattaa olla tehokkaan opiskelun esteenä. Tempus, vol 8, no. 19, 1984, p 8-10.

APPENDIX I

TEXTVERSTÄNDNISTEST (30 Fragen):

Madlene Clausen meldete sich umgehend und zum Entsetzen ihrer Eltern
35 zu einem Segelflugkurs an. Die anschließende Mitgliedschaft in einem
süddeutschen Segelflugverein machte ihr aber gar keinen Spaß: "Da waren
vor allem Opas drin, die abends am Biertisch über ihre Flugabenteuer
schwatzten", bemerkt sie heute noch voller Verachtung. Außerdem war
so ein Segelflugzeug ihrer Meinung nach viel zu langsam. Ein Propeller-
40 flugzeug war da schon was anderes, und so hatte Madlene Clausen 1975
den Privatpilotenschein in der Tasche.

Dies hatte Folgen für ihre Arbeit in der Münchner Flughafenverwaltung,
wo sie als Programmiererin beschäftigt war: "Weil ich nun Hobbypilotin
war und angeblich stündlich mit meinem Absturz gerechnet werden mußte,
45 durfte ich ab sofort nicht mehr an der Erweiterung von Computer-Pro-
grammen mitwirken, sondern mußte ausschließlich in der Dokumentation
arbeiten. 'Wenn Sie nicht mehr da sind, kommt ja niemand mit Ihren
Programmen zurecht', lautete die eigenartige Begründung. Und das
ausgerechnet auf einem Flughafen!"

50 Eine Minute später ist ihr Zorn verflogen. Madlene, schon wieder lächelnd,
meint: "Eigentlich muß ich diesen fliegerfeindlichen Herren ja dankbar
sein. Weil sie mir die Freude an der ohnehin langweiligen Arbeit am
Computer so gründlich verdorben haben, ist aus mir schließlich was
geworden."

55 Zunächst einmal half dem hübschen Mädchen ein Freund. "Er hat es mir
ermöglicht, viel zu fliegen und dafür sogar noch Geld zu bekommen.
Mit Beobachtungsflügen über den vollen Autobahnen für den ADAC
konnte ich seinerzeit massenweise Flugstunden sammeln." Die brauchte sie,
um ihren Berufspilotenschein zu machen und als Profi bei "Isarflug" in
60 München zu fliegen.

APPENDIX I (ctd)

7. Was wird über ihre Segelfliegerei gesagt?
   A Das Geschwätz alter Segelflieger gefiel ihr nicht
   B Ihre Eltern waren stolz darauf
   C Sie bewunderte die Abenteuerlust älterer Segelflieger
   D Sie fand die Maschinen des Vereins veraltet

(Z. 42-54)
8. Warum durfte sie keine Computerprogramme mehr machen?
   A Weil man sie für wichtigere Aufgaben brauchte
   B Weil ihre Programme unnötig geworden waren
   C Weil man ihren Tod befürchtete
   D Weil sie jetzt begonnen hatte, Fehler zu machen

9. Wofür ist sie den Herren dankbar?
   A Ohne sie hätte sie ihre Karriere nicht gemacht
   B Ohne sie hätte sie ihre heutigen Computerkenntnisse nicht
   C Sie haben sie fliegen gelehrt
   D Sie haben sie immer von Anfang an unterstützt

(Z. 55-74)
10. Was hat ein Freund getan?
    A Er hat sie auf einen Isarflug mitgenommen
    B Er hat ihr Fliegertalent entdeckt
    C Er hat ihr Geld geliehen
    D Er hat ihr Arbeit verschafft

APPENDIX II

ZUR AUSWERTUNG DES TEXTVERSTÄNDNISTESTS:

Item Nr.		Die besten Schüler					Alle Teilnehmer					Korrelation zwischen Item und Test	Die schwächsten Schüler				
		A	B	C	D	-	A	B	C	D	-		A	B	C	D	-
7	LKM	3291*	28	100	114	0	7551*	185	1315	769	0	.39	1466*	91	785	343	0
	%	93.2	.8	2.8	3.2	.0	76.9	1.9	13.4	7.8	.0		54.6	3.4	29.2	12.8	.0
	PIST	162.9	163.5	157.4	160.1	0.0	146.0	125.2	123.0	130.9	0.0		113.7	99.3	109.1	110.5	0.0
8	LKM	931	530	1578*	494	0	4137	1814	2480*	1389	0	.28	1343	610	370*	362	0
	%	26.4	15.0	44.7	14.0	.0	42.1	18.5	25.3	14.1	.0		50.0	22.7	13.8	13.5	.0
	PIST	159.1	160.7	165.9	160.9	0.0	136.9	136.6	152.4	141.0	0.0		113.8	108.9	109.5	109.2	0.0
9	LKM	3881*	104	6	42	0	6955*	1870	183	812	0	.52	1015*	1062	143	465	0
	%	95.7	2.9	.2	1.2	.0	70.8	19.0	1.9	8.3	.0		37.8	39.6	5.3	17.3	.0
	PIST	162.9	156.5	156.5	154.4	0.0	148.9	123.7	109.9	123.7	0.0		115.5	109.4	101.2	110.5	0.0
10	LKM	7	403	54	3069*	0	289	2698	413	6420*	0	.37	215	1086	229	1155*	0
	%	.2	11.4	1.5	86.9	.0	2.9	27.5	4.2	65.4	.0		8.0	40.4	8.5	43.0	.0
	PIST	159.4	157.3	160.2	163.4	0.0	110.5	133.0	123.3	147.4	0.0		100.5	109.4	101.2	110.5	0.0

LKM = Anzahl der Antworten; PIST = Durchschnittliche Punktzahl im Text- und Hörverständnis (Max. 180 Punkte).

Testteilnehmer	3533		Testteilnehmer	9820		Testteilnehmer	2685	
Durchschnitt*	84.4	= 93.8%	Durchschnitt*	72.8	= 80.9%	Durchschnitt*	55.9	= 62.1%
Streuung	3.0		Streuung	12.7		Streuung	10.0	
Reliabilität	-.38		Reliabilität	-.81		Reliabilität	.47	

*(Max. 90 Punkte)

AUFSATZTHEMEN:

Es wird erwartet, daß Sie einen Aufsatz von 100-150 Wörtern schreiben. Bitte möglichst nicht mehr. Die in der Anleitung genannten Stichwörter bzw. Gedanken sollen nicht alle behandelt werden, sie sind als Hinweise gedacht, aus denen Sie wählen können. Außerdem können Sie natürlich auch über solche Gesichtspunkte schreiben, die nicht in der Anleitung stehen, aber zu dem Thema passen. Folgende Themen stehen Ihnen zur Wahl:

1. *Es wäre schön, Erfolg zu haben!*
   - Sie können mehrere oder auch nur einen der folgenden Gesichtspunkte behandeln:
   Studium - Arbeit - Sport - Spiel u. a.

2. *Eine Flugreise*
   - Sie können über eine eigene oder eine frei erfundene Flugreise berichten. Sie können auch ganz allgemein schreiben:
   - Ist eine Flugreise nur eine Art, Menschen zu transportieren?
   - Was sieht man dabei - was sieht man nicht?
   - Fehlt dabei jede Spannung?
   - Was kann passieren?

3. *Einladung nach Finnland*
   - Schreiben Sie bitte einen Brief an Ihre Freundin / an Ihren Freund und laden Sie sie / ihn nach Finnland ein. Erzählen Sie, welche Pläne Sie für den Besuch Ihres Gastes in Finnland gemacht haben, was Sie gemeinsam unternehmen werden, was z. B. den Gast hier erwartet.

APPENDIX III

1. Es wäre schön, Erfolg zu haben

Die Schule ist sehr wichtig für die Jungen. Da wollen sie Erfolg haben. Wenn sie in der Schule Erfolg nicht haben, bekommen sie keine guten Arbeit.

Das Erfolg ist nicht bekannt für alle. Es gibt Menschen, die Angst für das Leben haben und sie versuchen nicht, Erfolg zu haben. Man kann sagen, dass alle ähnliche Möglichkeiten in seinem Leben haben.

Der Sport ist ein gutes Hobby. Wenn man kein Erfolg in seinem Leben hat, kann man Sport treiben. Der Sport ist eine gute Wahl, wenn man sein Lebenslust verbessern will.

Die Arbeit ist die wichtigsten Sache in dem Leben. Man sollte eine gute Arbeit haben, um Geld zu bekommen. Man kann auch Erfolg ohne Geld haben. Das Erfolg ohne Geld ist eine gute Familie.

2. Einladung nach Finnland

Niittysalo, den 1. April

Liebe Barbara!

Vielen dank für deinen Brief. Jetzt habe ich dir eine Frage. Könntest du nach Finnland kommen? Nun hättest du eine Möglichkeit, um Finnland an Ort und Stelle zu sehen.

Eine Reise nach Finnland möcht dir sicher Spass, denn nach meiner Meinung ist Finnland im Sommer am schönsten. Finnland ist reich an Wäldern und wir haben auch viele Seen. Du könntest auch in die Sauna gehen, wenn du willst.

Ich wohne auf dem Lande und wir haben sieben Kühe. Ich lehre dich melken, wenn du dich für Kühe interessierst.

Wir können auch Sehenswürdigkeiten, die in der Nähe sind, bewundern. Dann wenn du schon müde bist, kannst du ins Bett gehen.

Jeden Tag darfst du sagen, ob du etwas Besonderes tun willst. Ich mache mein Bestes, damit du sagen kannst, dass Finnland eine Reise wert ist. Willkommen in Finnland!

Mit grüssen

Deine Leena

P.S. Hoffen wir, dass die Sonne scheint, denn ab und zu ist das Wetter auch schlecht.

3. Eine Flugreise

"Guten Morgen, meine Damen und Herren! Dieser Flug 182 nach Frankfurt. Ihr Flugzeug ist in den sicheren Händen von Kapitän von Richthofen und seiner Besatzung. Gute Reise!"

So weit schien alles in Ordnung zu sein. Aber als die Fluggäste hörten, dass die Reise etwa sechs Stunden dauern würde, wurden sie verblüfft. "Frankfurt liegt ja nicht so weit von Hamburg", meint ein Mädchen. "Die Reise war sehr günstig, aber man durfte auch kein Gepäck mitnehmen." "Warum geht es nicht schneller?", klagte eine Frau. "Vielleicht hat es etwas mit diesem neuen, umgebungsfreundlichen Flugzeug zu tun", glaubt ein alter Herr. "Der Kapitän wird es schon erklären!"

Der Kapitän erklärte es auch: "Achtung, achtung! Um Energie zu sparen müssen wir leider um Ihre Hilfe bitten ..". Vor jedem Passagier wurden Pedalen, wie auf einem Fahrrad, langsam entdeckt. "Der Start ist sehr wichtig. Bitte alle teilnehmen! Eins, zwei, eins, zwei ..."

Eine historische Flugreise hatte angefangen. Der erste Pedalverkehrsflug war unterwegs.

APPENDIX IV

STRUKTURTEST (20 Aufgaben):

1) mistä
2) Präpos. + Art.?
3) minne
4) anfangen
5)
6) Sie + gehen
7–8) sitzenbleiben, Perf.
9)
10) Neutr.

11) Präpos. + Art.?
12)
13) Sie
14) folgen
15) erraten, Perf.
16) äkkiähän tullo
17) Präpos. + Art.?
18) sich ausziehen riisuutukaa
19) Präpos. + Art., Ienin.
20) Tinä

– Ihren Paß, bitte. Sie heißen?
– Mansfeld.
– 1) Woher kommen Sie?
– 2) Von Luxemburg.
– 3) Wohin wollen Sie jetzt?
– In den Taunus hinauf. Morgen 4) fängt die Schule an.
– 5) In welche Klasse 6) gehen Sie?
– 5) In die achte.
– Mit 21 Jahren?
– Ja.
– Dann 7) sind Sie dreimal 8) sitzengeblieben.
– Jawohl. Ich bin 9) ein sehr schlechter Schüler. Aber mein Vater verlangt, daß ich das Abitur mache.
– Das ist 10) Ihr ganzes Gepäck?
– Ja.
– Und alles andere?

– Habe ich 11) den Frankfurt gelassen. 12) Bei einem guten Freund. Der hat meine Sachen inzwischen zum Wohnheim hinaufgeschickt.
– Ich muß 13) Sie bitten, mir zum Zoll 14) zu folgen.
– Das 15) habe ich erraten.
– 16) Theden Sie nur nicht frech, junger Mann, ja? Leeren Sie, bitte, Ihre Taschen aus. Legen Sie alles 17) auf den Tisch. 18) Ziehen Sie sich aus bitte.
– Aber gern.
– Sie können sich setzen.
– Danke, ich stehe lieber.
– Sicherlich halten Sie das 19) für ein Schikane, Herr Mansfeld.
– Aber ich bitte 13) Sie!
– Ich tue nur meine Pflicht, glauben Sie mir. Sie können sich wieder anziehen.
– Ich danke 20) Ihnen, Herr Inspektor.

Evaluating speaking ability

Ray Clifford
Defense Language Institute, Monterey, USA

The views expressed in this article are those of the author and do not necessarily reflect official United States Department policy.

Introduction

The main three questions associated with language testing are: 'What to test, how to test, and why?' Before we can reasonably address the questions **What** and **How** to test, to assess speaking ability in a second language, we must first answer the question, '**Why** test speaking ability?' Ultimately it is why we are testing which will determine how to proceed and which criteria to use in the process.

As a profession, our reasons for administering speaking tests range all the way from a desire to punish or motivate our students to the more acceptable rationale of instructional programme evaluation. For purposes of this discussion, I would propose three general purposes for administering speaking and other language tests. These are to evaluate: (1) individuals' mastery of a course of instruction; (2) individuals' language adequacy for performance of specific jobs; or (3) individuals' competence in the target language relative to the ability of native speakers of that language. Underlying each of these purposes are significantly different theoretical perspectives on the relationship between the language to be tested and the real-world use of that language by first language speakers.

It does not seem that the profession at large is adequately cognisant of the distinction between the disparate domains of curriculum and real-world language use - nor is it fully aware of the implications of that distinction for language testing. In this paper I will be discussing the three testing purposes delineated above in relationship to real-world language needs, curriculum design, and teaching approaches.

Three types of testing

The testing of students' learning relative to a specific course of instruction is usually accomplished by **achievement tests**. These achievement tests, if they are good tests, systematically sample from the language curriculum which has been taught. However, it is not always recognised by students and teachers that the curriculum from which the test items were drawn represents only a subset of the language which a first language speaker would use within the same contexts. The degree to which the curriculum is representative of the most useful or most valuable language elements found in the native speaker's language domain is dependent on the skill of the curriculum developers. It is impossible for any textbook or curriculum to include the complete range of language options available to the native speaker, and since achievement tests sample only from the textbook, the decision to use achievement tests to assess language ability brings with it the decision to test only a subset of a subset of the language behaviours used by native speakers in the same situations. This perspective on language teaching is depicted graphically in Figure 1.

Figure 1

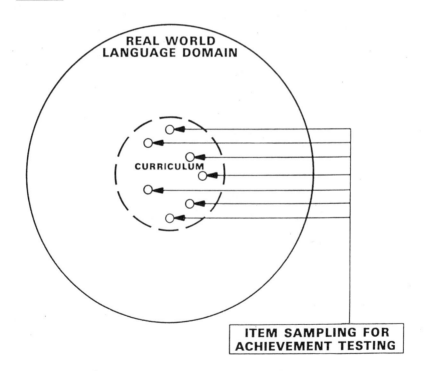

The second perspective or rationale for language testing is usually motivated by practical concerns such as, does an individual have sufficient control of the second language to be a vacuum cleaner salesman, a student at a foreign university, a cook in a restaurant, or to perform some other specific job or assignment. I call this approach to language testing **performance testing**. It is like achievement testing in that the test items are drawn from a subset of the total real-world behaviours of native speakers; however, it differs from achievement testing in one significant aspect. Whereas the curriculum for most courses - and therefore for most achievement tests - is selected to be as representative as possible of high frequency items from the total real-world domain, this is not the case with performance tests. The curricular subset from which performance tests items are drawn is purposely representative of situationally specific behaviours. These job- or assignment- specific language needs represent a narrowly defined slice of the real world, and while they may in part overlap with the curriculum of some general language courses, performance tests represent a significant divergence in philosophy from traditional achievement testing.

Figure 2

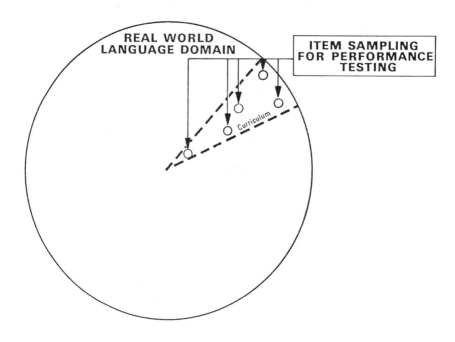

Achievement tests, if executed properly, result in test items which are a subset of a representative subset of the general language of the real world, but job-related performance tests, if executed well, consist of items which are a subset of a selected subset of real-world behaviours which is purposely non-representative of the larger domain of real-world behaviours. The comparison of Figure 2 with Figure 1 gives a graphic representation of the similarity and contrast between performance testing and achievement testing. Both approaches test from within restricted domains, but the domains are created based on different rationale.

The third approach to language testing is **proficiency testing**. As Figure 3 demonstrates, proficiency tests sample from the entire domain of language behaviours available to the native speaker and, if executed properly, are therefore a better representation of general real-world language ability than either achievement or performance tests. Because they sample from the entire language domain rather than from a restricted curricular domain, proficiency tests are therefore broader in scope than both achievement tests and performance tests.

Figure 3

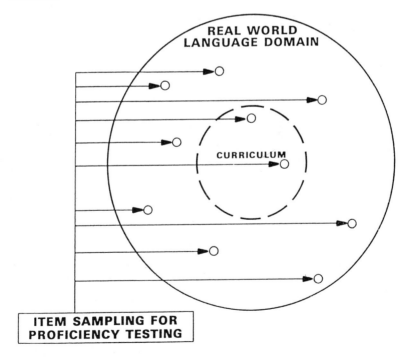

Other typologies of testing approaches are possible, but the main point is that teachers' decisions about which testing approach to use will influence their students' view of the world. Traditionally, in most language courses the curriculum or the textbook has been the students' entire world. Language for special purposes courses have followed a parallel philosophy that sought for congruence between a selected segment of the world and the classroom lessons. A proficiency approach, however, views the relationship between the language course and the world from the opposite perspective. In a proficiency-oriented course, the world is the course and the textbook serves as an aid in organising and addressing the broader real-world curriculum. These three testing perspectives might be summarised as follows:

> With achievement testing, the textbook is the world.

> With performance testing, the textbook is the only important part of the world.

> With proficiency testing, the textbook is a stepping stone to the real world.

The Defense Language Institute Foreign Language Center in Monterey, California, which provides language training each year for over 5,000 students from the Department of Defense and various other US Government agencies, has tried all three of these approaches to language teaching and testing.

ACHIEVEMENT TESTING

For over a decade an achievement testing approach linked with an instructional systems design model was followed. This model was built around the five logical steps of analysis, design, development, validation, and revision. While the logic of a systematic approach to developing courses based on an analysis of the graduates' language needs was overwhelmingly convincing, it was flawed in two ways. First, while this approach had been very successful for limited applications such as how to overhaul a carburettor, it had not been applied to functions as complex as language. At Figure 4 is a flow chart depicting the grammatical complexities involved in producing a simple prepositional construction in German. The length of this single diagram alone offers evidence that many of the approaches which systems engineers have successfully applied to other learning situations are not applicable when dealing with second language instruction, and when one considers the number of such problems in learning a second language the difficulty of applying such analyses to language becomes even clearer. The second serious deficiency in applying an instructional systems design methodology to languages was that the methodology never acknowledged that a severe non-congruence existed between the target language which had

Figure 4

PICKING THE RIGHT "THE" IN GERMAN

Task: While speaking, decline the definite article of a noun phrase following the preposition "in."

Conditions: Given a situation which requires the use of a subject, verb, the preposition "in" and an object noun preceded by a definite article.

Standard: Speak instantaneously so no hesitation in speech is perceived.

Cues: Flashcards/pictures/situation.

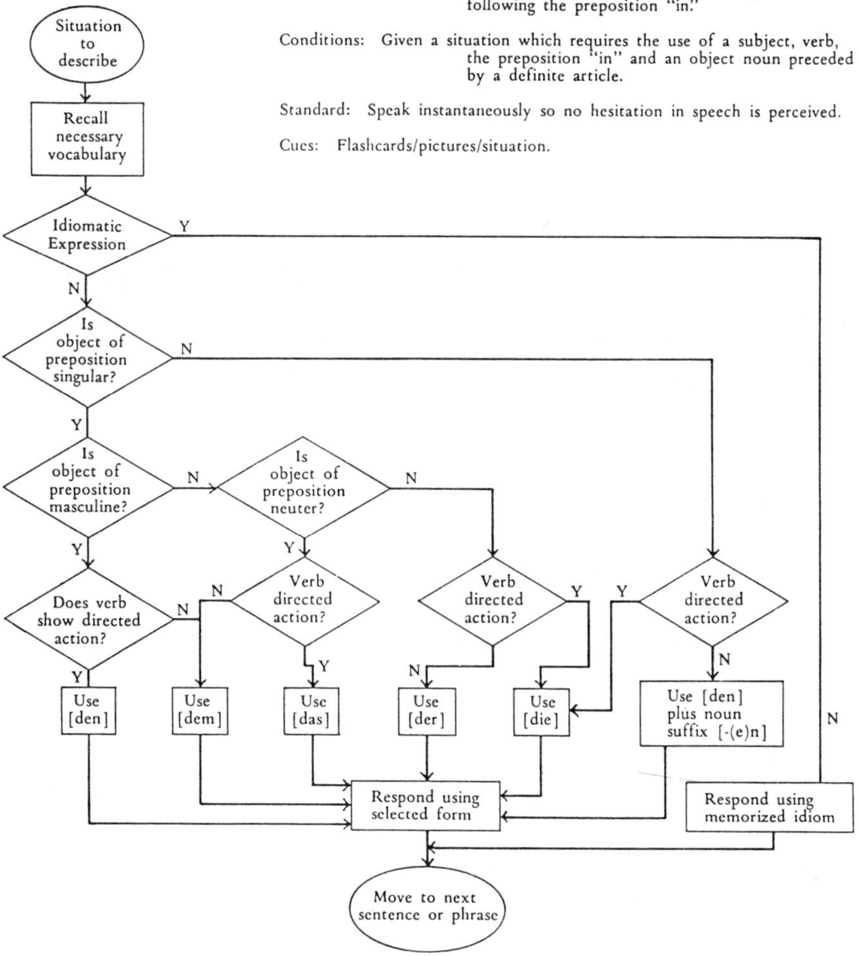

189

to be taught and the amount of language which could be contained in any given language textbook or language course. This had an impact both on course development and on teaching activities. Even within the intensive language courses of the Defense Language Institute, which include up to 1,400 instructional hours in the basic course sequence, it was still found that curriculum developers had to make choices about which of the language scenarios, functions, topics and specific linguistic elements that should be included, could be included. The systems development model did not address this contingency, so frequency counts and course-writer judgement were employed to make those decisions. Unfortunately, once the courses were developed, the instructional approaches used with these materials continued to reflect the rejected assumption of congruence between curriculum and target learning domain. Rather than recognising the experience of the course-writers, which demonstrated that such congruence was not possible in second language instruction, the teachers proceeded as if the textbook were the target learning domain. This situation was further complicated by the test developers, who likewise approached the curriculum as the target learning domain rather than viewing it as a subset of the broader real-world target domain from which it was drawn.

Given students' (and teachers') natural propensity to allow language tests to define the true objectives of any course, this led to an ever-narrowing instructional focus. The original intent of the instructional systems design approach was to define the language domain which needed to be taught, and then to teach the students those skills. However, application of the achievement testing approach resulted in testing (and ultimately in teaching) not the desired domain of real-world behaviours, and not even the subset of those behaviours represented by the curriculum, but rather only the subset of that textbook subset which happened to appear in the achievement tests. The result was students who received high marks but who did not have adequate linguistic skills to handle their various assignments after graduation.

PERFORMANCE TESTING

When this deficiency was recognised, a shift to job-related language teaching and testing was proposed. Separate courses were developed, each designed to prepare students for a specific job assignment. Again the logic behind this decision seemed unassailable. Since there was not enough time to teach all the skills needed to handle language behaviours across the entire target domain, it was felt that restricting instruction to that slice of the domain which was pertinent to a specific job would improve performance on the job. In fact, the planners were so confident of this fact, that course lengths were shortened by nearly 20% as part of selling this teaching approach to administrators. After a few years, it was determined that this approach was even less successful than the previous traditional approach. Graduates of the job-specific language programmes were so limited in their language abilities that they were unable to comprehend language outside of their own narrow range of training. Interestingly, where previous graduates had continued to learn on the job, these graduates plateaued or even retrogressed in their language ability after leaving the school. Unfortunately, no scientific attempt was made to systematically track and retest these students at intervals during their following assignments, but those students who returned for intermediate courses were consistently found unprepared to enter those courses and had to be either reassigned to basic courses of instruction or given extensive tutorial assistance. It was also found that graduates from job-related courses did not have sufficient breadth of linguistic skills to be reassigned from one job to another.

PROFICIENCY TESTING

In 1981 the Defense Language Institute began a major revision of its testing programme, which has led to another shift not only in our testing but also in our teaching philosophy. This revision is based on a proficiency-oriented philosophy of language testing. Major mid-course and end-of-course examinations have been, or are being developed, for all 40 of our basic language courses. It is important to note that while these tests are administered during and at the end of these courses, they purposely are not based on the contents of any specific course. By design, proficiency tests sample from the entire learning domain rather than from the curriculum alone. While some of the test items may relate to topics found in a particular course - since that course is drawn from the target domain as well - most of the test items will require the student to apply his or her functional language skills to situations which they have never encountered before. After three years of test development, we have end-of-course and some mid-course proficiency tests in place for all of our high enrolment languages, and already the results are quite promising. First and foremost we see improving student ability to communicate in the target language. Contributing to this improvement is a change in instructional approach. Instead of an ever-narrowing inward focus for teaching and learning, classroom activities now stress an expanding view of the language elements presented in the textbook. Each element introduced, whether it be related to a grammatical, semantic, or cultural aspect of the language, is now seen not as an entity to be learned in isolation, but rather as a means of increasing one's ability to handle the language of the world beyond the textbook.

Has the changing of testing philosophies alone been adequate to bring about this change in instructional practice? Since the introduction of proficiency testing was accompanied by concurrent teacher in-service training, the answer is not clear. Still, while it may be argued that changing testing alone would not be adequate to bring about changes in teaching learning approaches, I can say with confidence that any effort to change teaching methodology without a supporting congruency of philosophy in testing is doomed to failure.

Language skill levels

Having discussed the **Why** of language testing and having posed an argument in favor of proficiency testing, it is possible to look at the **What** and the **How** of testing speaking ability. One may do this by answering the questions: 'What is the speaker to accomplish by speaking? What is the topic and the context in which that task is to be accomplished? How well is it to be accomplished?' Language tests are no different from other tests in that an individual's test

Figure 5

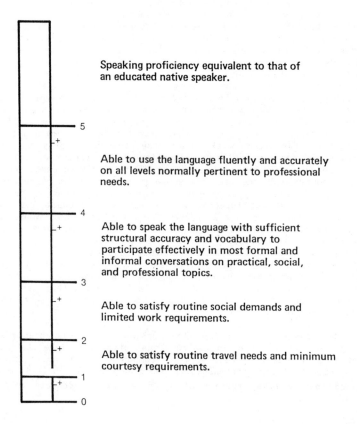

results are only interpretable either on a norm-referenced basis, i.e. against the performance of others, or on a criterion-reference basis, i.e. against an established standard.

In language testing, achievement tests tend to be norm-referenced and performance and proficiency tests tend to be criterion-referenced. I believe that the reason we do not see more criterion-referenced tests is the difficulty in setting measurable standards of language ability. To qualify as a standard, the performance level desired must include three essential components: task, condition, and required accuracy. It is interesting that the very first attempts by the Foreign Service Institute of the US State Department to quantify and measure the speaking ability of its employees did not consistently address all three of these components. The earliest standards developed in the mid-1950s were based on a five level system with each level defined by a single descriptive sentence. As you can see from Figure 5, the rating categories ranged from 'survival' to 'native' level ability. Perhaps because these original descriptions did not consistently define task, condition, and required accuracy, they were expanded in the 1960s to paragraph length descriptions. Later, it was the need to better define the third component of the standard, required accuracy, which forced an expansion of the scale from the basic six levels, zero through five, to an eleven-point scale by inserting a 'plus' level between each of the base levels. The plus level rating is assigned whenever the demonstrated speaking ability substantially exceeds the requirements of a given skill level, but does not fully meet the criteria for the next higher level. This most recent revision of the FSI language skill level descriptions was a joint effort of the members of the US Interagency Language Roundtable (ILR), and the revised standards are now referred to as the ILR Language Skill Level Definitions. The speaking skill section of these revised proficiency standards is appended.

Figure 6

TRISECTION OF ORAL PROFICIENCY LEVELS - PART I

LEVEL (ILR Speaking Levels)	TASK (Tasks accomplished, attitudes expressed, tone conveyed.)
5	Functions equivalent to an educated native speaker.
4	Able to tailor language to fit audience, counsel, persuade, negotiate, represent a point of view, and interpret for dignitaries.
3	Can converse in formal and informal situations, resolve problem situations, deal with unfamiliar topics, provide explanations, describe in detail, offer supported opinions and hypothesize.
2	Able to fully participate in casual conversations, can express facts, give instructions, describe, report on, and provide narration about current, past, and future activities.
1	Can create with the language: ask and answer questions, participate in short conversations.
0	No functional ability.

Figure 6 (ctd)

TRISECTION OF ORAL PROFICIENCY LEVELS - PART II

LEVEL (ILR Speaking Levels)	CONDITION (Topics, subjects areas, activities and jobs addressed.)
5	All subjects and situations.
4	All topics normally pertinent to professional needs in almost all professional situations including conferences, lectures, and debates.
3	Practical, social, professional and abstract topics, particular interests, and special fields of competence in formal and informal situations.
2	Concrete topics such as own background, family, and interests, work, travel, and current events in informal settings.
1	Everyday survival topics and courtesy requirements.
0	None.

Figure 6 (ctd)

TRISECTION OF ORAL PROFICIENCY LEVELS - PART III

LEVEL (ILR Speaking Levels)	ACCURACY (Acceptability, quality, and accuracy of message conveyed.)
5	Performance equivalent to an educated native speaker.
4	Nearly equivalent to an educated native speaker. Speech is extensive, precise, appropriate to every occasion with only occasional errors.
3	Errors never interfere with understanding and rarely disturb the native speaker. Only sporadic errors in basic structures.
2	Understandable to an native speaker NOT used to dealing with foreigners; sometimes miscommunicates.
1	Intelligible to an native speaker used to dealing with foreigners.
0	Unintelligible.

An overview of the tasks, conditions, and required accuracy required by the revised ILR speaking skill level descriptions is provided at Figure 6. It is important to note that the ILR standards form three separate hierarchical taxonomies which move in each case from the most limited or easiest requirements at Level 0 to the most extensive and demanding requirements at Level 5. It is also important to note that each rating level establishes its own distinct standard of performance. In order to be rated a Level 3, one must be able to perform the tasks at that level in the situations described with the specified degree of accuracy. Performing Level 3 tasks on Level 4 topics with Level 2 accuracy does **not** equal an average rating of Level 3 - nor does performing Level 2 tasks under Level 3 conditions with Level 4 accuracy. To earn the rating of Level 3 the test candidate must be able to perform Level 3 tasks under Level 3 conditions with at least Level 3 accuracy. This results in a rating scale which is simple to apply and interpret, but one which is clearly non-compensatory in nature.

Problems of scoring

The difference between compensatory and non-compensatory scoring becomes an important consideration when one shifts from norm-referenced to criterion-referenced testing. An example may be useful in demonstrating the difference between these two approaches to grading. Figure 7 shows the scores of three students on a hypothetical, traditional language test with two subtests. Each student has separate subtest scores from which overall compensatory and non-compensatory scores are computed. The most common computational methods for compensatory grading are to total or to average the subtest scores, but weighted totals or weighted averages are also possible. In Figure 7 the students' grades are first computed based on the totals of their part scores and then based on their lowest part score. The rank orderings of these students under each grading procedure differ so dramatically, because whenever scores are averaged or totalled, students' weaknesses can be hidden or at least mitigated by strengths in other areas. This compensatory process is usually acceptable in achievement testing, but it is not appropriate for proficiency testing.

Figure 7

COMPENSATORY VERSUS NON-COMPENSATORY SCORING

NAME	VOCABULARY	GRAMMAR
ALICE	50	20
BOB	30	30
CARL	10	70

STUDENTS RANKED BY COMPENSATORY GRADES

NAME	TOTAL SCORE
CARL	80
ALICE	70
BOB	60

STUDENTS RANKED BY NON-COMPENSATORY GRADES

NAME	LOWEST PART SCORE
BOB	30
ALICE	20
CARL	10

In proficiency testing the functional ability represented by each rating level exists as a separate standard of performance. Failure to meet that standard is not changed by strong performance in another area. Thus non-compensatory grading is essential to maintaining the criterion-referenced nature of any proficiency oriented testing system.

PERFORMANCE PROFILES

While non-compensatory rating is necessary to insure consistent interpretation of assigned criterion scores, it is also true that further scoring categories can also be informative. For instance, if a test candidate fails to meet the necessary accuracy requirements to be rated a Level 3 speaker of the language, is it possible to provide diagnostic information in addition to the overall functional ability rating? The answer is 'yes', and we have found that such information is often useful to both the student and the teacher. One way of providing additional diagnostic information is through the use of performance profiles such as the one shown at Figure 8.

In US Government language schools we have already begun to see patterns in the performance profiles of test candidates. One class of profiles is generally ascribed to a category of individuals called 'school learners' and another to 'street learners'. While 'school learners' usually have a fairly level profile on the elements shown in Figure 8, 'street learners' show a jagged or uneven profile with lexical ability rated fairly high and one or more other language aspects which have an impact on the accuracy of communication rated much lower. This is important information for teachers, because students with balanced profiles progress faster and further in standard instructional programmes, while others with uneven profiles need instructional programmes which address their demonstrated areas of weakness.

MAKING PEOPLE TALK

Next to rating standards, the most important concern of proficiency testing is elicitation technique. In speaking tests, this means that we must have some way of getting people to speak - and to speak naturally across a wide variety of tasks and conditions, even when the nature of the task makes it linguistically difficult.

Getting test candidates to speak is most easily accomplished by another person speaking to them, but other options are also possible. For instance, administrative and logistical considerations have forced the US Government to develop recorded tests of speaking ability. These indirect measures of speaking ability, which use prerecorded questions and picture stimuli, have been generally adequate substitutes for personal elicitation techniques at the lower end of the proficiency scale. Still, the most successful and reliable procedure for assessing speaking ability remains a face-to-face interview which includes not only question and answer exchanges, but also problem solving and role playing. The major disadvantage of such face-to-face assessment procedures is that the testers must be well trained. They must not only be thoroughly familiar with the performance standards and their component parts, but also be able to elicit those performances. At the Defense Language Institute the training of oral proficiency testers is a formal, full-time program lasting at least two weeks. Despite this rigorous course of instruction, which includes the supervised administration of many practice

Figure 8

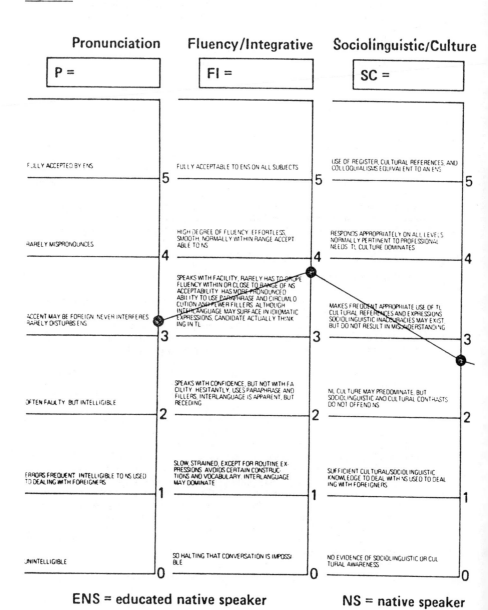

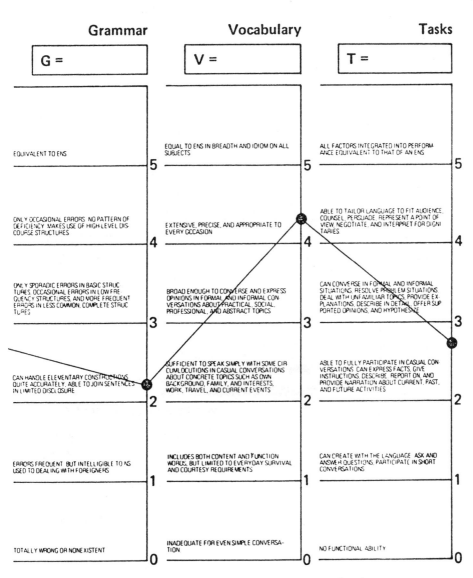

interviews, we have found that not all prospective testers are able to master the dual requirements of being able to internalise the rating standards and of demonstrating the appropriate interview techniques needed to elicit desired linguistic performances from test candidates.

ASKING QUESTIONS

One of the skills which testers of oral proficiency must master, if they are to be successful in eliciting ratable speech samples from test candidates, is the knack of asking questions. How a question is phrased has a definite impact on the type of response to that question. Figure 9 shows a sample of some of the question types which can be used and the performance levels for which they are most appropriate. Yes/no questions and alternative answer questions do not

Figure 9

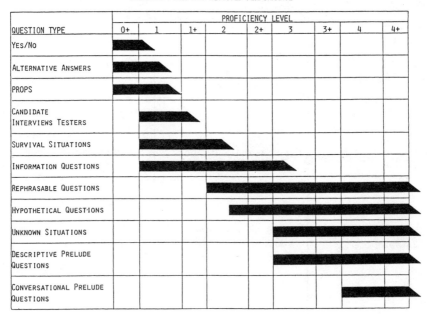

QUESTION TYPES AND ELICITED PERFORMANCE

generally result in expansive answers and so are generally more applicable at the lower end of the proficiency scale. They are, however useful in providing opportunities for limited ability speakers to participate in conversational exchanges. At the other end of the scale descriptive prelude and conversational prelude questions offer the best opportunities for high-level discourse because they provide the interviewers with a chance to establish models for register style, and sophistication to which the candidate should match his or her response. The other question types listed can also be readily linked to the types of behaviors described in the ILR proficiency standards.

COMMUNICATIVE EXCHANGE

However, being able to mechanically apply questioning and role playing techniques is not all that is required of an interviewer. During the process of an oral proficiency interview, the interviewer must concurrently handle several different aspects of the communicative and testing process. On the personal level the interview, although a test, must also be a positive communicative exchange. To accomplish this the interviewer must constantly be aware of the psychological, linguistic, and evaluative factors involved. The interview begins with a warm-up phase designed to accomplish three things: It should put the test candidate at ease; it should re-acquaint the candidate with the target language; and it should give the tester a preliminary indication of the candidate's speaking capabilities. Based on this preliminary assessment the interviewer then moves to tasks at an appropriate proficiency level and attempts to verify that the candidate can indeed perform at that level. Having once established a base level of demonstrated performance, the interviewer then probes for areas or linguistic functions which the candidate cannot handle. An iterative process follows moving between verification of performance and probing for non-performance until the candidate's highest level of sustained linguistic performance is established. The tester then returns to a linguistic level at which the candidate feels comfortable to conclude the interview. These four phases of warm-up, level check, probes, and wind-down are displayed along with their psychological, linguistic, and evaluative purposes in Figure 10. This is a very complex process, but test validity and reliability demand it.

Figure 10

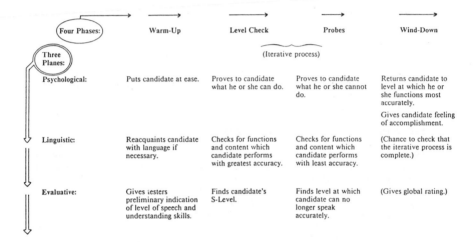

Conclusion

In this paper I have attempted to better define the theoretical rationale for oral proficiency testing and have provided a brief introduction to some of the complexities associated with this testing approach. ⁻roficiency testing is challenging to testers because of its complexity, and to teachers and students because it requires them to go beyond their textbooks to real-world applications. There is a saying in the teaching profession: 'Test what you teach'. I would contend that this aphorism does not apply to foreign language programmes. In the teaching and testing of foreign languages we should establish meaningful standards, decide how to test to those standards, and then teach not the test, but <u>in the same way</u> as we test. If we do not test language proficiency we fail to prepare students for the real world where language is neither entirely predictable nor a finite cor ҫ oᶠ lexical and morphological entities which can be captured on the static pages of a textbook.

References

ACTFL Provisional Proficiency Guidelines. Provisional Generic Guidelines - Speaking, Listening, Reading, Writing, Culture. New York: Hastings-on- Hudson.

BRUMFIT, Christopher. Communicative methodology in language teaching: the roles of fluency and accuracy. Cambridge: Cambridge University Press (1984).

HIGGS, Theodore, V, ed. Curriculum competence, and the foreign language teacher. Especially Theodore V Higgs and Ray T Clifford, The push toward communication, p 57-79. Skokie, Illinois: National Textbook Co (1982).

HIGGS, Theodore, V, ed. Teaching for proficiency: the organizing principle. Especially Alice C Omaggio, The proficiency-oriented classroom, p 43-84. Lincolnwood, Illinois: National Textbook Co (1984).

JAMES, Charles J, ed. Foreign language proficiency in the classroom and beyond. Especially Pardee Lowe, Jr, The ILR proficiency scale as a synthesizing research principle: the view from the mountain, p 9-53. Lincolnwood, Illinois: National Textbook Co (1985).

KOHONEN, Viljo. On instructional design in LSP. Finlance, vol 1, 1-37 (1981).

APPENDIX I

INTERAGENCY LANGUAGE ROUNDTABLE
LANGUAGE SKILL LEVEL DESCRIPTIONS
SPEAKING

Preface

The following proficiency level descriptions characterize spoken language use. Each of the six "base levels" (coded 00, 10, 20, 30, 40, and 50) implies control of any previous "base level's" functions and accuracy. The "plus level" designation (coded 06, 16, 26, etc.) will be assigned when proficiency substantially exceeds one base skill level and does not fully meet the criteria for the next "base level." The "plus level" descriptions are therefore supplementary to the "base level" descriptions.

A skill level is assigned to a person through an authorized language examination. Examiners assign a level on a variety of performance criteria exemplified in the descriptive statements. Therefore, the examples given here illustrate, but do not exhaustively describe, either the skills a person may possess or situations in which he/she may function effectively.

Statements describing accuracy refer to typical stages in the development of competence in the most commonly taught languages in formal training programs. In other languages, emerging competence parallels these characterizations, but often with different details.

Unless otherwise specified, the term "native speaker" refers to native speakers of a standard dialect.

"Well-educated," in the context of these proficiency descriptions, does not necessarily imply formal higher education. However, in cultures where formal higher education is common, the language-use abilities of persons who have had such education is considered the standard. That is, such a person meets contemporary expectations for the formal, careful style of the language, as well as a range of less formal varieties of the language.

Speaking 0 (No Proficiency)

Unable to function in the spoken language. Oral production is limited to occasional isolated words. Has essentially no communicative ability. (Has been coded S-0 in some nonautomated applications.) [Data Code 00]

Speaking 0+ (Memorized Proficiency)

Able to satisfy immediate needs using rehearsed utterances. Shows little real autonomy of expression, flexibility, or spontaneity. Can ask questions or make statements with reasonable accuracy only with memorized utterances or formulae. Attempts at creating speech are usually unsuccessful.

Examples: The individual's vocabulary is usually limited to areas of immediate survival needs. Most utterances are telegraphic; that is, functors (linking words, markers, and the like) are omitted, confused, or distorted. An individual can usually differentiate most significant sounds when produced in isolation, but, when combined in words or groups of words, errors may be frequent. Even with repetition, communication is severely limited even with people used to dealing with foreigners. Stress, intonation, tone, etc. are usually quite faulty. (Has been coded S-0+ in some nonautomated applications.) [Data Code 01]

Speaking 1 (Elementary Proficiency)

Able to satisfy minimum courtesy requirements and maintain very simple face-to-face conversations on familiar topics. A native speaker must often use slowed speech, repetition, paraphrase, or a combination of these to be understood by this individual. Similarly, the native speaker must strain and employ real-world knowledge to understand even simple statements/questions from this individual. This speaker has a functional, but limited proficiency. Misunderstandings are frequent, but the individual is able to ask for help and to verify comprehension of native speech in face-to-face interaction. The individual is unable to produce continuous discourse except with rehearsed material.

Examples: Structural accuracy is likely to be random or severely limited. Time concepts are vague. Vocabulary is inaccurate, and its range is very narrow. The individual often speaks with great difficulty. By repeating, such speakers can make themselves understood to native speakers who are in regular contact with foreigners but there is little precision in the information conveyed. Needs, experience, or training may vary greatly from individual to individual; for example, speakers at this level may have encountered quite different vocabulary areas. However, the individual can typically satisfy predictable, simple, personal and accommodation needs; can generally meet courtesy, introduction, and identification requirements; exchange greetings; elicit and provide, for example, predictable and skeletal biographical information. He/she might give information about

APPENDIX I (ctd)

business hours, explain routine procedures in a limited way, and state in a simple manner what actions will be taken. He/she is able to formulate some questions even in languages with complicated question constructions. Almost every utterance may be characterized by structural errors and errors in basic grammatical relations. Vocabulary is extremely limited and characteristically does not include modifiers. Pronunciation, stress, and intonation are generally poor, often heavily influenced by another language. Use of structure and vocabulary is highly imprecise. (Has been coded S-1 in some nonautomated applications.) [Data Code 10]

Speaking 1+ (Elementary Proficiency, Plus)

Can initiate and maintain predictable face-to-face conversations and satisfy limited social demands. He/she may, however, have little understanding of the social conventions of conversation. The interlocutor is generally required to strain and employ real-world knowledge to understand even some simple speech. The speaker at this level may hesitate and may have to change subjects due to lack of language resources. Range and control of the language are limited. Speech largely consists of a series of short, discrete utterances.

Examples: The individual is able to satisfy most travel and accommodation needs and a limited range of social demands beyond exchange of skeletal biographic information. Speaking ability may extend beyond immediate survival needs. Accuracy in basic grammatical relations is evident, although not consistent. May exhibit the more common forms of verb tenses, for example, but may make frequent errors in formation and selection. While some structures are established, errors occur in more complex patterns. The individual typically cannot sustain coherent structures in longer utterances or unfamiliar situations. Ability to describe and give precise information is limited. Person, space, and time references are often used incorrectly. Pronunciation is understandable to natives used to dealing with foreigners. Can combine most significant sounds with reasonable comprehensibility, but has difficulty in producing certain sounds in certain positions or in certain combinations. Speech will usually be labored. Frequently has to repeat utterances to be understood by the general public. (Has been coded S-1+ in some nonautomated applications.) [Data Code 16]

Speaking 2 (Limited Working Proficiency)

Able to satisfy routine social demands and limited work requirements. Can handle routine work-related interactions that are limited in scope. In more complex and sophisticated work-related tasks, language usage generally disturbs the native speaker. Can handle with confidence, but not with facility, most normal, high-frequency social conversational situations including extensive, but casual conversations about current events, as well as work, family, and autobiographical information. The individual can get the gist of most everyday conversations but has some difficulty understanding native speakers in situations that require specialized or sophisticated knowledge. The individual's utterances are minimally cohesive. Linguistic structure is usually not very elaborate and not thoroughly controlled; errors are frequent. Vocabulary use is appropriate for high-frequency utterances, but unusual or imprecise elsewhere.

Examples: While these interactions will vary widely from individual to individual, the individual can typically ask and answer predictable questions in the workplace and give straightforward instructions to subordinates. Additionally, the individual can participate in personal and accommodation-type interactions with elaboration and facility; that is, can give and understand complicated, detailed, and extensive directions and make non-routine changes in travel and accommodation arrangements. Simple structures and basic grammatical relations are typically controlled; however, there are areas of weakness. In the commonly taught languages, these may be simple markings such as plurals, articles, linking words, and negatives or more complex structures such as tense/aspect usage, case morphology, passive constructions, word order, and embedding. (Has been coded S-2 in some nonautomated applications.) [Data Code 20]

Speaking 2+ (Limited Working Proficiency, Plus)

Able to satisfy most work requirements with language usage that is often, but not always, acceptable and effective. The individual shows considerable ability to communicate effectively on topics relating to particular interests and special fields of competence. Often shows a high degree of fluency and ease of speech, yet when under tension or pressure, the ability to use the language effectively may deteriorate. Comprehension of normal native speech is typically nearly complete. The individual may miss cultural and local references and may require a native speaker to adjust to his/her limitations in some ways. Native speakers often perceive the individual's speech to contain awkward or inaccurate phrasing of ideas, mistaken time, space, and person references, or to be in some way inappropriate, if not strictly incorrect.

Examples: Typically the individual can participate in most social, formal, and informal interactions; but limitations either in range of contexts, types of tasks, or level of accuracy

APPENDIX I (ctd)

hinder effectiveness. The individual may be ill at ease with the use of the language either in social interaction or in speaking at length in professional contexts. He/she is generally strong in either structural precision or vocabulary, but not in both. Weakness or unevenness in one of the foregoing, or in pronunciation, occasionally results in miscommunication. Normally controls, but cannot always easily produce general vocabulary. Discourse is often incohesive. (Has been coded S-2+ in some nonautomated applications.) [Data Code 26]

Speaking 3 (General Professional Proficiency)

Able to speak the language with sufficient structural accuracy and vocabulary to participate effectively in most formal and informal conversations on practical, social, and professional topics. Nevertheless, the individual's limitations generally restrict the professional contexts of language use to matters of shared knowledge and/or international convention. Discourse is cohesive. The individual uses the language acceptably, but with some noticeable imperfections; yet, errors virtually never interfere with understanding and rarely disturb the native speaker. The individual can effectively combine structure and vocabulary to convey his/her meaning accurately. The individual speaks readily and fills pauses suitably. In face-to-face conversation with natives speaking the standard dialect at a normal rate of speech, comprehension is quite complete. Although cultural references, proverbs, and the implications of nuances and idiom may not be fully understood, the individual can easily repair the conversation. Pronunciation may be obviously foreign. Individual sounds are accurate; but stress, intonation, and pitch control may be faulty.

Examples: Can typically discuss particular interests and special fields of competence with reasonable ease. Can use the language as part of normal professional duties such as answering objections, clarifying points, justifying decisions, understanding the essence of challenges, stating and defending policy, conducting meetings, delivering briefings, or other extended and elaborate informative monologues. Can reliably elicit information and informed opinion from native speakers. Structural inaccuracy is rarely the major cause of misunderstanding. Use of structural devices is flexible and elaborate. Without searching for words or phrases, the individual uses the language clearly and relatively naturally to elaborate concepts freely and make ideas easily understandable to native speakers. Errors occur in low-frequency and highly complex structures. (Has been coded S-3 in some nonautomated applications.) [Data Code 30]

Speaking 3+ (General Professional Proficiency, Plus)

Is often able to use the language to satisfy professional needs in a wide range of sophisticated and demanding tasks.

Examples: Despite obvious strengths, may exhibit some hesitancy, uncertainty, effort, or errors which limit the range of language-use tasks that can be reliably performed. Typically there is particular strength in fluency and one or more, but not all, of the following: breadth of lexicon, including low- and medium-frequency items, especially socio-linguistic/cultural references and nuances of close synonyms; structural precision, with sophisticated features that are readily, accurately, and appropriately controlled (such as complex modification and embedding in Indo-European languages); discourse competence in a wide range of contexts and tasks, often matching a native speaker's strategic and organizational abilities and expectations. Occasional patterned errors occur in low frequency and highly-complex structures. (Has been coded S-3+ in some nonautomated applications.) [Data Code 36]

Speaking 4 (Advanced Professional Proficiency)

Able to use the language fluently and accurately on all levels normally pertinent to professional needs. The individual's language usage and ability to function are fully successful. Organizes discourse well, using appropriate rhetorical speech devices, native cultural references, and understanding. Language ability only rarely hinders him/her in performing any task requiring language; yet, the individual would seldom be perceived as a native. Speaks effortlessly and smoothly and is able to use the language with a high degree of effectiveness, reliability, and precision for all representational purposes within the range of personal and professional experience and scope of responsibilities. Can serve as an informal interpreter in a range of unpredictable circumstances. Can perform extensive, sophisticated language tasks, encompassing most matters of interest to well-educated native speakers, including tasks which do not bear directly on a professional specialty.

Examples: Can discuss in detail concepts which are fundamentally different from those of the target culture and make those concepts clear and accessible to the native speaker. Similarly, the individual can understand the details and ramifications of concepts that are culturally or conceptually different from his/her own. Can set the tone of interpersonal official, semi-official, and non-professional verbal exchanges with a representative range of native speakers (in a range of varied audiences, purposes, tasks, and

APPENDIX I (ctd)

settings). Can play an effective role among native speakers in such contexts as conferences, lectures, and debates on matters of disagreement. Can advocate a position at length, both formally and in chance encounters, using sophisticated verbal strategies. Understands and reliably produces shifts of both subject matter and tone. Can understand native speakers of the standard and other major dialects in essentially any face-to-face interaction. (Has been coded S-4 in some nonautomated applications.)[Data Code 40]

Speaking 4+ (Advanced Professional Proficiency, Plus)

Speaking proficiency is regularly superior in all respects, usually equivalent to that of a well-educated, highly articulate native speaker. Language ability does not impede the performance of any language-use task. However, the individual would not necessarily be perceived as culturally native.

Examples: The individual organizes discourse well, employing functional rhetorical speech devices, native cultural references and understanding. Effectively applies a native speaker's social and circumstantial knowledge. However, cannot sustain that performance under all circumstances. While the individual has a wide range and control of structure, an occasional non-native slip may occur. The individual has a sophisticated control of vocabulary and phrasing that is rarely imprecise, yet there are occasional weaknesses in idioms, colloquialisms, pronunciation, cultural reference or there may be an occasional failure to interact in a totally native manner. (Has been coded S-4+ in some nonautomated applications.) [Data Code 46]

Speaking 5 (Functionally Native Proficiency)

Speaking proficiency is functionally equivalent to that of a highly articulate well-educated native speaker and reflects the cultural standards of the country where the language is natively spoken. The individual uses the language with complete flexibility and intuition, so that speech on all levels is fully accepted by well-educated native speakers in all of its features, including breadth of vocabulary and idiom, colloquialisms, and pertinent cultural references. Pronunciation is typically consistent with that of well-educated native speakers of a non-stigmatized dialect. (Has been coded S-5 in some nonautomated applications.) [Data Code 50]

CONCLUSION

Where do we go from here?

Sauli Takala
University of Helsinki, Finland

Where have we come from?

I will base my paper on the following premise: We cannot know and and appreciate where we should go from here, if we do not have a valid assessment of where we are now, and, further, that we cannot do that if we do not now where we have come from. I am convinced that in order to make optimal progress, we must not be historical illiterates or contextual ignoramuses. We must have a historical sense in order not to be unwitting prisoners of history. If we are not aware of our past, we tend to repeat it, mistaking change for progress and rediscovery for discovery. Language teaching is no exception: we have many examples of re-inventing the wheel, feeling childish delight at something we thought was a genuine and original invention. Pedagogically, such a sense of personal discovery and invention is highly valuable and highly motivating in a school setting, but I believe that in university studies and in research we should try to work with really new problems and issues and be aware of previous work on them.

We are often in a situation where we are practising trial and error but not learning sufficiently from our mistakes; nor are we doing a very good job in building systematically on the experience of earlier generations, our predecessors. We are making uneconomical use of the past in the sense that the past is always invested with many exciting possibilities for future improvements, if only we were aware of those possibilities. So, my first theme is the importance of knowing the historical background of language teaching in general and the traditions of language teaching in our own countries. There is a good general account of language teaching in L G Kelly's Twenty-five centuries of language teaching, published by Newbury House in 1976. This analytical work can be excellently complemented by a selection of extracts from classical authors, edited by M G Hesse in his Approaches to teaching foreign languages, published by North-Holland in 1975. There is a history of modern language teaching in the United States before 1930, written by Bagster-Collins, and there are good shorter reviews in several books, such as William F Mackey's monumental Language teaching analysis (1965), and Eric Hawkins' Modern languages in the curriculum (1981). The Modern Language Journal has several useful articles in its earlier volumes, but regrettably that journal has joined the others in becoming quite a-historical.

As the first item of my list of future desirable lines of action, **where do we go from here?**, I would strongly recommend teacher educators to work to introduce or maintain a short and interesting course or section on the history of language teaching in the professional preparation of all future language teachers. I would also urge those who are supervising masters and doctoral theses to encourage graduate students to do historical studies of language teaching in their own countries. As a good example I wish to draw your attention to a thesis by Dr Elaine Degenhart, whose work provides a good model. She developed a theoretical framework within which she described the teaching of French in the United States in the early 1970s and compared the situation with that in England, New Zealand, the Netherlands and Sweden, contrasting it also with the situation of English teaching in the Netherlands, Sweden, Finland and Hungary. The dissertation was completed last year at the University of Illinois.

In addition to such academic work on the traditions of language teaching, we should encourage experienced teachers and teacher educators to write about their personal experience of how language teaching has developed in our countries during their professional careers. This could be a regular feature of language teachers' professional journals, like <u>Tempus</u>. Such first-hand accounts would be a valuable source of insight for young teachers and researchers and would be an appropriate way of honouring our predecessors.

It seems regrettable to me that we, as representatives of the broad spectrum of the whole language teaching enterprise, do not have a clear sense of the classical works on language teaching, be they books or journal articles or textbooks, international and national. Similarly, I think it is unfortunate and indicative of lack of professional self-esteem that we do not have a widely recognised list of pioneers or even heroes and heroines of language teaching. As a starting point for discussion on who our pioneers, heroes and heroines are, let me list a few candidates: Erasmus, Comenius, Pestalozzi, Henry Sweet, Otto Jespersen, Harold Palmer, Michael West, Charles Fries, Robert Lado, Mary Finocchiaro and John B Carroll. I am aware that my list is biased against recent experts and against those writing in a language other than English. I have listed people that I have benefited a lot from. If you agree with the tenor of my argumentation, I suggest that the Board of the FIPLV might conduct a survey of its member countries to determine which persons - say ten - past and living, are considered in each country to have made the most substantial contributions to our field. This should be accompanied by a list of their particularly significant works and give reasons for the choice. The results could be presented at the next World Congress, to be held in Australia in 1988.

I believe that such a historical orientation is useful and even necessary, but we need to be careful if we suddenly start delving into older books and textbooks. There is a danger that we might be tempted to judge older books and textbooks by contemporary standards and with contemporary language needs in mind. All too often you can hear or see older textbooks quoted out of their temporal, historical, context and without any regard for the objectives of the books. The object seems to be to expose the alleged silliness of such dated books and to show how much better we know how.

There is no need for such mistaken historical sketches nor for such misplaced ridicule. If we approach earlier works with an open and sympathetic mind, we can both learn from them and derive pleasure from them. They are valuable sources of cultural history, especially the early phrasebooks. Think of the delight of a teacher of Finnish who was going to Hungary and wanted to refresh her Hungarian. She got hold of a phrasebook, which was not very new but still on sale. She has never forgotten the first phrase she saw, which was related to travelling: 'I've lost my way in this fog. Please ask the scout to bring his horse here and ride in front of us'. Or consider the charming Hungarian <u>The English language master</u> by Kohanyi Tihamer. It has no publishing date, but it is probably from the beginning of this century and was intended for Hungarian immigrants going to or living in America. Anyone who has worked on functional-notional syllabuses and been involved in a communicative language teaching approach, as many of us have, is delighted on seeing the detailed sections Tihamer includes on a large amount of the basic concepts (notions), such as time and time expressions, colours, animals, trees and fruits, physical appearance and feelings, human characteristics, the city, the village, the field, women's clothing, men's clothing, etc. The book very nicely presents key vocabulary and then typical situational expressions, for instance, furniture - in the furniture store, the post - at the post office. Furthermore, it has systematic sections on a number of basic language functions, such as to ask, to answer, to remember, to thank, to refuse, to consent. It takes up various places where the immigrants might look for work and shows what they need to ask and say.

I would like to give you some examples to illustrate what we might learn from an early book like this. In teaching the auxiliary verbs, the book gives the following dialogue:

    What can I do for you?

    You can do a great deal, lend me your threshing machine.

Not only is the exercise nicely situated in a dialogue context, and in that sense 'modern', but it also tells us about the situation that was probably common to many Hungarian immigrants in the USA.

Or take some other examples:

- America is a fine country, but vintage festivals such as we have at home, she hasn't got.

- See my friend, at home they haven't any prohibitionists and apostles of cold water!

- I came to inform you, that since the morning a dead horse is lying at the corner of the 4th Street.

- Counselor, I want a warrant of arrest against Mrs Francis Hazay! She cut down our pulley-line end (sic!) all our laundried linen fell into the mire!

- Well indeed I have been a little bit tipsy, on my way home. I yelled once or twice, and the policeman arrested me.

Or what do we learn about what it seems to have been like on the trolley buses when all entries in the book are of this type:

- Why don't you stop on the corner?

- I told you to stop!

- I have already paid; shall I pay twice?

- You did not give me enough change!

- How much space do you want? One seat is not enough for you?

- This boy is not seven years old! -- I know it better, I am his father!

- Put the basket on the floor, not my lap!

- Excuse Miss, but I have at least as much right to this seat as your pet-dog.

- Shut the door!

- If you don't behave decently, I'll have you put off the car!

- If you expectorate again, I'll have you arrested!

- Don't push!

What do we learn about social customs, if we read these scenes taking place at a dance:

> – I do not want to flatter, but I tell you Miss, I never had a better partner!
>
> – Dont' laugh, it isn't proper, but that thickset bald fellow dancing with that pretty girl is indeed a ridiculous sight!
>
> – I see nothing ridiculous in the scene. Because he is old, fat and bald, hasn't he the right to enjoy himself?

What images come to our minds when we read what a mistress of a household says to a woman applying for a domestic job:

> – Every second Sunday afternoons you are free!

Similarly sobering scenes are played when the immigrants try to get a job on a farm, in a foundry, as a shoemaker or particularly when they are visiting a doctor.

In a section on 'Speaking English' the reader is told: 'The ear, the ear, that is the main thing!' He or she is advised: 'Frequent the theater, go to English lectures!' A good immigrant is always trying to learn more English. In the section 'At the mining', the newcomer says:

> – How is it, our 'gerenda' – beam I have already heard in English called girder, rafter, post and instead of lumber yard I have heard it called timber yard?
>
> – Well, that is the way: all the expressions are correct, but bring to me now the canthook, I have no time to give English lessons!

By all means let us laugh, but let our laughter be one of the delight and empathy. Let us also recognise that many textbook writers have frequently done an outstanding job in meeting the needs of a variety of language learners. Indubitably we can learn from our predecessors and it behoves us to make the effort.

Where are we now?

In trying to answer the question **Where are we now?**, I will mainly talk about where we are in language in Finland. We have heard excellent general reviews by outstanding experts and I see no reason to try to summarise or comment on them. I could of course refer to current literature, but I do not know what the actual situation is in foreign-language classes in different countries. I'm afraid that there is not much factual data on how foreign languages are actually taught in schools. I thought that if I presented a case study of Finland, drawing on the research done by my colleagues and myself, I would be able to make some concrete point that, <u>mutatis mutandis</u>, might be applicable to other circumstances as well. In this paper I will only deal with the Finnish-medium school system. This is a choice which I regret, but I fear that if I always refer to the Swedish-medium system as well, you will be thoroughly confused. I will also make no distinction between second and foreign language teaching and learning.

First some history. Foreign language teaching has been the subject of continuous discussion from the beginning of the establishment of our modern secondary schools. If our language teachers at the present time feel that they are fighting to safeguard the conditions of language teaching, this is really nothing new. In public discussion, it is frequently stated that we have, or are saddled with, a 'heavy language teaching programme' in school. If you were to give a word association test among the educational profession, and presented them with the stimulus word 'heavy', I would not be surprised if the majority would make a syntagmatic association by answering 'foreign language programme', and vice versa. This familiar phrase is not new, however. It was used by our highly esteemed national philospher Johan Vilhelm Snellman, whom you can see on our 100-mark bill. This phrase is celebrating its 130th anniversary, almost challenging our national epic, the Kavevala, which was published 150 years ago. Snellman also complained about the poor standards achieved in foreign language teaching.

Foreign language teachers have not been very successful in this kind of verbal game. To my knowledge they have been mainly on the defensive. They have not pointed out that the term 'heavy' is a negative one and implies a clear value judgement. A more neutral term might be 'a language programme commensurate with our needs and linguistic situation' or a 'needs-based language teaching programme'. Foreign language teachers could take a cue from our mother tongue teachers, who have managed to improve their situation by asserting that 'Finland is the country with the fewest lessons for mother tongue teaching in the whole world'. (I once wrote a whole page of slogans and sent it to SUKOL. I remember that a few of them were in English: 'Monolinguism is curable'. 'Split infinitives not atoms'. 'English teachers are novel lovers'.)

What has happened to foreign language teaching in Finland during the last few decades? I will first discuss the developments in time allocation and try to explain the reasons for the changes. I will then take the changes in the clientele of language teaching. I will conclude this section by giving an account of how learning outcomes have developed.

First, teaching time. I think it is highly desirable in reporting on time available for teaching foreign languages to indicate how many years each language is studied and in what grade levels (age levels), how many lessons a week, and finally to indicate the total absolute number of lessons and convert that to (real) hours. If this were standard procedure, it would be much easier to have comparable data from country to country.

Table 1

Development of time allocation (number of lessons)

SWEDISH	570	+	342	912	
					− 301 (33%)
	345	+	266	611	
ENGLISH	650	+	456	1106	
					− 232 (21%)
	570	+	304	874	
GERMAN	−		304	304	
					+ 114 (37,5%)
	190	+	228	418	

It is obvious that the amount of teaching time for Swedish has diminished by almost 40% from the older junior secondary school to the comprehensive school (570 lessons vs. 345, a difference of 225 lessons). In the case of English, there has been a 12% cut, from 650 lessons to 570 (a difference of 80 lessons). The cuts in the upper secondary school have been some 22% for Swedish, 33% for English and 25% for the second world language. (Swedish: 342 vs. 266, −76 lessons; English: 456 vs. 304, −152 lessons; second world language: 304 vs. 228, −76 lessons. Total: Swedish: 912 vs. 611, English: 1106 vs. 874; other world language: 190 + 228 = 418).

Why have there been such continuous cuts in the number of hours available to foreign language teaching? There is no definite answer to this, but we can suggest a few possible answers. First, foreign languages, in addition to mathematics, were the primary reason for the fact that 8% of all students in the secondary school had to repeat a grade each year in the 1960s, and another 20% were conditionally promoted and had to do extensive make-up work in the summer and pass a test. Foreign languages have the reputation of being very difficult subjects, and students received very low grades in them. This reputation was certainly one of the main reasons why the earliest advocates of the comprehensive school pressed strongly for a policy of having only one compulsory modern language in the new school. Two languages were made compulsory in a political compromise, which has not been fully accepted, as a couple of recent seminars have indicated. I believe that the traditional reputation of foreign languages as difficult and theoretical subjects, has probably contributed more to the eagerness to make cuts rather than, for instance, a view that one foreign language is enough in Finland. Second, the reputation of being theoretical and difficult was the main reason why mathematics, as well as the two foreign languages, has been streamed during the last three years (grades 7-0) - English after four years of study and Swedish from the very beginning. Streaming came under heavy attack almost from the beginning. The problem was that streaming was not only a pedagogical measure; the choice of the easiest set meant that students making such a choice could not continue in the senior secondary school, and some lines of vocational schools were also shut off. These students were mainly boys and there was also more of a tendency to choose low sets at the periphery than in large population centres. This administrative ruling continued making foreign languages appear more responsible for educational blind alleys than the system which had in fact introduced this unholy linkage. I attempted to expose this fact and place the blame where it belonged, on the decision-makers, with little success. Perhaps I managed to cause some irritation. The full story of the introduction and subsequent dismantling of streaming awaits its historian, who will need to be a veritable Sherlock Holmes or Hercule Poirot in order to expose 'the enigma wrapped within a mystery', to quote Winston Churchill freely. It is like a Russian wooden doll, <u>matryoshka</u>, which has several smaller dolls inside it.

We have seen, then, that when the study of foreign languages was extended to the whole age group in the comprehensive school, and when about half of them then continued in the academic senior secondary school, the amount of class time available to the study of foreign languages was clearly cut. This is, naturally, highly problematic from our point of view, since the need for foreign language skills is not expected to diminish. Quite the contrary.

But there is also the other side of the coin: in spite of the fact that the teaching of foreign languages was becoming established in the former primary school and in its upper grades (called the continuation school) when the comprehensive school reform started, only half of the students who stayed in that school (i.e. who did not go to the junior secondary school) were studying a foreign language in the early 1970s. The situation was, therefore, quite varied: of all Finnish fourteen-year-olds in 1971, about 10% had studied English for one year or less, 20% for two years, 4% for three-four years, 28% for five-six years, and 1-2% for more than seven years.

According to a rough estimate, then, the comprehensive school brought to a substantial proportion of students an opportunity for a systematic and much longer exposure to English in class. (For those who could have gone to the junior secondary school, had it been preserved, the opportunity to study was curtailed in terms of class time, as we have seen.)

Another point to consider is that the study of the other national language, in this case Swedish, was made compulsory for every student. Although the time available for this is clearly smaller than in the previous junior secondary school, the decision was a clear safeguard for Swedish, which was being almost totally crowded out by English as the students' first choice. Now, for the first time in the history of our compulsory education, we are in a situation where the entire Finnish-speaking majority will have at least an elementary knowledge of the minority language and thus has made a start at being able to communicate with other Scandinavians in a Scandinavian language.

A third point to keep in mind when we are trying to assess the present as against the previous situation, is that a further foreign language, usually German (67.6% in 1983-1984; French 10.1%; Russian 7.6%; English 4.5%; Latin 1.9%; and Saame 0.2%) became an optional subject in grades 8 and 9. This was another clear improvement over the previous junior secondary school, where this option normally was not available. This optional world language course, which was taken by one third of the students in 1983-1984, gives the chance of a five-year course of study in a widely-used language other than English for those students who enter the senior secondary school.

Up till now, I have been discussing only one factor, the opportunity for the whole age-group or certain sections of the age-group to have organized language teaching services in school. This opportunity to learn is naturally a central determinant of learning actually taking place. But the ultimate question is: to what extent have our students learned foreign languages? Are the resources - student class time and the cost of teacher salaries, textbooks, tapes, etc - in fact well spent? It is by no means easy to answer such a question, but try to answer it we must. Despite all our efforts, one of the biggest problems in all education is that it is difficult to show whether we are now doing a better job in teaching than before. Yet the general public and educational decision makers are justified in asking for such evidence. It is, therefore, regrettable that extensive work on language testing has been so much preoccupied with a search for ideal test types, with exploring the structure of language ability, etc, that it has neglected to develop a methodology of getting reliable generalisations of what students in a given school system have actually learned. Parents and decision makers are not interested in the best types of testing language proficiency. They expect us to know what good tests look like, and they want to know whether students are learning better or worse in the new system than in the old one. They are also interested in knowing how good a job we in Finland are doing in language teaching in comparison with other countries.

Thanks to the systematic work on language testing and assessment of learning outcomes carried out by a research team at the National Institute for Educational Research for the last twenty years or so, we are in a position to provide some answers to such questions.

Finland has also been actively participating in international comparative studies of educational achievement for about twenty years. On the basis of this, we know that when the old school system was being phased out, more exactly in 1971, the relative performance of Finnish fourteen-year-olds was clearly below the international average. This was due to the extremely poor performance of those students who had not transferred to the junior secondary school and whose duty of English was not so well organised. Students in the selective junior secondary school were, however, at the average international level in reading and listening comprehension and above average in speaking and writing. Pre-university, college-bound students who were about to take the matriculation exam ('A' level, Abitur), were somewhat above average. This comparative perspective at the last stage of the older school system was largely reassuring: we were doing a fairly good job in language teaching. Among a host of other interesting results, I will just mention the fact that while 11% of fourteen-year-olds were rated as having done well or very well on the speaking test, only 5.5% of pre-unversity students were so rated. This is an intriguing result and is probably explained by the fact that the external matriculation examination then consisted of only a translation test. Teachers - and, perhaps even more so, students - were practising translation and neglecting other skills, and this was clearly reflected in the results.

Thus, we conclude that fifteen years ago, before the comprehensive reorganisation, the teaching of foreign languages to the **whole age-group** was not organised in a satisfactory way during the period of compulsory education and this was reflected in the learning outcomes. The selected senior secondary school had long traditions and was doing a good job. The junior secondary school, as a well-established selective school, was also doing a creditable job.

What is the situation now that the whole school system has been reorganised? We have no data concerning the senior secondary school. The external matriculation examination is not so constructed that it would be possible to compare performance across time. This is unfortunate and something ought to be done about it.

The situation is better with regard to the comprehensive school. A first large-scale national assessment of progress in the new comprehensive school was carried out a few years ago. The data was gathered in 1979, when the comprehensive school had been introduced in the whole of the country. Students' knowledge of English, Swedish, mother tongue and mathematics was assessed. There have been some changes since then, particularly concerning the dismantling of streaming and time allocation. We are in a good position now to carry out a second national assessment, perhaps in 1990, and see what has happened since the latest changes.

In studying students' knowledge of English, I used a number of the same items in 1979 as were used in the international study in 1971. These were related to listening and reading comprehension. I illustrate the results in Table 2. The results show that if we are talking about the **whole age group**, the average percent correct figures were about 40% in both listening and reading comprehension in 1971 (fourteen-year-olds), while they were about 60% in 1979. Thus there has been an improvement of some 20 percentage points. This has to be taken with some caution, due to the complexity of all comparisons. Twenty is the upper estimate and 10 percentage points a lower estimate. Still, it is clear that the whole age-group was doing better in the comprehensive school than in the older school system, as far as listening and reading are concerned.

Table 2

Listening and reading comprehension

	READING % correct	LISTENING % correct
1971	40.3	40.4
1979	59.4	62.7
Set A	80.1	81.7
Junior secondary	65.7	63.0
Set B	55.2	56.7
Set C	33.3	42.1
Continuation school	15.0	18.0

The above figures are averages, and we all know that some students were doing much better and some much worse. To give a more detailed picture, I have broken down the results by type of school and by set (stream).

What generalisations can we validly draw from these figures? I will just point out a few. First, the introduction of the comprehensive school, thereby giving all students an opportunity to learn two 'foreign' languages systematically, has not meant a general decline in standards, as has sometimes been suggested. On the contrary, when all students have been able to study English as a regular school subject, the national standard has improved. This is one of the best illustrations of the importance of the concept 'opportunity to learn' (OTL) that I know of. Given the opportunity, students will learn a foreign language to a certain extent, and when all are given such an opportunity, the mean level will go up. On reflection, this may appear self-evident, and the result may smack of what in Finland has been called 'zero research', i.e. research which is trivial, since it only shows what everybody knows anyway. But anyone familiar with the debate on comprehensivization in all countries concerned knows that there have always been sharply divided opinions about what happens to educational standards. The famous French psychologist and educator, Alfred Binet, said some seventy years ago in a charming book, Les idées modernes sur les enfants, that in education everything has been claimed and nothing proved. The situation is not much changed since his day: we are still in sore need of facts about education. By contrast, opinions are readily available.

Second, the figures also show how great the difference is in learning results. This is neither new nor surprising. I claim, however, that at least here in Finland, we have been too much preoccupied with variability in performance, considering it to be a serious failure. I suggest that we should pay more attention to the fact that, when provided an opportunity, all students have been learning a foreign language, and should regard this as an achievement that both teachers and students should rightly feel proud of. In other words, I feel that we should start paying more attention to ensuring that each student is individually making progress and – which is equally important – that each perceives that he or she is improving, albeit at his or her own rate, than to regarding individual deviation from the ideal of an identical rate of progress and the same learning outcomes ('mastery learning') as a failure. We should be more interested in the actual learning improvement of each student than in differences in the rate and amount of learning. If each student makes steady progress, standards will automatically rise!

Third, if we look at the results by type of school and type of set (stream), we see that Set A was clearly making the best progress, followed by the previous junior secondary school and Set B. Set C was also ahead of the previous continuation school students.

Although we should regard the figures I have quoted with some caution, they do suggest that our English teachers have managed the rapid transition to the new system surprisingly well. I believe that this is due to their high professional skills and to the serious and dedicated efforts made by them. I have no reason to doubt that our teachers of Swedish and our teachers of the optional world language have done an equally good job. Results from pilot schemes with non-streamed teaching of English and Swedish, which is going to be introduced into the whole country, suggest that the results do not give any cause for alarm. We seem to be able to tackle the new situation with the reassurance that it is highly probable that our teachers will continue doing a good job of teaching students foreign languages.

I have been giving you comparative data: in other words, I have illustrated how well our national school system, our different school types and sets/streams within the comprehensive school are doing in comparison with each other. Such comparative data are extremely important and useful, but they are not enough. We should try to get more absolute indicators of students' language skills. A colleague of mine, Mrs Kaija Kärkkäinen, and I wanted to try to get some absolute estimates of that kind, and we selected vocabulary as the object of our first effort. One reason was that several studies clearly show that, in spite of lack of interest in vocabulary within the second language research community and perhaps also by some teachers, vocabulary is the single best predictor of reading and listening comprehension. Another reason for the choice was that it is easier, although very laborious, to get absolute estimates of the size of students' vocabulary than it is to assess their level of, say, reading and listening comprehension.

After an intensive period of planning and preparation, which took years – remember, we had no models but had to learn to do this kind of research almost from scratch – we were able to collect data which was fully representative not only of our whole student population but also of the whole taught vocabulary. As regards Swedish, my colleagues showed that the average size of students' passive vocabulary (tested with a multiple-choice item format) was 1,380 words (girls 1,510, boys 1,205). Students in the more advanced set had learned almost twice as many words as students in the basic set (1,590 vs 870). The results were obtained after three years of studying Swedish, with a total of some 340 lessons, or some 225 real hours of class time. Students also had had four years exposure to English before they started learning Swedish.

In my dissertation, I estimated students' vocabulary sizes in English after seven years of English, with some 600 lessons or 450 real hours. Using a representative sample of 39 schools, including 2,400 students, I presented several test versions to the students in each class. Each student answered only 40-50 word items, but through careful item rotation I was able to have a sample of 950 words tested. One reason for having such a large word sample was that we wanted to build a computerised vocabulary item bank for subsequent use. I tested both active and passive vocabulary knowledge, using the following types of test formats. The data contained 115,000 answers that had to be scored. Interrater agreement was above 90%. The results are presented in Table 3.

Table 3

English vocabulary size by set

	Original estimates		Corrected estimates	
	'Passive'	'Active'	'Active'	'Passive'/con-text-aided
SET A	1 550	1 450	2 000	2 200
SET B	950	850	1 025	1 050
SET C	450	550	450	–

SWEDISH VOCABULARY SIZE (340 lessons, 225 clock hours)

| BASIC SET | 870 | ADVANCED SET | 1 590 | | |
| BOYS | 1 205 | GIRLS | 1 510 | ALL | 1 380 |

What did the results look like? They showed that there was no appreciable difference in students' active and passive vocabulary knowledge. There were clear differences between sets (average about 1,000 words) of about 500 words from lower to the next highest set. The vocabulary first taught during the lower stage (i.e. during the first four years) was known better than vocabulary taught more recently. Most of the vocabulary items known by Set C students (i.e. the weakest students) were those introduced in the early grades. Students did not learn much of what was covered in grades 7-9.

There was another somewhat surprising result, in addition to the finding that the active and passive vocabulary sizes were almost equal. It was shown that students' word building ability, i.e. knowledge of the basic morphology of English, was poorly developed. Thus the estimates need to be corrected only by 45% (Set A), 17% (Set B) and 7% (Set C). These are low figures, since in the mother tongue we are normally talking about 300-400%. In the other words, knowing only the basics of morphology - even in a language like English, whose morphology is much less productive than that of, say, Finnish - would increase the vocabulary size by a factor of 3 or 4. So, instead of our students knowing 1,000 words, they would know 3,000 or 4,000 words.

Two recommendations suggest themselves for consideration and testing: (1) it might be useful to increase the size of vocabulary taught in our lower stage (the first four years) from 1,000 to 1,500 or even 2,000, and to introduce fewer words during the upper stage (last three years); (2) during the upper stage, teach students the basic word formation and give them practice in guessing (or inferring, if you do not like the word 'guess') word meanings on the basic of morphological analysis and contextual cues. Perhaps other countries might want to consider and test such an approach as well.

In sum, I consider that in Finland we have a good chance to plan where to go from here. We are getting to be more aware of our traditions and we have a fairly good picture of how well our students have been learning foreign languages in the past fifteen years or so. Thanks to intensive work, we have modern syllabuses and modern, motivating textbooks. Our pre-service and in-service training of teachers has been intensively developed. Certainly, it will not be easy to maintain the conditions of language teaching, let alone improve them. There will always be competition among school subjects for class time. Foreign languages will be able to succeed in this only if they can bring forth convincing evidence that they are educationally valuable and practically useful, and that the time is well spent in the sense that teaching produces skills which correspond to national needs in foreign language skills.

Where do we go from here?

Let me begin by outlining where, in my opinion, we in Finland should go. Perhaps foreign colleagues will, after my case study review, be able to better understand how my views might be applicable to them.

First, I would like to emphasise that we need to continue and strengthen the work on language planning and language teaching policy that we started ten years ago. Despite some worrying developments, we have accomplished something potentially very important: (1) For the first time in our history, we have been able to produce a national plan, regional plans, and local plans for teaching foreign languages. During this process, thousands of people have been involved in thinking about the role that foreign languages should play nationally, regionally and locally. We now have basic documents, which we can build on in our further work. (2) Last April, a Centre for the Study of Language Learning and Teaching was established, as the Numminen Commission recommended six years ago. This gives us a chance to strengthen our research and development work and thus produce more facts to balance and influence opinion. I believe that each country should have or develop a national language teaching policy and keep it up-to-date. The Ministry of Education has published a summary of the Numminen Commission in English.

Second, I think it is very important that we learn to see language teaching and language learning in systemic terms, as Christopher

Brumfit has also recommended (in his introduction to this volume). The Numminen Commission outlined some clear principles for such an approach, but we now need to give life to the abstract principles. To put this more concretely, in all countries we should see language learning and language teaching as an activity which extends from school to working life. Here in Finland, we must realise that we have a sequence of language teaching provision: (1) from comprehensive school to senior secondary school to university; and (2) from comprehensive school to vocational schools and institutes. We also have language teaching in adult education, organised by business and industry. The work of preceding and receiving schools should be carefully integrated, and teachers at different levels should have regular and active contact with each other. We must make sure that there is always a second, third or further chance to begin to learn foreign languages or to complement language skills. As there are many ways to skin a cat, so there are many ways to fulfil the needs for foreign language skills. Promoting such contacts across levels of education and across types of school will be one of my priorities as we start making plans for the newly founded Centre for the Study of Language Learning and Teaching.

Third, I strongly believe that we should actively try to understand the nature of our work, as representatives of the language teaching enterprise, so that we are asking the right questions and promoting research and development work that is relevant to our questions and concerns. In this, too, I fully agree with Brumfit. It may be that it is not very exciting to work on questions like: What should or can we teach to our students? How can we best teach the passive to our Finnish students, who are used to a radically different passive in their Finnish mother tongue? What should be the best way of providing feedback and correction to our students? How many words do our students know in each grade level? How can we build up a good programme of teaching our students word formation skills, from comprehensive school to university? etc. Such questions are not perhaps of interest to many researchers who are working on second language acquisition studies. Yet, they are important questions to those who are actually responsible for planning and implementing a national language teaching programme.

It is important that research in all countries contribute, as much as possible, to making foreign language classes an educationally rewarding experience for students and teachers alike and a practically useful place for learning tools for communication and interaction skills.

I had thought of making several recommendations for those who are doing research on language teaching and learning or are otherwise involved in developing our field, but I will only make one suggestion: I hope that we will all practise what we preach! We are pleading the need to know foreign languages and give arguments to support our case. Yet, when you read our current literature, what do you see? Most often all the references at the end of articles, books, etc, are only in English. I suggest that this is bordering on scandal - some might even call it cultural and linguistic imperialism. I therefore urge that we, as representatives of foreign language teaching, expect that those who seek to develop our own theory and practice through professional books and articles, become familiar with and cite major works written in at least two languages other than their own mother tongue. If we do not bother to read what is written in other languages, how can we expect others to take a recommendation to do so seriously?

Lastly, let me remind you of the section on 'Foreign Languages and Civilization' of the Final Act of the Conference on Security and Cooperation in Europe.

Extract from the Helsinki Final Act

To encourage the study of foreign languages and civilisations as an important means of expanding communication among peoples for their better acquaintance with the culture of each country, as well as for the strengthening of international co-operation; to this end to stimulate, within their competence, the further development and improvement of foreign language teaching and the diversification of choice of languages taught at various levels, paying due attention to less widely-spread or studied languages, and in particular:

- to intensify co-operation aimed at improving the teaching of foreign languages through exchanges of information and experience concerning the development and application of effective modern teaching methods and technical aids, adapted to the needs of different categories of students, including methods of accelerated teaching; and to consider the possibility of conducting, on a bilateral or multilateral basis, studies of new methods of foreign language teaching;

- to encourage co-operation between institutions concerned, on a bilateral or multilateral basis, aimed at exploiting more fully the resources of modern educational technology in language teaching, for example through comparative studies by their specialists and, where agreed, through exchanges or transfers of audio-visual materials, of materials used for preparing textbooks, as well as of information about new types of technical equipment used for teaching languages;

- to promote the exchange of information on the experience acquired in the training of language teachers and to intensify exchanges on a bilateral basis of language teachers and students as well as to facilitate their participation in summer courses in languages and civilisations, wherever these are organised;

- to encourage co-operation among experts in the field of lexicography with the aim of defining the necessary terminological equivalents, particularly in the scientific and technical disciplines, in order to facilitate relations among scientific institutions and specialists;

- to promote the wider spread of foreign language study among the different types of secondary education establishments and greater possibilities of choice between an increased number of European languages; and in this context to consider, wherever appropriate, the possibilities for developing the recruitment and training of teachers as well as the organisation of the student groups required;

- to favour, in higher education, a wider choice in the languages offered to language students and greater opportunities for other students to study various foreign languages; also to faciliate, where desirable, the organisation of courses in languages and civilizations, on the basis of special arrangements as necessary, to be given by foreign lecturers, particularly from European countries having less widely-spread or studied languages;

- to promote, within the framework of adult education, the further development of specialised programmes, adapted to various needs and interests, for teaching foreign languages to their own inhabitants and the languages of host countries to interested adults from other countries; in this context to encourage interested institutions to co-operate, for example, in the elaboration of programmes for teaching by radio and television and by accelerated methods, and also, where desirable, in the definition of study objectives for such programmes, with a view to arriving at comparable levels of language proficiency;

- to encourage the association, where appropriate, of the teaching of foreign languages with the study of the corresponding civilizations and also to make further efforts to stimulate interest in the study of foreign languages, including relevant out-of-class activities.

I think that we agree that these principles are not limited to the European nations, as is shown by the fact that the Act was also signed by Canada and the United States. I believe that the principles apply to all countries of the world. I therefore recommend that the FIPLV regularly conduct an assessment of how the principles have been implemented in each member country and that a report be presented at each world conference. This could be called the 'Helsinki Review' or some other appropriate title. As language teachers we can serve as models of co-operation across cultures and languages, and help others to acquire the tools for and an attitude of co-operation and negotiation.

References

BAGSTER-COLLINS, E W. History of modern language teaching in the United States. In E W Bagster-Collins (ed), Studies in modern language teaching, p 3-96. New York: MacMillan (1980).

DAGENHART, R E. The teaching of French in the United States in the early 1970's: A descriptive and comparative study. PhD. thesis, University of Illinois at Urbana-Champaign (1984).

HAWKINS, E. Modern languages in the curriculum. Cambridge: Cambridge University Press (1981).

HESSE, M G. Approaches to foreign language teaching. Dordrecht: North-Holland (1975).

KELLY, L G. 25 centuries of language teaching. Rowley: Newbury House (1969).

KARKKAINEN, K. Havaintoja peruskoululaisten ruotsin kielen sanaston ja rakenteiden osaamisesta (Some observations on the comprehensive school students' knowledge of Swedish vocabulary and grammar). In V Hirvi (ed), Peruskoulun kehittäminen tutkimustulosten perusteella, p 58-66. University of Jyväskylä, Institute for Educational Research, Bulletin no. 209 (1983).

MACKEY, W F. Language teaching analysis. London: Longman (1965).

TAKALA, S. Evaluation of students' knowledge of English vocabulary in the Finnish comprehensive school. University of Jyväskylä, Institute for Educational Research (Tech Rep No 350) (1984).

TIHAMER, K (nd). The English language master.

APPENDIX

THE INTERNATIONAL FEDERATION OF MODERN LANGUAGE TEACHERS (FIPLV)

FIPLV stands for <u>Fédération Internationale des Professeurs de Langues Vivantes</u> - International Federation of Modern Language Teachers. The aims of the FIPLV are, among others, to promote and encourage friendly and fraternal relations between modern language teachers in all parts of the world and to co-ordinate the efforts and research work of the profession for the purpose of improving methods of foreign and second language teaching and learning. To achieve these aims the FIPLV holds international multilingual congresses at regular intervals. The 15th World Congress took place in Helsinki, Finland, in 1985 with the theme of 'Confidence through Competence'. This had been chosen on purpose: 1985 was the United Nations International Year of Youth, and since language teachers are increasingly concerned with promoting co-operation between nations and thus securing international understanding, it had been the wish of the congress organisers to focus particular attention on the two components of the congress theme: confidence - in the abilities of young people, 'thereby giving them greater willingness to act more boldly in foreign languages as well', as Pirkko-Sisko Häkinen, President of the Finnish Modern Language Association, put it; competence - to be achieved through confidence, and also by effective teaching, the application of research in the field, and by learning strategies that support language acquisition for the multilingual citizen of tomorrow.